The

John Whitmer

Historical Association

JOURNAL

The
John Whitmer
Historical Association
JOURNAL

———————— • ————————

Edited by William D. Morain

Spring/Summer 2018
Volume 38, Number 1

About This Journal

The *John Whitmer Historical Association Journal* is published semi-annually by the John Whitmer Historical Association. The association's purposes are to create and encourage interest in Latter Day Saint history, especially the history of the Community of Christ, to promote communication, research, and publication in the field of Latter Day Saint history, and to provide vehicles for the dissemination of scholarly research to persons interested in Latter Day Saint history. For more information, visit the association website: *www.jwha.info*.

Papers for consideration will be reviewed by the editorial committee and should be submitted in a digital file (preferably Microsoft *Word*) using the most current *Chicago Manual of Style* format. Send all submissions and queries to the editor via email: *anplsurg@grm.net*.

Painting of Nauvoo Temple ruins by David Hyrum Smith.
Cover design and typesetting by John C. Hamer.

The John Whitmer Historical Association Journal

Spring/Summer 2018, Vol. 38, No. 1

COURTESY OF COMMUNITY OF CHRIST ARCHIVES

John Whitmer (ca. 1870)

Table of Contents

The John Whitmer Historical Association Journal

Articles

Exploring RLDS Identity in the 1960s: The Joint Council
Seminars of 1967
    Peter A. Judd...1
In his Presidential Address, Peter Judd provides a detailed first-hand
review of matters surrounding the eventful 1967 RLDS Joint Council
Seminars, a critical episode in the church's fractious transition from
its traditional "one true church" stance to a more inclusive institutional
posture.

The Divergent Memories of Joseph Smith's Restoration
Movement
    Michael Scott Van Wagenen..38
For his Richard Howard lecture, Mike Van Wagenen interviewed 25
members from each of 10 restoration traditions to gather collective
memory beliefs and compare them to authentic history. His rich
anecdotal findings portray a colorful spectrum of antagonisms,
misconceptions, and tribalisms unique to each group.

Anointed Queens and Priestesses: Alpheus Cutler's Plural
Wives
    Danny L. Jorgensen and Andrew Leary..55
Danny Jorgensen and Andrew Leary carefully document what is known
of Alpheus Cutler's six polygamous wives in addition to his first. The
authors further describe how nascent Mormon polygamy failed to evolve
into a formalized structure of normative behavior as a result its short
duration.

Historical Empathy for Early Mormon Nauvoo, Illinois,
1839-1846
    Richard P. Howard..80
Dick Howard asks readers to empathize with the Nauvoo Mormons in
their situation-appropriate decisions concerning baptism for the dead,
the Nauvoo legion, and plural marriage.

I Know What You Said Last Time: Reflections and
Cogitations by a 46-year JWHA Charter Member
    Paul M. Edwards..87
JWHA Charter Member Paul Edwards describes his annotated
summary of all presentations from past JWHA meetings with
an accompanying critical assessment of the tedious focus on the
foundational period. He offers an impassioned plea for new areas of
investigation, including more recent Community of Christ events and
outreach activities.

The Relationship of Oliver Cowdery with Joseph Smith
    William Shepard and H. Michael Marquardt.........................95
Bill Shepard and Mike Marquardt chronicle in detail the many-faceted
decline in the relationship between Joseph Smith and Oliver Cowdery,
resulting in Cowdery's permanent separation from the church he
helped to found.

The Appeal of Mormonism to Norwegian-American
Immigrants: A Case Study
    Thomas J. Morain..131
Tom Morain traces the Hayer family's emigration to America as a
paradigm of Norwegian familial and religious traditions and how this
foundation melded so seamlessly into Mormon culture.

The Tragedy of William Hodges
    William Shepard..142
Bill Shepard details the final two tragic months of the life of William
Hodges who, with his brother and two outlaw companions, carried
out a homicidal robbery, leading to a bumbling aftermath of judicial
retribution and a celebrated public hanging. Shepard focuses
on William's cognitive deficiency as a contributing factor to his
vulnerability to making unfortunate choices.

The Nauvoo Council of Fifty Minutes

 H. Michael Marquardt 168

Mike Marquardt draws upon the 2016 release of the minutes of
the Nauvoo Council of Fifty to provide a direct chronicle of events
surrounding this new theocracy, beginning with Joseph Smith's ascent
to kingship and culminating with emigration to the West. Many of
the ambitious projects outlined within the minutes would never come
to fruition.

The Historical Attachment of Nauvoo for Community of
Christ

 Mark A. Scherer 180

Community of Christ Past-Historian Mark Scherer traces his
institution's evolving views about early Nauvoo from its former anti-
LDS posture to one in which the brutality of that era now testifies to
the new Community of Christ belief in the banality of violence.

Book Review Article

Michael W. Homer, *Joseph's Temples: The Dynamic
Relationship Between Freemasonry and Mormonism,* and
Angela Pulley Hudson, *Real Native Genius: How an Ex-
Slave and a White Mormon Became Famous Indians*

 Reviewed by Newell G. Bringhurst 187

Book Review

Gregory A. Prince, *Leonard Arrington and the Writing of
Mormon History*

 Reviewed by Paul M. Edwards 196

Peter A. Judd, JWHA President 2016–17

Exploring RLDS Identity
in the 1960s:
The Joint Council Seminars of 1967

Peter A. Judd

I BEGIN BY ACKNOWLEDGING the assistance of Rachel Killebrew and Barbara Bernauer of the Community of Christ Archives who helped me find source materials, as well as former church historians Richard Howard and Mark Scherer who read a draft of this paper and offered valuable suggestions. Their help contributed greatly.

A Changed and Changing Church

Few if any persons with even a passing acquaintance with the RLDS church/Community of Christ over the last sixty years will deny that this denomination has undergone significant change during that time. Abundant evidence exists that this church, from its beginning in 1830, has always been changing. But my purpose in this paper is to address the significance of the 1960s and specifically a series of meetings of the church's top leaders in 1967—fifty years ago this year—referred to as Joint Council Seminars.[1] This year marks the fiftieth anniversary of those seminars, so I find it timely to explore them now.

What I will present here is really just a small piece in the story of a religious movement that has been, and continues, on a journey of discovery and mission—a journey that has been marked by far more changes and transitions than it has sameness and familiarity. So in the broader scheme of things, the 1967 Joint Council Seminars are a small piece but, as I hope to show, an important, even pivotal, piece.

---

1. The three seminars addressed in this paper were not the only ones held during this time frame. Indeed, the Joint Council held at least one other seminar during that same year. This council held other seminars during this decade and those that follow. See Duane E. Couey, "Historical Review of the Joint Council Seminar Program," September 1980, Duane Couey papers, Community of Christ Archives.

The Importance of the 1960s

The 1960s, I suggest, are significant because of the major programs and events during that decade that gave impetus to change in the church. These all occurred under the presidency of W. Wallace Smith, grandson of the founding prophet, Joseph Smith Jr. W. Wallace took office in October 1958 following the accidental death of his half-brother Israel A. Smith. It has been observed by Mark Scherer and others that one of W. Wallace Smith's most significant contributions from the presidential chair was in three persons he appointed to the Council of Twelve Apostles in the first two years of his presidency: Clifford Cole, Charles Neff, and Duane Couey. Scherer refers to these three leaders as change agents.[2] The contribution of each as a navigator of change in the 1960s and later cannot be overstated.

I identify five programs and events of the 1960s pertaining to the developing identity and theology of the church as being most significant.

I. The Basic Beliefs Committee

This committee was formed in 1960 to address the need to restate the church's basic beliefs in a way that more adequately reflected the church's place in the contemporary world. At that time, the church still used the "Epitome of Faith" authored by Joseph Smith Jr. more than a hundred years earlier.[3] And, as Richard Howard has pointed out, the major published work on church beliefs, on which church leaders and members had depended heavily from its first publication in 1936, was F. Henry Edwards's *Fundamentals*.[4]

Edwards, a member of the First Presidency from 1946 to 1966, recognized the need to continually examine and rearticulate the faith and beliefs of the church. He served as the first chair of the Basic Beliefs Committee. On Edwards's retirement in 1966, Council of Twelve president Clifford Cole took that role. Committee members included Percy Farrow, Harry Doty, Reed Holmes, Charles Davies, Cecil Ettinger, Clifford Buck, Russell Ralston, Alfred Yale, Will Timms, Merle Guthrie, Geoffrey Spencer, and Jacques Pement. The committee worked throughout the decade culminating in the 1970 publication of *Exploring the Faith*,[5] which contained a new nineteen-paragraph statement of belief, each paragraph accompanied by an explanatory

---

2. Mark A. Scherer, *The Journey of a People: The Era of Worldwide Community, 1946 to 2015* (Independence, MO: Community of Christ Seminary Press, 2016), 155.

3. See *Times and Seasons* 3, no. 9 (March 1, 1842): 709–10.

4. F. Henry Edwards, *Fundamentals: Enduring Convictions of the Restoration* (Independence, MO: Herald Publishing House, 1936). See Richard P. Howard, *The Church Through the Years*, vol. 2 (Independence, MO: Herald Publishing House, 1993), 359–60.

5. *Exploring the Faith* (Independence, MO: Herald House, 1970).

chapter. The text of this book was serialized in the church's periodical *The Saints' Herald* in 1968 and 1969.[6]

II. Church Expansion into Non-Western Nations

Before 1960, the Reorganized church was officially established in ten countries: United States, Canada, Great Britain, Australia, French Polynesia, Netherlands, Norway, New Zealand, Germany, and Cayman Islands. Only one of these, French Polynesia, could be considered non-Western. But that year the Joint Council sent apostles Blair Jensen and Charles Neff to the Orient to explore the possibility of planting the church there. This led to the church being officially established in Japan that same year and the Neff family living there for four years. By the end of the 1960s, the church had been officially established in an additional eleven countries in Asia, Africa, and Central and South America: Japan, Korea, Mexico, Brazil, Peru, Nigeria, India, Philippines, New Caledonia, Haiti, and Fiji.

Neff's experience in Japan quickly led him to ask questions that required church leaders to consider the purpose and role of the church in new ways. In a letter to the Basic Beliefs Committee, he asked: "What is the central message of the gospel? Surely it must be something beyond the differences between the RLDS church and other churches. In a non-Christian culture, is it possible to see other Christians more as allies than as adversaries?"[7]

III. Statement on Objectives for the Church

This statement was introduced at the 1966 World Conference. It presented five goals:

1. Clarify the theology of the church and unify the membership in their faith.
2. Deepen the effectiveness of worship within the church.
3. Develop world church concepts and procedures in evangelism and administration.
4. Decentralize the administration of the church.
5. Interpret the Zionic concept for our day in world terms and aggressively pursue the implementation of Zionic development.[8]

---

6. Articles on the separate belief statements were included starting in the 1968 issues and on into the 1969 issues of *The Saints' Herald*, the official periodical of the Reorganized Church of Jesus Christ of Latter Day Saints.

7. Summarized from an unpublished presentation given by Clifford Cole to a Joint Council Seminar at Park College (September 18, 1976), 5–6. Community of Christ Archives. As reprinted in Howard, *The Church Through the Years* 2, 359.

8. W. Wallace Smith, "Statement on Objectives for the Church," *World Conference Bulletin* April 18, 1996, 238–40. Reprinted in *Saints' Herald* 113, no. 10 (May 15, 1966): 18–19. This statement was also published in pamphlet form under the same title.

IV. Joint Council Seminars of 1967

These seminars were planned to get the church's top leaders to address the first goal in the Statement on Objectives for the Church: "Clarify the theology of the church and unify the membership in their faith."

V. Position Papers[9] and the New Curriculum

Concurrent with the three joint council seminars, church leaders made plans to produce an entirely new church school curriculum for children, youth, and adults. The staff of the church's Religious Education Department prepared a series of "position papers" covering various topics. These papers were presented to a Curriculum Consultation Committee for review and discussion with the intent of receiving input and suggestions for what would serve as the foundations for the forthcoming curriculum. Curriculum planning and writing followed with release of the first course books in a three-year cycle in 1972. These church school materials reflected less sectarian, more ecumenical views of the church and its mission.

Leading Up to the Seminars

Three Joint Council Seminars focusing on the identity and mission of the church were held at the church headquarters' Auditorium in 1967. They emerged from an identified lack of clarity and purpose of the church that had contributed to low morale among the church's full-time appointee ministers. Morale issues had been reported to and observed by members of the Council of Twelve Apostles as they interacted with appointees in their respective fields. This led to the decision in 1965 to form a Committee on Appointee Morale, composed of apostles William Timms (chair), Duane Couey, Charles Neff, and Reed Holmes. Subsequently, this committee crafted and distributed a survey asking appointees a broad range of questions related to their effectiveness as appointee ministers.[10]

Out of a total of 225 surveys sent out, 197 were returned, 186 in time to be tabulated for a report presented to Clifford Cole, president of the Council of Twelve, on January 6, 1966.[11] After discussion in that Council on February 2, Cole forwarded the

---

9. These papers are variously referred to as study papers or discussion papers. I use the term "position papers" here as this was used at the time in correspondence among Religious Education Department staff members, between the department director and the members of the Curriculum Consultation Committee, and on drafts of some of the papers, P111 f88, f92, and f93, and Donald Landon papers, Community of Christ Archives.

10. A search of the Community of Christ Archives and Council of Twelve files was not successful in locating a copy of the survey instrument; so it is not possible to identify any of the specific questions asked.

11. The Committee on Appointee Morale to Clifford A. Cole, January 6, 1966. See Council of Twelve Minutes February 2, 1966, Community of Christ Archives.

committee report to the First Presidency, along with a summary of the report's findings and recommendations. This summary concluded:

> The primary cause of low morale to which all other factors are secondary is that the men lack a sense of destiny and direction, which vagueness gives them little to point toward and nothing of significance by which to gauge the effectiveness of their efforts. Consequently, their sense of worth and even of calling is sacrificed to what they consider to be expediency and indecision in the leading councils.
>
> The survey indicates clearly that appointee morale reflects directly the effectiveness or ineffectiveness of leadership. Primary solutions of the morale problem rest squarely on the shoulders of the Joint Council.[12]

The full report puts it this way: "There is persistent evidence throughout the responses from appointees that direction is indecisive and that it is, in fact, irrelevant because of lack of clear definition of where the church is going and what role the church should be fulfilling."[13] Some respondents to the survey went as far as identifying the problem to be at the top level of church leadership. One expressed concern over "prophetic paralysis and preoccupation."[14] At a special joint council of presidency and twelve held on March 2 and 3, 1966, to discuss the report on appointee morale, Council of Twelve president Clifford Cole said "the Council of Twelve felt very deeply about item number 1 'prophetic paralysis and preoccupation' under the objectives of the church. He stated that this is the major problem we are facing and we need to concentrate on this one subject, and the remaining points will fall into place."[15]

A First Presidency-Council of Twelve committee was quickly formed to address the issue of lack of clear objectives or goals for the church. This committee was composed of the three members of the First Presidency: W. Wallace Smith, F. Henry Edwards, and Maurice L. Draper, and apostles Clifford A. Cole, Charles D. Neff, and Duane E. Couey. They met on March 10, 11, and 16, 1966. By March 18, they had presented to the Council of Twelve their "Report of the Committee on Church Objectives to the Joint Council of the First Presidency and Council of Twelve."[16] This report identified five areas for consideration as church objectives. The first was "To clarify the theology of the church and unify the membership in their theological commitments." Under this objective, the first intermediate objective was "To develop a planned seminar program for the Presidency, Twelve, and Presiding Bishopric to

---

12. Clifford A. Cole to The First Presidency, February 2, 1966. See Council of Twelve Minutes, February 2, 1966, Community of Christ Archives.

13. Committee on Appointee Morale to Clifford Cole, 3.

14. Committee on Appointee Morale to Clifford Cole, 3.

15. "Joint Council of the First Presidency and Council of Twelve" [a transcript of the 2 and 3 March 1966 sessions], 2, P94 f129, Community of Christ Archives.

16. A copy of this report can be found in with the Joint Council Minutes in Community of Christ Archives. See also Council of Twelve Minutes, March 18, 1966.

clarify theological understanding and unify the members of this Joint Council in their theological commitments."[17] This started the ball rolling on preparation and planning for the seminars held in 1967. It recognized the all-important step of getting the top leaders of the church on board and unified first, prepared then to lead implementation throughout the church.

This report also identified four other main objectives identified earlier in this paper. After minor refinement and approval by the full Joint Council on April 14, 1966, these five objectives were presented to the World Conference as the "Statement on Objectives for the Church." Apostle Charles Neff, who read the statement to the conference on April 17, 1966, later recalled his role in its development this way:

> The members of the Council of Twelve kept talking to the Presidency about objectives for the church and . . . finally, the Presidency . . . [said] "Why don't you produce a list." That was a very big challenge to me, and I went home that night and burned a little midnight oil and . . . drafted the 1966 Statement of Objectives. I came back and bounced them off Cole, who suggested a minor change or two and we went back to the Presidency. I remember Brother Edwards saying, "This is far better than I had any reason to believe it could be."[18]

Preparing for the Seminars

A significant transition in church leadership occurred at the April 1966 World Conference. Francis Henry Edwards, who had served in the First Presidency and Council of Twelve for a combined forty-four years retired at the age of sixty-eight. He was succeeded in the First Presidency by Apostle Duane Couey. Just two weeks after the close of that world conference, President Couey initiated the planning of the seminars by proposing to his colleagues in the presidency that a committee comprised of members of the presidency and twelve be formed to begin planning.[19] Because Couey had served on the church objectives committee it was natural that he should spearhead the planning of seminars at which the Joint Council would begin the process of clarifying the church's theology.

On June 8 the First Presidency sent a memo of invitation to apostles Clifford Cole, Charles Neff, and Aleah Koury to serve with them on a steering committee to

---

17. Report of the Committee on Church Objectives, 1. This intermediate objective echoed Cole's expression to the Presidency in January of that year: "We now need to bring the Joint Council of the Twelve and Presidency together in discussion of [our theology] until we are unified and enthused with our message," Clifford A. Cole to The First Presidency, January 28, 1966, P94 f129, Community of Christ Archives.

18. Charles D. Neff, "An Oral History Memoir," 84–85, Community of Christ Archives.

19. Duane E. Couey to The First Presidency (W. Wallace Smith and Maurice Draper) May 9, 1966, RG 29-2 f132, Community of Christ Archives.

plan the mechanics and procedures of the seminars.[20] Within this memo is reference to another committee that would be dealing with the subject matter of the seminars; this committee would consist of the First Presidency and apostles Clifford Cole, Reed Holmes, and Charles Neff.[21]

A question that surfaced quickly in the discussions of the planning committee dealing with subject matter pertained to who else should be involved in the seminars with the Joint Council, providing facilitation or input and also as participants. During the summer of 1966 the committee decided to explore the possibility of involving faculty members from the nearby Saint Paul School of Theology in leading the seminars. This seminary was located just five miles west of church headquarters, in Kansas City, Missouri. It was, and still is, sponsored by the United Methodist Church. Several headquarters staff members had attended classes there since its opening in 1959. These included Richard Lancaster and Clifford Buck starting in 1959; both received their BD[22] degrees in 1965. Other headquarters staff members taking classes at Saint Paul were Edna Easter, Hazel Imrie, James Lancaster, Athol Packer, and Wayne Ham (MDiv 1969). Also Bill Russell studied there between 1961 and 1966 while serving as an assistant editor at the church's publishing division, Herald House. Russell finished his Saint Paul MDiv in 1967 after joining the Graceland College faculty.[23] Richard Lancaster recalls that Apostle Clifford Cole encouraged him and other church staff members to attend Saint Paul and arranged for the church to pay their costs.[24] These individuals had become well acquainted with several of the professors who taught there.

Richard Lancaster, who had served as director of the church's Religious Education Department since October 1963, was asked by the committee to contact the seminary and explore possibilities. He recalls that Clifford Cole was a primary voice in suggesting the use of Saint Paul.[25] In late July 1966 Lancaster met with a committee at the seminary "to discuss ways they could assist in a program of education for church leadership."[26] The principal contact at the seminary was the school's president, Dr. Don Holter. From this meeting, Lancaster reported: "They all agreed to give every assistance possible. There seemed to be no real reservations once it was clear

---

20. The First Presidency to Apostles C. A. Cole, C. D. Neff, and A. G. Koury, June 8, 1966, RG 29-2 f132, Community of Christ Archives.

21. See also "Joint Council Committees," a listing of various committees of the Joint Council, dated June 1966. Community of Christ Archives RG29-2 f132.

22. The bachelor of divinity was the standard seminary degree at that time. These degrees were later "converted" to the master of divinity (MDiv).

23. Information on the Saint Paul students was provided by Bill Russell. Telephone interview, August 26, 2017.

24. Telephone interview with Richard Lancaster, August 29, 2017.

25. Lancaster 2017.

26. Richard Lancaster to Duane Couey August 2, 1966, RG 29-3 f14, Community of Christ Archives.

that we had serious and deep intent."[27] In a memo addressed to fellow members of the subject matter planning committee, Duane Couey refers to a subsequent meeting between him, Clifford Cole, and Richard Lancaster and the Saint Paul president, Don Holter. Couey confirms the positive response received: "The reception given to us was excellent, and after Dr. Holter became convinced that we were very serious in our quest, he and other members of the faculty warmed to the possibility of this dialogue."[28]

Lancaster's involvement with planning the seminars was short-lived, however. He had applied for and received a leave of absence to pursue doctoral studies starting in the fall of 1966. His successor as department director and seminar planning liaison was Donald Landon who had served in various roles as a church appointee since 1951.[29]

FIGURE I: *Donald Landon*

Couey's memo to his committee colleagues just mentioned indicated the need for further consultation with the Saint Paul staff. To aid in these conversations, Couey proposed his colleagues review a six-page paper he, Cole, and Landon had compiled titled, "Proposed Outline of Purpose for Joint Council Studies."[30] Landon's contribution to this important document is evidenced by its inclusion of key elements from a memo he wrote to Couey the day before its distribution to the other committee members.[31] This paper consisted of three sections: an introduction, objectives for the study, and subject matter. Highlights include acknowledgment that

The Reorganized Church of Jesus Christ of Latter Day Saints today confronts a growing problem of theological disunity within its ranks. This disunity has been caused by the impact of the so-called liberal thought upon a basically conservative

27. Lancaster 1966.

28. Duane E. Couey to Presidents W. Wallace Smith and Maurice L. Draper, and apostles Clifford A. Cole, Reed M. Holmes, and Charles D. Neff, September 9, 1966, RG 29-2 f132, Community of Christ Archives.

29. Landon credits Lancaster with doing much of the spade work. Interview with Donald Landon, August 31, 2017.

30. Couey to Smith, Draper, Cole, Holmes, and Neff, September 9, 1966, with attachment, "Proposed Outline of Purpose for Joint Council Studies," Duane Couey Papers, Community of Christ Archives.

31. Donald Landon to President Duane Couey, September 8, 1976, Donald Landon papers, Community of Christ Archives.

people, by the changing image which the church has of its role in today's world, and by the changing world in which the church operates.[32]

The objectives section included:

1. To help the Joint Council develop a sound and unified image of the Reorganized Church of Jesus Christ of Latter Day Saints and its mission in relation to the historical movement of Christianity.

2. To help the Joint Council develop a greater clarity of understanding and unity of thought regarding the mission of the church in relation to the world of today.

3. To help the Joint Council deepen its theological perception of God and the problems of man, thus seeing more clearly the task to which God has set his hand and commit the church more fully to the divine eschatology toward which all creation moves.

4. Through this discipline, searching and worship to prepare the way for the generation of renewed spiritual power which was felt in the inception of the Restoration Movement but which has diminished in more recent years.[33]

Under subject matter, the proposed outline suggested three areas:

1. We first need help in seeing the church as it has tried to express its calling and mission through the stream of history. . . .

2. We shall need to restudy and re-evaluate the history of [our church] as it has developed in the nineteenth and twentieth centuries. . . .

3. We shall . . . need to see the world in which the church is cast today with its needs, and in light of these needs seek to discern as best we can the will of God regarding this world and the role of the church in bringing to pass the will of God.[34]

In reference to the first and third elements under subject matter, the outline emphasized the need for church leaders to receive help from persons outside the denomination. The proposal concludes, "It is our hope that the testimony of the Holy Spirit will be present to guide us altogether, and that the experience will be basically a spiritual experience in its totality."[35]

---

32. "Proposed Outline," 1.

33. "Proposed Outline," 4.

34. "Proposed Outline," 5.

35. "Proposed Outline," 7. What is presumably the final copy of this paper—the version subsequently shared with the Saint Paul personnel who would assist in leading the seminars—was titled "Outline of Purpose for Joint Council Studies," and is essentially the same as the earlier proposed outline from which these quotations were taken, P118 f246, Community of Christ Archives.

The Joint Council

The term "joint council" had been used in the RLDS church from at least as far back as 1905. In fact, the need for the leading councils of the church to confer together is found in Doctrine and Covenants 122 accepted by the church in 1894.[36] It most commonly refers to a council or meetings of the three leading councils of the church: The First Presidency, The Council of Twelve Apostles, and The Presiding Bishopric. However, as in the case of discussions leading up to the development of the 1966 objectives and the 1967 seminars, a joint council of the presidency and twelve met. The term joint council has largely fallen into disuse since President Grant McMurray instituted the World Church Leadership Council in 1996. This council, which continues to the present day, includes all three of the previously mentioned leading councils as well as other world church officers.

In 1967, this joint council consisted of the three members of the First Presidency, eleven members of the Council of Twelve Apostles, and three members of the Presiding Bishopric. There was one vacancy in the twelve. The age of these individuals ranged from sixty-six to thirty-seven and averaged fifty; their average tenure as general officers of the church was nine years. Over the previous three years, seven of these individuals were new to the council and four others were new to their specific roles. Only three had tenures of twenty years or more. This three-year period had seen the retirement of eight joint council members with an average of just over twenty-five years of service each.

Consideration was had to adding additional persons as attendees at the seminars. But that did not occur, because, according to The First Presidency, "The presence of other personnel could have some limiting influence on the discussions, and we would want to avoid that."[37] An exception was made with Donald Landon who had served as the primary organizer of the seminars and liaison with the Saint Paul faculty.[38] Landon attended all seminar sessions.[39]

36. See Maurice L. Draper, "The Nature and Function of the Joint Council of First Presidency, Council of Twelve, and Presiding Bishopric," P118 f246, Community of Christ Archives.

37. The First Presidency to Elder Richard B. Lancaster, August 29, 1966, RG 29-3 f14, Community of Christ Archives.

38. First Presidency to Donald D. Landon, February 22, 1967, Donald Landon papers, Community of Christ Archives.

39. Interview with Donald D. Landon, August 31, 2017.

FIGURE 2:
CHURCH PRESIDENT

FIGURE 3: COUNSELORS IN THE
FIRST PRESIDENCY

W. Wallace Smith

Maurice L. Draper

Duane E. Couey

FIGURE 4: THE COUNCIL OF TWELVE APOSTLES

Clifford A. Cole

Reed M. Holmes

Donald O. Chesworth

Donald V. Lents

Charles D. Neff

Cecil R. Ettinger

Russell F. Ralston

William E. Timms

Aleah G. Koury

Earl T. Higdon

Alan D. Tyree

FIGURE 5: THE PRESIDING BISHOPRIC

Walter N. Johnson

Francis E. "Pat" Hansen

Harold W. Cackler

FIGURE 6: *Saint Paul School of Theology Professors*

E. Dale Dunlap   Carl Bangs   W. Paul Jones

The First Seminar: March 1967[40]

After some conversation with the Saint Paul School of Theology representatives, it became evident to the First Presidency that a single week of meetings would be quite inadequate to address the range of concerns identified.[41] However, they decided to schedule a one-week seminar and then determine subsequent meetings after that. This first seminar was held March 6 through 10, 1967, in the music room of the church's headquarters Auditorium. This room was chosen as it had capabilities for audio recording of the sessions. Evidence that at least some of the sessions were recorded is found in memos from the presidency to Don Landon acknowledging receipt of tapes sent to their office.[42] However, a search of the church archives and First Presidency records has so far failed to find any of the tapes.

The First Presidency sent details of this first seminar to joint council members. Details included times of the meetings and the names of the guests from Saint Paul: Dr. E. Dale Dunlap (professor of theology and acting dean), Dr. Carl Bangs (professor of historical theology), and Dr. W. Paul Jones (associate professor of philosophical theology).[43] Copies of the agenda for the week[44] and biographical data on the three guests were included.[45]

---

40. A brief overview of the 1967 Joint Council seminars can be found in W. B. "Pat" Spillman, "Taking the Road More Traveled," *John Whitmer Historical Association Journal* 24 (2004): 140–42.

41. Presidency to Lancaster, August 29, 1966.

42. The First Presidency to Don Landon, December 26, 1967; Donald Landon to Duane Couey, December 26, 1967; and The First Presidency to Donald D. Landon, December 28, 1967, Donald Landon Papers, Community of Christ Archives.

43. First Presidency to Joint Council, February 27, 1967, RG29-2 f133, Community of Christ Archives.

44. "Orientation Seminar," Donald Landon papers, Community of Christ Archives.

45. These biographical statements can be found in RG 29-4 f23, Community of Christ Archives.

The committee responsible for planning the agenda concluded, "The essential task confronting us is that of helping the church find and clarify its mission in this present day world. . . . If we are to be the church of Jesus Christ, we must be relevant to the central mission Christ lays upon the church."[46] The theme of the first seminar was: "The Church and the World."

The March 1, 1967, *Saints' Herald* carried an editorial over the names of W. Wallace Smith for the First Presidency, and Clifford Cole for the Council of Twelve, announcing the first seminar. This talked about the seminar as the first of a series that would address implementation of the objectives presented at the previous year's world conference. The editorial admitted the considerable time and effort required of church officers but said the importance of the task justified the effort. It was indicated that this seminar would address "the theological heritage which we have as a church and to what that heritage and the present resources of the church should contribute to the world in which we live." Mention was made that knowledgeable persons from various fields would be invited to "meet with us to help us see the nature of the problems confronting us as clearly as possible."[47]

In addition, this first seminar was announced to church headquarters staff in the weekly *The Auditorium Log*. The March 8, 1967, issue carried a short paragraph saying the seminar was focusing on "the theological heritage of the church."[48]

Prior to the March 1967 seminar, on behalf of the planning committee, Don Landon provided the Saint Paul professors with a bibliography, an extensive portfolio of articles and other material that would provide them with adequate background on the RLDS church,[49] and photos and biographical information on each of the seventeen joint council members.[50] In turn, the professors provided a bibliography of eight books they thought would be helpful for the joint council members to read in advance.[51] Dale Dunlap followed up in February 1967 with a proposal on how the three Saint Paul professors would use the time during the week.[52]

46. Two-page report from planning committee, Donald Landon papers, Community of Christ Archives.

47. W. Wallace Smith and Clifford A. Cole, "The Joint Council Studies World Church Objectives," *Saints' Herald* 114, no. 5 (March 1, 1967): 149.

48. *The Auditorium Log*, March 8, 1967. This was an internal publication to disseminate information to church headquarters' employees.

49. This material consisted of a twelve-page bibliography and 177 pages of articles from church periodicals and related sources. A copy of these materials is in a notebook titled "Joint Council Seminars" in the Community of Christ Archives.

50. P94 f223, Community of Christ Archives.

51. E. Dale Dunlap to Donald D. Landon, December 12, 1966, Donald Landon papers, Community of Christ Archives,.

52. E. Dale Dunlap to Donald D. Landon, February 17, 1967, RG 29-4 f2, Community of Christ Archives.

The schedule for the week was:

MONDAY: "The Mirror of History." Major questions addressed were: How do we do history? Are there different modes of truth? By what authority do we operate? Presentations were by Bangs, Dunlap, and Jones.

TUESDAY: "The Early Church and the World." Major questions addressed were: What was the intent of the early church? What did the early church consider central in its faith? How did church forms develop? What problems did the Constantinian crisis occasion? Presentations were by Bangs, assisted by Dunlap and Jones.

WEDNESDAY: "Protestantism and the World." Major questions addressed were: What did the major Reformation groups take to be their justification for coming into being? How did this affect the understanding and structure of the church? Presentations were by Bangs, assisted by Jones and Dunlap.

THURSDAY: "Church, Sect and the World." Major questions addressed were: What gave rise to Protestant sectarianism? What factors helped to shape this movement? How has this affected these churches? Presentations were by Dunlap, assisted by Bangs and Jones.

FRIDAY: "The Nature and Ministry of the Church in the World." Major questions addressed were: What is the church? What is the church's mission? How does the world affect the shape of the Church and Mission?[53] Presentations were by Jones, assisted by Bangs and Dunlap.

The month before this first seminar, President Maurice Draper communicated by interoffice memo to President Smith his thinking regarding who should preside and lead the sessions. Draper suggested that Smith should open the sessions and then ask President Duane Couey to direct the meetings, on account of Couey's role as chair of the steering committee that planned the seminar.[54] On the first day, President Smith opened the seminar by referring to the "Outline of Purpose for Joint Council Studies" distributed earlier saying he found it "lucid and quite complete." He continued: "The questions posed furnish springboards for discussion designed to head us to valid conclusions on which we can base our future course among religious bodies. We hope it will help determine what our posture s.[should] b.[be] as a religious entity. ... We hope our explorations will be productive."[55] Smith then turned the presiding role over to Couey.

Following a brief opening worship, input was provided each morning by the Saint Paul professors. Typed copies of their presentation papers and notes are lo-

---

53. "Orientation Seminar," Donald Landon papers, Community of Christ Archives.

54. M. L. Draper to W. Wallace Smith, February 6, 1967, RG 29-2 f133, Community of Christ Archives.

55. Taken from W. Wallace Smith's handwritten notes, P94 f227, Community of Christ Archives.

cated in the church archives.[56] Discussion of what had been presented occurred each afternoon. Presidents Smith and Couey, Apostles Ettinger and Tyree, Bishop Hansen, and Donald Landon took extensive and detailed notes.[57]

In August 1968 Duane Couey prepared a sixteen-page typed "Review of Joint Council Seminar Program." This summarized the subject matter addressed in all three 1967 Joint Council Seminars.[58] A Summary was shared with church members in the March 15, 1968, *Saints Herald*.[59] Couey later expanded his summary paper to include seminars held in the 1970s.[60]

Wading through the papers and notes from just the first seminar is a challenging and time-consuming task. It is beyond the space-limits of publication in the *JWHA Journal* for me to attempt even a summary of the more intriguing conversations. But I will recount one of the most significant and interesting pieces. During the first seminar, the presenters provided background that showed the RLDS church in a broader context than the previously dominant emphasis on the church having exclusive authority to represent Christ. On at least one occasion that week, the question was raised of whether the church was primarily focused on Jesus Christ or on the founder, Joseph Smith Jr. During the Thursday afternoon session, President Smith offered the following observation, quoted here from Alan Tyree's hand-written notes:

> [A] feeling that I picked up [is] whether or not there is a centrality of [Joseph Smith] or [Jesus Christ] in our [movement]. We do not hold [Joseph Smith] up as [the] central figure [of] our [movement]. . . . We believe [Joseph Smith] [was an] inspired servant [of] God, = one of a [number of movements] that came out of [the] same time— perhaps we feel like we have a little edge on others. . . . [Christ] is head [of the] church & not [Joseph Smith]: he was [the] instrument that gave rise to this particular belief.[61]

Immediately after this statement by Smith, guest presenter Paul Jones asked three questions:

   1. Is [Joseph Smith's] relationship to [the] RLDS faith [the] same kind as Luther's to Lutheranism?

---

56. See Donald Landon papers; see also W. Wallace Smith President Emeritus Papers, P94 f224, f227, f228, Community of Christ Archives.

57. These notes can be found in the Community of Christ Archives. See Alan D. Tyree "Joint Council Seminar on Theology #1 notebook,"; W. Wallace Smith President Emeritus Papers, P94 f227; Duane E. Couey Papers; Ettinger notes are found in black three-ring notebooks, "Joint Council Seminars" and "Joint Council Seminars Book 2," Francis Hansen's notes are in RG 28 f91; and Donald Landon Papers.

58. A copy can be found in P94 f227, Community of Christ Archives.

59. "Joint Council Seminars," *Saints' Herald* 115, no 5 (March 15, 1968): 16–17.

60. Duane E. Couey, "Historical Review of the Joint Council Seminar Program," September 1980, Duane Couey papers, Community of Christ Archives.

61. Alan D. Tyree, "Joint Council Seminar on Theology #1," handwritten notes, 53; notebook; Community of Christ Archives.

2. Do you see the Bible and [Book of Mormon] as equals, or [Christ] as [the] norm for evaluation of the [Book of Mormon] & [Doctrine and Covenants] as well as [the] Bible?

3. [Do you see the] Bible as [the] norm against which other scriptures are evaluated[?]

Tyree's notes indicate that President Smith answered "yes" to each question.[62]

Paul Jones later recalled an exchange on this topic at the seminar. He remembered asking W. Wallace Smith: "If our mutual studies of Christianity and the RLDS Church were to discover that there was a discrepancy between what Jesus taught and what Joseph Smith taught, which would you accept?" Jones recalled a profound silence settling in the room. He observed that "time stopped." Everyone seemed to understand the implications of the question. All eyes stared at the prophet, who took a long breath, did not falter, but said with poise: "We would have to go with Jesus." There was a great sigh of relief, recalled Jones. He concluded that W. Wallace's answer became the foundation for their work together from that point on.[63]

On March 20—ten days after the first seminar ended—Don Landon joined the planning committee to evaluate what had occurred. They agreed not to prepare a complete transcription of the proceedings but that Landon would attempt to obtain copies of as many of the presented papers as he could for those participants who would like them. The committee concluded that "the greatest value of the seminar was that it left a certain impression in the minds of all those who participated." It was also acknowledged that "in some instances there may have been a desire to express different points of view than those which seemed to predominate . . ." But it was agreed that "to open up these subjects again out of context would not be particularly helpful."[64]

At this same meeting, the committee identified two areas for consideration at future seminars: "evaluation of our church history" and "the church in the present-day world." The dates of November 26 to December 1, 1967, and January 8 to 12, 1968, were recommended for those seminars.[65]

Don Landon's summary of this meeting, preserved in his handwritten notes, includes Clifford Cole's observation that the three Saint Paul professors would not be the ones to provide input in the future seminars. Charles Neff referred to them

---

62. Tyree, 54.

63. Taken from an email from W. Paul Jones to Andrew Bolton, May 4, 2001. Quoted in Mark A. Scherer, *The Journey of a People: The Era of Worldwide Community, 1946 to 2015* (Independence, MO: Community of Christ Seminary Press, 2016), 296.

64. "Minutes" [of Committee on Theology, March 20, 1967], P94 f227, Community of Christ Archives.

65. "Minutes", P94 f227.

as "too ivory towered. Their concept of mission is too academic." However, Duane Couey thought "Dr. Jones can be helpful."[66]

Subsequently, Don Landon contacted the Saint Paul professors requesting copies of their papers and notes.[67] They were quick to oblige.[68] And in the case of Carl Bangs, he also sent copies of notes he took of the discussions among the joint council members following the presentations.[69]

At the end of the seminar, the three Saint Paul professors sent a letter to the joint council:

> We wish to express our very great appreciation to the Joint Council for your creativity and honesty in planning and executing the consultation of this week. As the guest participants we have been sensible of your genuine acceptance of us and of our presentations, and we have rejoiced in the openness of your receptivity and response. In providing this occasion in which we have wrestled together with the difficulties and challenges which face us all, you have placed us in your debt. We acknowledge the benefit which God has granted us as we have been knit together in the Christian community which has been embodied here this week, and we are now bound to you in the newnesss of the love of Christ which has been vouchsafed to us here together.
>
> Dated: March 10, 1967.   Signed: Carl Bangs, W. Paul Jones, E. Dale Dunlap[70]

On March 13, The First Presidency, in turn, sent letters of appreciation to the guest presenters as well as to Dr. Don Holter, Saint Paul president.[71] This exchange of letters suggests the collegiality and mutual benefit that was experienced by all parties.

The Second Seminar: November–December 1967

The steering committee composed of presidents Smith, Draper, and Couey and apostles Cole, Holmes, and Neff continued its work of planning the subsequent two seminars. The committee decided to invite Dr. Carl Bangs to be a resource at the seminar on church history and Dr. Paul Jones at the seminar on the church in the present-day world. The committee asked Don Landon to continue to serve as liaison

---

66. "Evaluation Session: March 20, 1967," Donald Landon papers, Community of Christ Archives.

67. Donald D. Landon to Dr. Dale Dunlap, March 22, 1967. Similar letters were sent to Drs. Bangs and Jones, Donald Landon Papers, Community of Christ Archives.

68. For example, see "Notes by W. Paul Jones 3/10/67," in "Joint Council Seminars," black notebook, Community of Christ Archives.

69. Donald Landon Papers, Community of Christ Archives.

70. Donald Landon Papers, Community of Christ Archives.

71. The First Presidency to Dr. Carl Bangs, March 13, 1967, RG 29-4 f2, Community of Christ Archives. Identical letters were sent to Drs. E. Dale Dunlap and W. Paul Jones. Also, The First Presidency to Dr. Don Holter, March 15, 1967.

FIGURE 7: *Second Seminar Speakers*

Robert Flanders   *Geoffrey Spencer*   *Richard Howard*

with the Saint Paul faculty.[72] Landon quickly requested that the two Saint Paul faculty members named be available.[73]

The committee selected three RLDS-member resource persons to join Carl Bangs in making presentations at the second seminar. These were Dr. Robert Flanders of the Ohio State University history faculty, Geoffrey Spencer, director of the RLDS Religious Education Department's Church School Division, and Richard Howard, RLDS church historian.[74] The committee invited Bangs, Howard, and Landon to be present for the entire week of meetings. Flanders and Spencer attended only those sessions where their presentations were considered.[75]

According to Landon's notes taken at a meeting of the steering committee immediately before the second seminar, Duane Couey observed: "After the seminar on church history we will be aware that the church in Utah is a logical extension & projection of Jos[eph] Smith's theology & thinking. The Reorg[anization] is an attempt to re-enter orthodox Christianity and carry into it those ideas which commend them-selves to us." At this meeting, the discussion, according to Landon, included the observation: "We have assumed that everyone is able and interested in intellectual & theological ruminations. We may need to learn that our people want to do something rather than believe something. Is it possible to express emerging

---

72. The First Presidency to Donald D. Landon, June 1, 1967, Donald Landon Papers, Community of Christ Archives.

73. Donald D. Landon to Dr. Dale Dunlap, June 16, 1967, Donald Landon Papers, Community of Christ Archives.

74. The First Presidency to Richard P. Howard, June 1, 1967, Donald Landon Papers, Community of Christ Archives.

75. Duane E. Couey to Members of the Joint Council, November 17, 1967, RG 29-4 f23, Community of Christ Archives.

theological viewpoints in concrete programs without asking everyone to know & accept the theological premises?"[76]

The agenda for the second seminar's week of meetings was:

MONDAY, NOVEMBER 27: morning: a general orientation for the week

TUESDAY AFTERNOON: input by Carl Bangs focused on the nineteenth-century situation to which the Latter Day Saint movement was related.[77]

TUESDAY, NOVEMBER 28: morning input by Geoffrey Spencer focused on the nature and significance of the church's founding experiences. Spencer gave particular attention to three aspects: "1. The relation of these experiences to the environment and temper of the times, 2. The connection between the founding experiences and the movement's understanding of authority, and 3. The significance of the founding experiences for the church today."[78]

TUESDAY AFTERNOON: input by Richard Howard focused on the theology of revelation held by the early church and its expression in the Book of Mormon, Doctrine and Covenants, and Inspired Version of the Bible.[79]

WEDNESDAY, NOVEMBER 29: input by Carl Bangs focused on the doctrinal development within the movement from its inception to the early twentieth century.[80]

THURSDAY, NOVEMBER 30: input by Robert Flanders focused on the historical roots of the idea of Zion in the early church. Flanders discussed approaches to Latter Day Saint historical studies, the kingdom and gathering in early Latter Day Saint history, and the kingdom of God in Nauvoo.[81]

FRIDAY, DECEMBER 1: input by Carl Bangs focused on the significance of historical heritage. How shall it be used? How can we achieve objectivity without repudiating our history?[82]

76. "Committee 11/22/67," Donald Landon Papers, Community of Christ Archives.

77. Carl Bangs, "Nineteenth Century Backgrounds of the Latter Day Saint Movement," P94 f224, Community of Christ Archives. This file also contains a number of other papers Bangs used and distributed to participants in his presentations during the second seminar.

78 Geoffrey Spencer, "Seminar Session, Tuesday morning, November 28," P94 f224, Community of Christ Archives.

79. Richard P. Howard, "Theology of Revelation Disclosed in the Origins and Development of Latter Day Saint Scriptures," P94 f224, Community of Christ Archives.

80. See papers by Bangs, P94 f224, Community of Christ Archives.

81. Flanders's papers used and distributed during this session were, "Propositions for Approaching Latter Day Saint Historical Studies," "Some Reflections on the Kingdom and the Gathering in Early Mormon History," and "The Kingdom of God in Illinois—Politics in Utopia," copies, P94 f224, Community of Christ Archives.

82. "Joint Council Seminar #2, Church History" [outline and schedule], Donald Landon Papers, Community of Christ Archives.

Each presentation was followed by discussion among the seminar participants. Notes of the discussions were taken by Alan Tyree, W. Wallace Smith and Richard Howard. As in the notes from the other two seminars, summaries of comments are identified by the initials of the speakers.[83]

As with the first seminar, resource persons prepared bibliographies of books and articles they recommended that participants read. Landon distributed these lists ahead of the seminar meetings. So that Bangs could be adequately prepared in terms of the historical background of the church, Landon asked Church Historian Howard to prepare a bibliography of books and articles to send to Bangs.[84]

This seminar, like the first, was brought to the attention of headquarters staff through an announcement in *The Auditorium Log*. Unlike the announcement of the first seminar, however, this description included mention of the resource persons by name and that Carl Bangs was on the faculty of Saint Paul. It was described as a seminar on church history.[85]

It is not known which joint council members completed the extensive recommended reading or how much of it they got through. Nor is it known, for the most part, what their reaction was to the books and articles they read. My search of the church archives did, however, discover one letter of interest. After receiving the reading list for the second seminar, Apostle Russell Ralston communicated to Don Landon his concern over one recommended volume: "My one hope is that the other books on the list will be more authoritatively documented than the one by Flanders. . . . he arrives at conclusions which can only be supported by very questionable Mormon history which the church has never accepted as factual and which I hope it never will." Ralston continued, "I deeply regret that we shall give this questionable book the implication of Joint Council approval by its use. . . . Frankly I can take the implications of the liberal theologians in better spirit than I can take this book."[86]

The Third Seminar: December 1967

Although the third seminar had been scheduled for January 1968, this was changed to December 1967 because the chosen resource person, Dr. W. Paul Jones from Saint Paul School of Theology, was unavailable for the January dates.[87] The

83. Alan D. Tyree, "Joint Council Seminar #2," notebook; W. Wallace Smith, P94 f224; Richard P. Howard, "Joint Council Seminar 1967," folder in Richard Howard Papers, Community of Christ Archives.

84. These lists are found in Donald Landon Papers, Community of Christ Archives.

85. *The Auditorium Log*, November 29, 1967.

86. Russell F. Ralston to Donald D. Landon, October 3, 1967, Donald Landon Papers, Community of Christ Archives.

87. Don Landon to Duane Couey, July 12, 1967, Duane Couey Papers, Community of Christ Archives.

steering committee had considered inviting additional resource people, but Jones felt it was better that he carry that responsibility entirely.[88]

This seminar carried the theme "The Church in the 20th Century," with the objective: "To explore the mission of the church in the contemporary world." Don Landon distributed to joint council members copies of two books Jones had recommended for this third seminar, both written by Colin Williams: *Where in the World?* and *What in the World?*

After introducing the principle that form follows function, Jones led the seminar through major theological categories according to two diverse approaches: evangelical or conservative Christianity and secular Christianity. This took most of the first two days. On Wednesday, Jones focused on the challenge of reaching a theological consensus in the then-current era of cultural crisis. This was followed by discussion of the technological revolution, automation, knowledge and population explosions, leisure, generational crises, and the issue of power and the human tendency toward idolatry.[89]

The Thursday sessions highlighted Zion as theonomous community: dynamic and integrally connected with society. Paul Jones challenged the joint council to look for new creative ways for Zion to become real in signal communities.[90] He emphasized the need for membership education, a new religious education program, seminary programs, and continuing education for joint council members. Jones's concluding statement that day called for three things:

1. A First Presidency Pronouncement giving a clear and compelling vision of Zion as a "kairoi," or "intoxicating symbol" to move the church beyond lethargy to a "Christ transforming culture posture."

2. A clear and consistent program of education including the work of the Basic Beliefs Committee, new religious education material, an RLDS seminary house in connection with an outside institution, and continuing education for leaders.

3. All of this focuses in Mission—in the world and with the world, not apart from it.[91]

On the concluding day, Friday, Jones suggested there was a "mandate to the First Presidency by the Joint Council to give clear and charismatic leadership." He suggested the presidency prepare a list of action items from the Joint Council to present

88. Don Landon to Maurice Draper, December 11, 1967, Duane Couey Papers, Community of Christ Archives.

89. Typed outline summaries of Monday, Tuesday and Wednesday sessions, Duane Couey Papers, Community of Christ Archives.

90. Typed outline summary of Thursday session, Duane Couey Papers, Community of Christ Archives.

91. "Summary of Statement Made Thursday by W. P. Jones" in "Joint Council Seminar #3, softcover notebook, Community of Christ Archives.

to a future council session for decision on follow-up. Next Jones called for several theological affirmations including that incarnation is the key paradigm of revelation, that the Joseph Smith event is an illumination of Jesus Christ—transparent and not opaque or idolatrous—and that the church should communicate the ecumenical dimension of Christian faith.

Jones went on to enumerate a number of practical implications of the theological affirmations, including the need to de-Americanize missions abroad.[92]

This seminar was also announced to headquarters staff. The description included the name Dr. Paul Jones of Saint Paul as resource person. It was described as a seminar on the church in the twentieth century.[93]

Seminar Follow-up

On January 16, 1968, just three-and-a-half weeks after the end of the third seminar, the presidency sent a draft of a proposed communication to the elders of the church to the heads of the two other quorums involved in the seminars: Clifford Cole and Walter Johnson. The presidency asked for suggestions to be returned to them as quickly as possible.[94] Making few if any changes, the First Presidency sent this communication summarizing what had occurred in the seminars to the elders under the date of January 1968. This was published in the March 15, 1968, issue of the *Saints' Herald*.[95] These communications offered four affirmations to summarize the seminar conclusions; they bore a resemblance to the emphases Paul Jones had made on the last day of the third seminar:

1. The great and central revelation of the gospel of Jesus Christ is what God has done in him for the sake of mankind.
2. The witness of the prophet Joseph Smith is an illumination of God's revelation in Jesus Christ.
3. Scripture of all kinds is not the primary truth itself. It is the inspired interpretation of the great central truth which is found in the meaning of the Incarnation.
4. Zion is seen as the corporate life of the faithful in communities wherever they may be.[96]

---

92. "Joint Council Seminar III, Friday, December 22, 1967, typed Outline Summary of Jones's presentation, Duane Couey Papers, Community of Christ Archives.

93. *The Auditorium Log,* December 20, 1967.

94. The First Presidency to Apostle C. A. Cole and Bishop Walter N. Johnson, January 16, 1968, RG 29-4 f23, Community of Christ Archives.

95. "Joint Council Seminars," *Saints' Herald* 115, no. 6 (March 15, 1968): 16–17.

96. "Joint Council Seminars," 17.

Immediately after the conclusion of the third seminar, the presidency invited each member of the joint council to communicate his suggestions for implementation. In opening a meeting to receive suggestions, President Smith said: "We are charged with doing something concrete about the matters we have considered over the past three seminars. We are charged with implementing what we have talked about." All seventeen members offered suggestions. Included were those of Don Landon and Paul Jones.[97] It is unclear whether these two individuals were present at the meeting or had offered their suggestions separately.

The suggestions for follow up were numerous and varied. Couey's list contained seventeen distinct items and Jones's and Landon's were extensive. It is impossible within the scope of this paper to either present a complete list or to even highlight the suggestions that came from the largest number of participants. However, it is possible to say joint council members were very aware that if their deliberations were to have impact on the church they would need to work diligently on helping local church leaders and members catch the importance of the conclusions they had reached—conclusions that defined a new identity and mission for the church. A widespread educational program would be essential.

The April 1968 world conference provided an opportunity for church leaders to share the outcome of the seminars. The First Presidency's report to the conference shared information about the seminars, including the four conclusions published earlier in the March 15 *Saints' Herald*. These were preceded by reference to the need to "gain a better understanding of the world and the church's mission in it." The report made reference to the use of resource persons but did not give their names or any indication of their association with a local seminary.[98] President W. Wallace Smith made reference to the seminars in his conference sermon delivered on March 31, 1968. He indicated that in their studies, the joint council had "moved in the spirit of the School of the Prophets by searching for truth, light, and understanding."[99] The seminars were also mentioned in the Council of Twelve report to the conference.[100]

---

97. [untitled], "SMITH: We are charged . . . ;" From these notes it is obvious they were taken at a meeting of the joint council. But no date is given. The following are lists of suggestions prepared individually by those named: Duane E. Couey, "Program Recommendations Growing Out of Joint Council Seminar III," dated 12/28/67; Earl T. Higdon, "Education, Research and Development," undated; Alan Tyree, [untitled], "1. For our immediate attention, . . ." 22 December 1967; Reed M. Holmes, "Suggested procedure:," undated; and Fred L. Young to The First Presidency, December 26, 1967, RG 29-4 f23, Community of Christ Archives. Young was the world church secretary at the time. There is no evidence that he attended any of the seminar sessions.

98. "Report of the First Presidency," *World Conference Bulletin*, April 1, 1968, 222–23. Reprinted in *Saints' Herald* 115, no. 9 (May 15, 1968): 8–9.

99. W. Wallace Smith, "Men Are that They Might Have Joy," *World Conference Bulletin*, April 1, 1968, 210. Reprinted in *Saints' Herald* 115, no. 9 (May 15, 1968): 14.

100. 1968 "Council of Twelve," "To the Presidency and World Conference," *World Conference Reports*, 66; reprinted in "Report of the Council of Twelve," *Saints' Herald* 115, no. 9 (May 15, 1968): 12–13.

The July 1, 1968, *Saints' Herald* carried a photo of the Council of Twelve and Council of Presidents of Seventy meeting on May 8–10 that year for the purpose of giving "the presidents an opportunity to explore with the Twelve some of the implications of the recent Joint Council Seminars."[101] The church archives do not seem to contain any record of this meeting.

The years 1967 and 1968 were busy ones for Donald D. Landon, director of the church's Religious Education Department. Not only did he carry primary responsibility for arranging the three joint council seminars, but his department was in the middle of preparing for a new church school curriculum. During these years, under Landon's direction, his staff wrote drafts of "position papers" that were reviewed by their peers at staff meetings in preparation for consideration and response by the Curriculum Consultation Committee.[102] An interesting overlap between the joint council seminars and the preparation of position papers was the involvement of Dr. Carl Bangs of Saint Paul School of Theology. On at least one paper topic—revelation—he was asked to meet with the Religious Education Department staff for consultation.[103]

Richard Howard, in the second volume of his *The Church Through the Years*, comments on the connection between the seminars and the new curriculum: "Hand in glove with the Joint Council seminars, preparation for the new curriculum involved looking at some of the same issues from an educational perspective." Howard adds: "Questions addressed by the five objectives of 1966 and the resulting Joint Council seminars illuminated issues of theology, church history, mission, and scriptural interpretation for the curriculum planning process."[104]

And as previously mentioned, January 1968 saw the first of the monthly serialization of the work of the Basic Beliefs Committee with an article on "God the Father."[105] An introductory statement to the series, authored by committee chair Clifford Cole, appeared on the editorial page of that issue of the *Saints' Herald*. This editorial referenced the new "Statement of Belief" that provided the basis for the series of articles.[106] The resulting work carried a distinctly ecumenical and mainstream Christian flavor and was therefore compatible with the direction of the church being identified in the work of the joint council seminars. This Christ-centered, rather than RLDS church-centered emphasis could also be found in the new *Church School*

101. *Saints' Herald* 115, no. 13 (July 1, 1968): 7.

102. Copies of these papers and correspondence related thereto are found in P111 f88, f89, f90, and f91, Community of Christ Archives.

103. Don Landon to Executive Staff, January 22, 1968, P111 f90, Community of Christ Archives.

104. Richard P. Howard, *The Church Through the Years*, vol. 2: "The Reorganization Comes of Age, 1860–1992" (Independence, MO: Herald Publishing House, 1993), 365–66.

105. Basic Beliefs Committee, "God the Father," *Saints' Herald* 115, no. 1 (January 1, 1968): 17–20.

106. Clifford A. Cole, "Basic Beliefs Series," *Saints' Herald* 115, no. 1 (January 1, 1968): 3.

Handbook announced on that same editorial page.[107] In this book's introduction, Religious Education Department Director Don Landon said religious education

> is not disseminating information. Rather, it is the process of creating new persons in Christ Jesus. Such a process may well include careful consideration of our traditions and history but not as ends in themselves. Such material must be a tool facilitating the personal encounter of the learner and God in an experience of revelation. In such an experience the learner learns of himself and of God's will for him. Such an encounter issues in growth and change.[108]

Such an approach to the role of the church school was much different from what had previously dominated RLDS materials and congregations. It would fit well with the image of the church that emerged from the seminars and could be found in the new basic beliefs statement.

Perhaps ironically this same issue of the *Herald* included an article by Presiding Evangelist Roy Cheville on the church's distinctives—a dearly cherished theme among more conservative members, those resistant to change.[109]

The Aftermath

Throughout the 1960s a number of RLDS members in the United States and other western nations were sensing that some church leaders and other individuals were supporting a move away from the church seeing itself as the only body authoritatively representing Christ in the world—the "one true church" compared to all others. These persons felt the church's true identity was being threatened and they became suspicious of church leaders, their motives and actions.

The papers and discussions from the 1967 Joint Council seminars were not made available for church members' review and the summaries made available through the *Herald* lacked specifics. However, in 1968 and on into 1969, the work of the Basic Beliefs Committee published in the *Saints' Herald* was found to lack emphasis on the distinctives so near and dear to conservative members. This bothered some.[110] But even more distressing to traditional members was what they read when they got their hands on leaked copies of the position papers developed in preparation for the new church school curriculum. Although the Curriculum Consultation Committee had been told the papers were confidential, they were duplicated and circulated quite widely. The papers addressed modes of revelation, the nature of scripture, the value

107. Geoffrey Spencer, "New Church School Handbook" *Saints' Herald* 115, no. 1 (January 1, 1968): 3.

108. Department of Religious Education, *Church School Handbook* (Independence, MO: Herald Publishing House), 14.

109. Roy A. Cheville, "What Distinctives Count Today?," *Saints' Herald* 115, no. 1 (January 1, 1968): 8–10, 25.

110. D. E. C [Duane E. Couey], "The Purpose of the Basic Beliefs Series," *Saints' Herald* 115, no. 5 (March 1, 1968): 3.

of the Book of Mormon, church history, the nature of the church, Zion, the role of Christian education, and other topics.[111] They suggested that some traditional views on these subjects should not be included in the new church school curriculum.

Suspicion that new ideas were being promoted can be seen in a resolution adopted by the Center Stake of Zion Conference on November 19, 1967, for consideration at the next world conference. The resolution resolved: "We affirm that the Inspired Version of the Bible, Authorized [1908 edition] Book of Mormon, and the Doctrine and Covenants are the scriptures of the [church] and any teachings, writings, or activities that are not consistent with these scriptures shall not be tolerated in the church, its organizations, publications, or institutions."[112] Publication of this resolution created a lively exchange in the "Letters" column of subsequent issues of the *Herald*.[113] At the April 1968 World Conference, after this resolution was called up for consideration, two substitute resolutions were offered. However, the matter was disposed of when a resolution to table the matter was adopted.[114]

Evidence that church leaders were intending to minimize or remove cherished church distinctives was now in people's hands. Some saw this movement to have originated with the non-RLDS resource persons who had provided input at the joint council seminars: professors from the Methodist-sponsored Saint Paul School of Theology. With the April 1968 world conference now passed, troubled members looked to the 1970 conference to make their point.

A delegate to this conference asked from the floor for information to be provided on any payments made by the Religious Education Department for outside consultants.[115] Don Landon responded that no funds from the Religious Education Department budget had been paid to Dr. Paul Jones or any other consultants.[116] On a follow-up question, Chairman Draper said,

> We know of no fees paid to Dr. Paul Jones or others under the circumstances you described.... Prior to this ... inter-Conference period, the Joint Council did call in some consultants for which we paid the school. . . . we did pay some modest fees for some consultations during the Joint Council seminars which were reported to the church.[117]

---

111. "Position Papers," P11 f88, Community of Christ Archives.

112. "RLDS Scriptures," *Saints' Herald* 115, no. 2 (January 15, 1968): 3.

113. See "Letters" columns in *Saints' Herald* 115, no. 2 (January 15, 1968): 2; *Herald* 115, no. 4 (February 15, 1968): 4–5; *Herald* 115, no. 5 (March 1, 1968): 5, 26; and *Herald* 115: no. 7 (April 1, 1968): 5.

114. *World Conference Bulletin*, April 7, 1968, 285.

115. "Official Minutes of Business Session, Wednesday, April 8, 1970," *World Conference Bulletin*, April 9, 1970, 292.

116. *World Conference Transcript*, April 8, 1970, 151.

117. *Conference Transcript*, 152.

However, the matter did not end there. Additional information was leaked from the church's confidential files: confirmation that Jones had been paid directly by the church. According to Richard Price, this documentation was a copy of a check from the church made payable to Paul Jones for his services as a seminar consultant.[118] Word of this evidence spread around the conference causing President Draper to read a prepared statement to the conference on April 11. Here he acknowledged he had previously spoken from memory and was at that time unaware of the payment directly to Jones. He lamented that confidential information about the payment had been leaked and how this constituted a "serious breach of trust."[119] Following his statement, Draper recognized presiding bishop Walter Johnson for an additional statement. In it Johnson supported Draper and indicated "that an investigation will be made into the matter of divulging confidential information and that appropriate measures will be taken."[120]

Church records show that a check for $1870 was paid to Saint Paul for the services of professors Bangs, Dunlap, and Jones at the March 1967 seminar.[121] A further $500 was paid to Carl Bangs for the second seminar, and the same to Paul Jones for the third.[122] A total of $108.20 was paid to Robert Flanders to cover his expenses in getting from his home in Ohio to Independence and back for the second seminar.[123] The funds were approved by the joint council to come from the church's Missionary Reserve Fund.[124] This total expense of $2,858.20 was reported to the 1968 World Conference in the report of the Presiding Bishopric with the description "Joint Council Seminar."[125] No payments were made to Geoffrey Spencer and Richard Howard as they were church employees.

118. Richard Price, *Saints at the Crossroads* (Independence, MO: Richard Price, 1974), 201.

119. "Official Minutes of Business Session April 11, 1970, *World Conference Bulletin* April 12, 1970, 325; *Bulletin*, Final Issue, 1970, 338–40.

120. "Official Minutes of Business Session April 11, 1970," *World Conference Bulletin*, April 12, 1970, 325–26. The full transcript of Johnson's remarks is in *1970 World Conference Transcript*, April 11, 1970, 353–54.

121. Donald D. Landon to President Duane Couey, March 8, 1967; Duane E. Couey to Dr. E. Dale Dunlap, April 18, 1967, Donald Landon Papers, Community of Christ Archives.

122. Carl Bangs to Donald D. Landon, November 2, 1967; The First Presidency to Dr. Carl Bangs, November 22, 1967, RG 29-4 f23, Community of Christ Archives. General Ledger records, "Joint Council Seminar," Community of Christ Fiscal Services Office, copy in author's possession.

123. Robert Flanders to Mr. Donald D. Landon, December 15, 1967; The First Presidency to The Presiding Bishopric, December 28, 1967; W. N. Johnson to Dr. Robert Flanders, January 5, 1968, Donald Landon Papers, Community of Christ Archives.

124. The subcommittee on the seminar in theology to The First Presidency, March 9, 1967; W. Wallace Smith to The Joint Council, March 21, 1967; W. Wallace Smith to The Joint Council, November 15, 1967. See "Joint Council Minutes," March 21, 1967 and November 21, 1967, Community of Christ Archives.

125. "Missionary Reserve Fund Balance Sheet, December 31, 1966 and 1967," *World Conference Bulletin*, March 31, 1968, 184.

Brief mention should be made here that in *Saints at the Crossroads*, Richard Price, a strong opponent of change in the church, laid much of the blame for changes on the influence of Saint Paul School of Theology professors through their role as consultants at the joint council seminars and in their other contacts with church leaders. He also pointed to their influence on church headquarters staff members who had attended that school as students. Price believed these professors were instrumental in changing the church into a "Protestant denomination."[126]

Unlike Bill Russell who believes Price was right, I disagree with Price on almost everything. But I must admit that reading parts of his book did help me organize sections of this paper and even point to a few sources I might not have otherwise found. The copy of his book

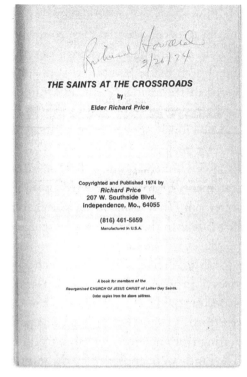

FIGURE 8: *Title page of Richard Price book*

I used is in the Community of Christ headquarters library. Interestingly enough it has the autograph of Richard Howard on the title page, along with the date 3/26/74, the year of its publication. Dick must have run quickly to obtain a copy as soon as he heard it was available. But the absence of any other markings on the book's pages leads me to wonder if he ever read it. Well! I never thought I, or anyone else for that matter, would mention Russell, Howard, and Price in the same paragraph.

While considering those joint council members who were participants in the seminars, I find myself identifying three great thinkers of the church who were not there. First is F. Henry Edwards, mentioned earlier as the author of *Fundamentals*, the book that strongly influenced the members for three decades before the seminars. General officer in the church for forty-four years, Edwards also influenced members through his other writings and speaking. He had retired less than a year before the first seminar and so was not invited to attend.[127] Second is Arthur Oakman, apostle

126. Price, *Saints at the Crossroads*, iv.

127. For an overview of Edwards's life, his contributions as a church leader, and a complete list of his publications see Paul M. Edwards, *F. Henry Edwards: Articulator for the Church* (Independence, MO: Herald Publishing House, 1995).

for twenty-six years, whose writing and preaching was rivaled by none in their appeal to members across the church. He was retired from the twelve in 1964 at the young age of fifty-nine.[128] These two leaders, both British by birth and upbringing, were largely self-educated but widely read.

Third is Roy Cheville, since 1958 presiding patriarch of the church. By contrast, Cheville was an academic with a PhD in religion from the University of Chicago and was a longtime faculty member in religion at the church's Graceland College.[129] Elbert A. Smith, his predecessor under the presidencies of Frederick M. Smith and Israel A. Smith, attended a number of joint council meetings.[130] But Cheville, under W. Wallace Smith, was never included and not invited to the seminars. Like Edwards and Oakman, he was a prolific writer, his books and articles having wide influence. Richard Lancaster credited Cheville's 1942 doctoral dissertation[131] as being "the key to the beginning of the transformation of the RLDS Church."[132]

We can only speculate what difference the presence of these three men might have made in the discussions. But these three giants had made their contributions, and their impact continued for years to come. 1967 was a new time with new leadership and new ideas.

However, former general officers of the church were kept informed of what was going on in the church, including actions of the joint council. For example, the First Presidency included a lengthy paragraph on the first seminar in their March 1967 letter to retired joint council members.[133]

The Significance of the Seminars

I wish now to present some observations of seminar participants from each one's later recollections. These are taken from their oral histories and other reflections.

128. For an overview of Oakman's life, his contributions as a church leader, and a complete list of his publications see Maurice L. Draper, *Arthur A. Oakman: An Artist with Words* (Independence, MO: Herald Publishing House, 1997).

129. For an overview of Cheville's life, his contributions as a church leader, and a complete list of his publications see Malcolm L. Ritchie, *Roy Cheville: the Patriarch Years* (Lamoni, IA: Center for Christian Leadership, Graceland College, 1997).

130. See "Joint Council Minutes," 1938 to 1958, Community of Christ Archives.

131. Published by the RLDS church as *The Role of Religious Education in the Accommodation of a Sect* (Independence, MO: Herald House, 1942).

132. Richard B. Lancaster, "The Gathering Storm Part 1: 1954 to 1966: An Insider's View of the Transition from Sect to Denomination within the Reorganized Church of Jesus Christ of Latter Day Saints," *Restoration Studies* 14 (2013): 17.

133. The First Presidency to Elder F. Henry Edwards, March 28, 1967, RG 29-2 f133, Community of Christ Archives. The copy of this letter in the archives indicates the same letter was sent to retired general officers G. L. DeLapp, C. R. Hield, D. B Jensen, P. E. Farrow, R. E. Davey, E. J. Gleazer Sr., H. L. Livingston, and A. A. Oakman. It appears that this kind of update was sent monthly to retired general officers, based on similar letters for other months of 1967 found in the same file.

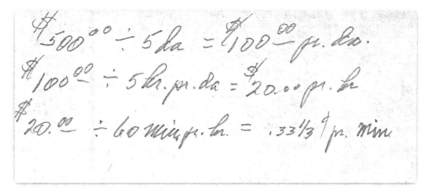

FIGURE 9: *W. Wallace Smith's calculations*

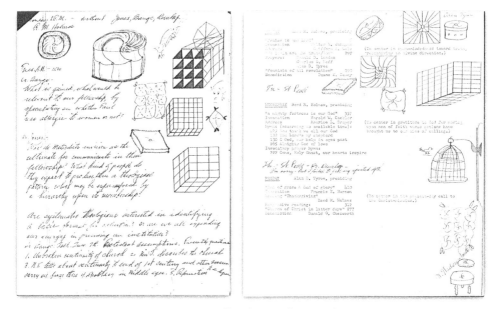

FIGURE 10: *Doodles of W. Wallace Smith*

President W. Wallace Smith

New members of the Joint Council felt that we needed to approach our theology in an organized manner.

. . . we were advised that seminars utilizing outside personnel would be a helpful way to see ourselves.

. . . we didn't lose any members of the Joint Council over the seminar studies. . . . The overwhelming majority of our church membership, after they finally understood what we were trying to do, were agreeable to the fact that we had made these kinds of studies. . . .

I had a little slip of paper . . . that evidently indicated how much we were paying one of these consultants . . . $500 for five days . . .[equals] a hundred dollars a day . . .

for five hours a day was [makes] $20 per hour ... [that] equals 33 1/3 cents per minute. There were people that questioned whether or not we were getting our money's worth. ... I think we did. ... This was just another doodle, I guess, along with other things to occupy my mind when I wasn't particularly interested in what was going on."[134]

Asked if he thought the seminars had brought theological consensus among the Joint Council, Smith responded, "I'd say that maybe we got seven-and-a-half out of ten."[135]

President Maurice L. Draper

I think the whole series of seminars was very significant. It did a great deal to break us out of traditional modes of thinking and to give new meaning to our heritage.

... there's nothing about these seminars that caused us to reject our heritage or to debunk it.[136] It is not surprising that for many of us these sessions produced some tensions. In retrospect, however, that tension was alleviated in the remarkable spirit of good fellowship that developed."[137]

President Duane E. Couey

we realized ... in many cases our understanding of the Christian church was very distorted and inaccurate. We realized that doctrine should not be absolutized, or ecclesiology nor any thing else that had been traditionally absolutized by church members over the years, but that the only thing that is worthy of universalizing is God, and the implications of this in Christ and His mission. ...

The simple, fundamentalist doctrine and historical tradition that had characterized our stance for many years as a church, literally fell apart at that time. ...

Our general officers needed up-dating in their education, particularly in theological matters ...

The entire Joint Council needed to go through some kind of experience which would open us to the areas of understanding that we needed to acquire, but also in the process to bring a unity about our purposes and our work that had never been present in the Joint Council before. ... Wallace's support of that whole endeavor was excellent."[138]

Apostle Charles Neff

in reference to the first of the five 1966 objectives: "We said, 'How can the membership of the church become unified in the faith except the leaders shall first become unified in

---

134. W. Wallace Smith, "An Oral History Memoir," 119, 124, Keith Henry, interviewer, June 3, 1980, Community of Christ Archives.

135. Smith, "An Oral History Memoir," 125.

136. Maurice L. Draper, "An Oral History Memoir," 646, L. D. Harsin, interviewer, June 6, 1984, Community of Christ Archives.

137. Maurice L. Draper, "Footnotes" vol. 3, 154, Acc. #8699, Community of Christ Archives.

138. Duane E. Couey, "An Oral History Memoir," 144, 202, 209, 215, L. D. Harsin, interviewer, November 7, 1991, February 5, 1992, Community of Christ Archives.

the faith?' And we were very sober in our recognition of the fact that we were not unified in the faith."[139]

What we did in the Joint Council Seminars would have been absolutely impossible in previous Joint Councils.

. . . the church was probably losing its witness quality [and] had to update its approach to the world, its understanding of the world."[140]

Bishop Walter Johnson

There was a need for education on the part of the Joint Council. The men had gone their separate ways before, and they had not come to any great unity, and so there was divergence among them.

. . . most of the Joint Council just listened. None of them seemed to have any great convictions about what they believed. . . .

The move, of course, was to liberalize the church, it seemed to me"[141]

Bishop Francis E. "Pat" Hansen

I had some problems with the seminars in the 1960s. . . . My concern was the need to have balance. We brought Dr. Carl Bangs and Dr. Jones and others to make presentations. . . . We had men like Brother [F. Henry] Edwards, Henry Livingston, Roy Cheville, Arthur Oakman, and others available. I think their participation would have balanced the presentations made . . .[142]

I think . . . we were trying to make a change in the course of the church too rapidly. I think it needs to be done slowly."[143]

Apostle Don Lents

I can well remember Paul Jones telling the Council that we ought to recognize what we really have and should not hesitate in sharing this conviction in our preaching, teaching, and testimony. He counseled us not to be ashamed of our message.

. . . there were some thoughts shared that I had a most difficult time working into my theology and thinking."[144]

---

139. Charles D. Neff, "An Oral History Memoir," 85, Keith Henry, interviewer, December 18, 1980, Community of Christ Archives.

140. Neff, "An Oral History Memoir," 87.

141. Walter N. Johnson, "An Oral History," 102, L. D. Harsin, interviewer, October 17, 1972, Community of Christ Archives.

142. Francis E. "Pat" Hansen, "An Oral History Memoir," 230, Paul M. Edwards, interviewer, May 4, 1995, Community of Christ Archives.

143. Hansen, "An Oral History Memoir," 229–30.

144. Donald V. Lents, "An Oral History Memoir," 142, March Scherer, interviewer, October 29, 1966, Community of Christ Archives.

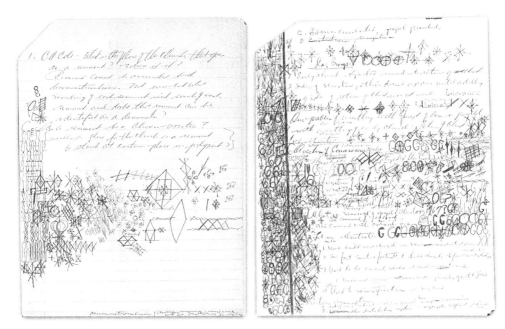

FIGURE 11: *Doodles of Pat Hansen*

Apostle Clifford Cole

Many of the members of the twelve did not feel the same need for the seminars that some of us did.

. . . the ultimates for us are really the ultimate faith in God and the ultimate faith in the worth of human persons.

The seminars were part of a very big movement that was growing and happening in the church.

. . . the seminars opened up the thinking of general church officers.

. . . if we could bring some unity and understanding and mutual support at the level of the Joint Council that was the first step in helping to unify the rest of the church.[145]

Apostle Will Timms

The contribution those seminars made for us was that, in my judgment, if we would listen to what was being said it would cause us to evaluate more carefully our sense of mission, our purpose, and our theologican [sic] foundations. I think that was a benefit.

I had a deep appreciation for the contribution of particularly Carl [Bangs] from St. Paul's . . . he did challenge our leaders to a broader perspective.

I found [the seminars] stimulating."[146]

---

145. Clifford A, Cole, "Oral History," 128, 130, 132, 133, Keith Henry, interviewer, September 15, 1980, Community of Christ Archives.

146. William E. Timms, "Interview #8," June 18, 1981, Tom Mountenay, interviewer, Oral History Interview Collection, Community of Christ Archives.

Apostle Alan Tyree

I have fond memories. I welcomed the seminars due to the different theological positions within the joint council. They addressed questions I had: What is our place within Christianity: mainstream or not? What should our mission be? Bangs and Jones assured us we were in the mainstream. And Jones said "Your concept of Zion intrigues me—keep pursuing it. You are advantaged as your top leaders are liberal and can lead change."

I heard no criticism of the seminars from council members, although I suspect some were uncomfortable.

Although there was no formal follow-up, we were affirmed and felt confident in moving ahead in new directions.[147]

Donald Landon

I was astonished during the seminars to see the role [President Smith] took in them. Probably no one at the seminar took more notes than President Smith.

There were several members of the Joint Council who I'm sure struggled very hard with some of the content presented during the seminar. They did not respond openly hostile or react in any overt ways during the discussions but there were nuances in the breaks and so forth that made it apparent that some of them listened with a great deal of skepticism.[148]

Paul Jones made efforts to build bridges between traditional Christianity and the RLDS.

Clifford Cole was strategically reserved. He contributed little but gained much.

Wallace Smith was uncomfortable. Much seemed new to him.[149]

. . . so far as the Joint Council is concerned, I don't think there was that much progress made toward either clarifying or unifying.

The production of [the] position papers and their reading and discussion by the curriculum consultation committee subsequently was to my knowledge the only concrete, constructive result of the seminar sessions.

. . . the Joint Council itself . . . never did really come to terms with what happened in that seminar. . . . much of the conflict that has resulted over the [Religious Education] department's work has been caused by virtue of the fact that the Joint Council never did come to any conclusions about what it heard in the seminars, any formal conclusions.[150]

Robert Flanders

I'm sure I must have been elated to be invited.

147. Interview with Alan Tyree, September 7, 2017.

148. Donald D. Landon, "An Oral History Memoir," 96, 97, Daniel T. Muir, interviewer, June 9, 1970, Community of Christ Archives.

149. Interview with Donald Landon, August 31, 2017

150. Donald D. Landon, "An Oral History Memoir," 98, 99.

I have absolutely no recollection of having been asked to give a paper, or having delivered a paper.

I have very particular memory of Dr. Bangs and his presentation. . . . He was an extremely skillful man . . . it was a *tour de force*, a masterful presentation. . . . The man himself was gracious, appropriately self-effacing in a difficult situation. . . . He handled himself beautifully.

It was a lovely experience for me. . . . I'm sure I felt vindicated. . . .I felt that I had ruled myself out of the intellectual fellowship of the church. . . . my feeling [was] . . . well, **I was invited**. I did not experience anything there but the kindest, most friendly fellowship.[151]

Richard Howard

Carl Bangs . . . gave us some very good insights into our own history and theology by just looking at it from the outside; [as] an informed outsider, who understood something of the Latter Day Saint movement in the cultural context of North America in the nineteenth century. So that was a very valuable experience for me, to hear that coming from him.

. . . . the discussion was engaged in by a minority of members of the Joint Council. . . . we heard from [Draper, Couey, Cole, and Neff] rather frequently. . . .

I . . . thought, President Smith isn't that interested in the history of the church. He never said very much at all through that whole [church history] seminar.[152]

After I had completed my presentation at the seminar, we took a break. I was packing up the projector I had used and, while passing close to me, W. Wallace Smith said, "Well, I'm sure glad this nonsense is over." I simply responded, "Me, too."[153] Apostle Timms was not happy with what happened in the seminars.[154]

Paul Jones

We started out guarded and tentative because we didn't know each other. Then things became easier.

The Joint Council members were very receptive; they seemed to be hungering for permission to reflect on the possibilities.

It was like the RLDS Vatican II; we were the catalysts giving permission for them to dream.

Wallace was dignified and quiet; he didn't talk much. He was like a Sphinx— you didn't know what he was thinking. Anything he might say would be seen as a pronouncement.[155]

---

151. Robert Bruce Flanders, "An Oral History Memoir," 132. Barbara J. Bernauer, interviewer, January 16, 2004, Community of Christ Archives.

152. Richard P. Howard, "An Oral History Memoir," 153–54, 155, 156. L. D. Harsin, interviewer, January 24, 1995, Community of Christ Archives.

153. Interview with Richard P. Howard, August 29, 2017.

154. Interview with Richard P. Howard, 2017.

155. Interview with Paul Jones, August 31, 2017.

A Fourth Seminar?

Although not usually included as part of the trio of 1967 seminars, a fourth seminar, held in May 1968, must surely be considered in relationship with them, because of its theme: "What We Believe." This seminar included all seventeen Joint Council members who had attended the previous three plus the new apostle who had, at the April 1968 World Conference, filled the vacancy in the twelve: Howard S. Sheehy Jr. No resource people were used at this fourth seminar.

This seminar, like the previous three, was held in the Auditorium music room. It lasted from Monday morning, May 13, through Friday noon, May 17. The format was also similar to that of the previous seminars: presentation of papers followed by discussion. After a quick review of the content of the three 1967 seminars[156] and worship each day, the topics addressed were:

"What We Believe About God," by Apostle Earl T. Higdon

"What We Believe About Man, by Apostle Russell F. Ralston

"What We Believe About Christ," by Apostle Clifford A. Cole"

What We Believe About the Church," by Apostle Charles D. Neff

"What We Believe About Scripture," by Apostle Cecil R. Ettinger

"What We Believe About Zion," by President Maurice L. Draper, and

"How Do We Communicate Our Understanding." by Apostle Reed M. Holmes[157]

Notes taken at this seminar by President Smith, Bishop Johnson, and Apostle Tyree can be found in the church archives.[158]

Conclusion

I may disappoint some when I confess that I cannot offer a crisp summary of the impact of the 1967 Joint Council seminars on the church, either in the years immediately following 1967 or at any time in the last fifty years. Instead I will conclude by going back to the words of one of the vital change agents of the 1960s: Charles Neff. For I know of no greater cause driving leaders to examine the church's theology,

---

156. Walter N. Johnson, handwritten notes of the May 13–17, 1968 seminar, P67 f51, Community of Christ Archives.

157. "Agenda for Joint Council Seminar IV," in Alan D. Tyree, "Joint Council Seminar #4 on What We Believe" [notebook], Community of Christ Archives.

158. W. Wallace Smith notes in P94 f227, f228; Walter N. Johnson notes in P67 f51; Alan D. Tyree notes in Tyree, "Joint Council Seminar #4," Community of Christ Archives.

history, and mission in the 1960s than the start of the church in the Orient, led by Neff. In a November 1967 *Saints' Herald* article, "What Shall We Teach?" he said: "A prophetic church is one that discerns the signs of the times and speaks to the present age. Prophetic ministry is possible only on these terms. It must be a work of mission rather than revivalism. It must acknowledge that God is creator of the universe and not the God only of the church." Neff went on, "The prophetic church must speak to [the world's] needs." In referring to Christ announcing his own mission in Luke 4:18–19, Neff asserted, "This is the mission of the church also."[159] This affirmation portended what recently has become Community of Christ's byline: "Christ's Mission, Our Mission."[160]

We are who we are today in Community of Christ because of much of what preceded us. This church's identity, mission, and message would not now be centered on following and serving Christ had we been unwilling to listen to Neff's observation from almost fifty years ago: "We must expect the church to change, because the entire world is changing."[161] I wonder where we will be fifty years from now. I just know I will not be around to see it.

PETER JUDD is s native of England and has lived in the USA for the last 56 years. He holds degrees from Graceland University, the University of Kansas, and Saint Paul School of Theology from which he earned the MDiv and DMin. Peter served as a world church minister for Community of Christ for 34 years including as a member of that church's Council of Twelve Apostles and First Presidency before retiring in 2005. He has written ten books published by the church and edited many publications.

---

159. Charles D. Neff, "What Shall We Teach," *Saints' Herald* 114, no. 21 (November 1, 1967): 6–7, 9. This article received the 1967 Elbert A. Smith Memorial Award for best *Saints' Herald* article for the year. See "Oakman and Neff Share Elbert A. Smith Award," *Saints' Herald* 115, no. 6 (March 15, 1968): 30.

160. See cover of *Herald* 164, no. 2 (March/April 2017).

161. Charles D. Neff, *Mission Mission Mission* (Independence, MO: Herald Publishing House, 1968), 19.

The Divergent Memories of Joseph Smith's Restoration Movement

Michael Scott Van Wagenen

IN THE SPRING OF 1988, I was an LDS missionary serving along the US-Mexico border in South Texas. On one typically hot day, my companion and I were biking along Ocean Boulevard in Los Fresnos. This small town was not our home base, so we did not know the area very well. We approached a small blue chapel which appeared to be nothing more than another Protestant church in the overwhelmingly Mexican-Catholic borderlands. As I glanced up, however, I noticed the name "Reorganized Church of Jesus Christ of Latter Day Saints" on its curbside sign. My companion and I screeched to a halt pondering what strange parallel world we had wandered into. After all, we had just passed a Mexican-American Elvis impersonator's version of Graceland so it seemed anything was possible in this small town. Intent on solving this mystery, my companion and I walked up to the front door of the church and knocked. In this flipped universe I half expected young women in black shirts and white name tags to greet us. Much to our disappointment, no one answered the door, and we left contemplating the meaning of this "reorganized" version of ourselves. I know this must seem strange to many of you that two twenty-year-old Mormon missionaries had never heard of the RLDS church, but neither of us had been raised particularly devout in our faith. I never attended seminary and rarely visited Sunday school during my high school years. Frankly, I had never given thought to the fate of Joseph Smith's family and had assumed they all came west along with my pioneer ancestors.

Like many missionaries, my understanding of the Mormon past was not so much informed by actual history as it was by what we historians call "collective memory." Collective memory (sometimes shorthanded to simply "memory") is a fascinating mix of truth, fiction, folklore, and propaganda that is far more influential than history for most people. In my last book, *Remembering the Forgotten War*, I explained the subtle differences between the two. "History is an academic discipline that uses critical analysis to interpret and explain the past. Memory, on the other hand, is the socially negotiated reconstruction of past events to correspond with the needs of groups in the present. History often challenges popular assumptions about the past, while memory regularly enshrines them and grants them contemporary relevance." In other words, Richard Bushman's *Rough Stone Rolling* is history while Gerald Lund's *The Work and the Glory* is collective memory. Similarly, Benjamin Park's presentation tomorrow "The Relief Society and Political Mobilization" will be history. The countless faith-promoting pioneer stories shared each month at LDS fast and testimony meetings are largely collective memory.[1]

When I was invited to give the Richard P. Howard Lecture several months ago, I considered the theme of this conference "Restoration Diaspora: All Roads Lead From Nauvoo" and thought that a comparative memory study of the divergent branches of the restoration would be an appropriate interpretation. In particular, I wanted to consider my own experiences as a member of the Church of Jesus Christ of Latter-day Saints. How has collective memory influenced my understanding of theology and religious history? While I was very aware of polygamists growing up, why did it take two decades for me to realize that there were hundreds of thousands of followers of Joseph Smith who did not consider themselves "Mormon"? I also wanted to know how memory shaped these other branches. How have they interpreted us, and how have they interpreted each other? Ultimately I wanted to understand the greater meaning behind the memories we have created.

To accomplish this I interviewed twenty-five individuals from ten different branches that grew from the roots of Joseph Smith's religious movement. The denominations included were: The Church of Jesus Christ of Latter-day Saints, Reorganized Church of Jesus Christ of Latter Day Saints as well as its modern iteration as the Community of Christ, Independent Restoration Branches, Conference of Restoration Elders, The Church of Jesus Christ (Bickertonite), Church of Jesus Christ of Latter Day Saints (Strangite), Church of Christ (Temple Lot), Apostolic United Brethren (The Order), and most controversially, the Raelian Movement.

Scholars largely agree that the primary reason collective memory exists is for the development of identity. Memory is constructed on multiple levels. Each person has their own "individual memory" that shapes their sense of self. These individual memories become the building blocks of "group memory." Essentially, groups sort through the personal memories of their members. Individual recollections that support the needs of the whole are synthesized into the group's memory of itself, while those which conflict with a group's values are discarded and forgotten. This process

---

1. Michael Scott Van Wagenen, *Remembering the Forgotten War: The Enduring Legacies of the U.S. - Mexican War* (Amherst: University of Massachusetts Press, 2012), 240; Richard Lyman Bushman, *Joseph Smith: Rough Stone Rolling* (New York: Knopf, 2005); Gerald N. Lund, *The Work and the Glory: A Pillar of Light* (Salt Lake City: Bookcraft, 1990).

can be expanded, in some cases, to an even larger level where countries sift through group memories to create a national "public memory."[2]

My twenty-five interviewees shared both individual and group memories with me. Very telling was that most were uncomfortable recalling the collective memories of their childhood. They and the groups they belonged to had changed. Their values, and even sense of self, had evolved. They were, at times, embarrassed recounting the folktales of their youth, which clearly demonstrates that collective memory is a dynamic process that is more of a shifting mosaic than a static portrait. It progresses across time. So while some of the interviewee's statements may sound inflammatory, they need to be understood in the context of their time, and do not necessarily reflect the current beliefs of my informants or their churches. Also consider that this is merely a survey of some of the larger trends within the churches, and individual experiences may vary.[3]

To begin, I would like to focus on the role of collective memory in creating group identities. Since I am also a player in this study, I will frame my analysis within my own life experiences. So allow me to share another story—one that will be familiar to those who grew up LDS. I was raised in Los Angeles by parents who were casual in their devotion to the church. In fact, I would define my family's Mormonism far more in terms of culture than I would theology. Still, I attended church enough in my youth to grow fat on a steady diet of LDS group memory. While this may sound a bit reductionist, speaking as a member of the LDS church raised in the 1960s and 70s, we based our identity primarily on the fact that we were the only true and living church upon the face of the earth with which the Lord was well pleased. The absoluteness of our claim was ingrained in us from childhood as we dutifully lined up to recite our pre-rehearsed testimonies once a month in sacrament meaning. While rivalries with other branches of the restoration likely crept into the consciousness of our ancestors, we had no such distraction. We were correct, so there was no particular need to dwell on other denominations. There is one major exception to this, which I will address in a moment.

For those branches either thriving or languishing in the shadow of the much larger LDS church, they did not have the luxury of ignoring the source of their eclipse. Out of necessity, their identity was forged in opposition to their western cousins. One Bickertonite lamented the fact that his people were constantly mistaken for Mormons. They "cringed at being called Mormon. It was the equivalent of being called something you don't agree with." The common mantra of his youth was I'm a Member of the Church of Jesus Christ, not Latter Day Saints.[4]

---

2. Van Wagenen, *Remembering the Forgotten War*, 4–5.

3. All interviews were conducted in confidentiality. To distinguish between them, initials and dates are cited. Exceptions are made when the interviewees are specifically named in the text.

4. Interview with DS, August 19, 2017.

For those raised RLDS, the longtime rivalry with the mountain saints helped forge their identity as well. One church member born in the 1950s recalled that "the focus of a lot of our conversation was that we were not Mormon. We defined ourselves by who we weren't rather than who we were." Another brother recalled the necessity to maintain the "boundary distinctions between us. They are Mormons, we are not." Yet another pointed out that "the LDS can grow up not knowing about RLDS, but the converse is not true." Perhaps ironically, as some of these members joined restoration branches following the RLDS schism of the 1980s, their rivalry shifted from the LDS to the more present Community of Christ.[5]

Other branches of the restoration have also chafed under their associations with the larger RLDS and Community of Christ churches. One member of the Church of Jesus Christ of Latter Day Saints (Strangite) remembered that in the 1940s "the RLDS were a major threat to the church so there was a built in paranoia about them—far more than the LDS." Competing for sacred space in Independence, Missouri, members of the Church of Christ (Temple Lot) likewise viewed themselves in opposition to the RLDS church. One brother recalled that in earlier times "We tried with the RLDS but that didn't work." Instead they now define themselves as entirely independent from the Community of Christ. Their early split from the mainstream of the restoration has allowed them to not feel "affinity with the other churches. . . We are the church of Christ, and we don't make a point to advertise."[6]

I'd like to return a moment to the LDS. I mentioned that there was one distinct exception to defining ourselves in terms of other restorationists. For over a century there has been a broad confusion with the splinter polygamist groups in the West and the mainstream church. Indeed, American history classes struck cold fear into the hearts of many of my generation as the polygamy issue would undoubtedly be trotted out and examined. I recall clearly one lesson on the Overland Trail devolving into accusations of Mormon murder, cults, and, of course, polygamy. A woman of my generation likewise remembered a high school English vocabulary list that included the word "polygamy" along with the usage "The Mormons practiced polygamy." This unexpected evoking of her unconventional history made her want to sink into her desk and disappear.[7]

Halfway across the continent, the RLDS had carefully and deliberately separated themselves from the legacy of plural marriage. Still, their mistaken affiliation with polygamists persisted for decades. One church member in Independence noted that visitors sometimes confused the RLDS with the FLDS. He claimed that "one

---

5. Interview with AS, August 20, 2017; Interview with DH, August 14, 2017.

6. Interview with WS, August 23, 2017; Interview with HS, September 15, 2017.

7. Interview with MD, September 11, 2017.

of the benefits of changing our name to Community of Christ is that we are not as likely to be mistaken as the polygamous Mormons."[8]

Polygamists also feel the pressure of mistaken identities? Members of the Apostolic United Brethren originally found themselves overshadowed by the mainstream Mormon Church, but as times have changed, their struggle for self-definition has evolved. One woman in her forties recalled that they were raised to fear both Mormons and other fundamentalist groups. She complained that Mormons see no difference between the various polygamist groups. Events surrounding the Yearning for Zion Ranch in Texas have upped the stakes of the AUB defining themselves apart from Warren Jeffs's Fundamentalist Church of Jesus Christ of Latter-Day Saints. Such pressures prompted this sister wife to compare LDS feelings toward them to her feelings about the FLDS. "The Mormons lump us all together with Warren Jeffs. We're an embarrassment, and they just want us to go away. But maybe that's the way we feel about the other sects too."[9]

While theologians and scholars have broadly accepted the branches of the restoration already discussed in this talk, the Raelians are far more controversial. Before you cast stones, let me explain that the theology of this so-called "UFO cult" is based, in part, on a firm belief in the prophetic mission of Joseph Smith. They draw from both his cosmology and his experiments with non-traditional marriage. Worldwide, seventy thousand Raelians accept that Smith has been resurrected through cloning and continues his work with alien life forms to bring peace to this earth. So, far out on the margins of the restorationist universe, the Raelian Movement has forged a unique identity that borrows from the followers of Joseph Smith without drawing distinctions between the varied branches. One member of their church explained how Smith fits into their religious identity. "When the atomic bomb was dropped in 1945, the Elohim (Creators) decided to send the last prophet Rael who is the son of Yahweh. Joseph Smith was an earlier prophet. So the basic ideas of Mormonism fit with our theology... I am particular to Joseph Smith because he is one of our prophets, and I feel a kinship to him." He also attended the Hill Cumorah Pageant and loved both the dramatic stage production and the spectacle of the anti-Mormon protestors outside. He further explained that Smith's First Vision was an alien encounter similar in nature to Rael's first meeting with alien lifeforms. Critics of the Raelian Movement have viciously attacked the group over its forty-three-year history, so unflattering comparisons to the LDS are of little matter to them.[10]

The memory, ideas, and folklore of the varied restorationists are useful beyond self-identity. A vital component of group cohesion is the demarcation of borders and

8. RR, email message to the author, September 8, 2017.

9. Interview with CB, July 6, 2017.

10. Interview with HH, September 14, 2017.

the self-policing of those boundaries. Many of the people I spoke with remember church lessons, informal family discussions, and community lore that established firm boundaries between their particular branch and those of their cousins in the restoration. As I previously mentioned, growing up I was only aware of one other group associated with Joseph Smith—the polygamists. No summer of my childhood was complete without a visit to my grandparents' home in Provo, Utah. They lived on Center Street, across 400 East from the historic Knight-Mangum House which at the time was occupied by polygamist members of Ervil LeBaron's murderous Church of the First Born of the Lamb of God. During the 1970s, my grandfather took great joy in chatting with the many children who played on the sidewalk in front of his house and watching them scatter when he asked them who their father was. To me, these mysterious children, secretive women, and absent fathers were all part of a monolithic polygamist church. The nuance that could mean life or death to these furtive Mormons, was completely wasted on me and many other LDS. United by archaic conjugal bonds, they were a relic of our past to be ignored and shunned.

As I learned Mormon history as an adult, I became aware that much of the disdain toward these polygamists was built upon two LDS folktales. The first was that polygamy was instituted to provide for widows of the hundreds or perhaps thousands of men killed during the persecutions. The second was that Joseph Smith had never taken plural wives. Oddly, this latter myth was one of the greatest points of contention between the LDS and RLDS for generations. Yet by the time I was growing up, it was a convenient shortcut for rank-and-file members that supported the lie that plural marriage was merely a benevolent form of church welfare. Many of the middle-aged Latter-day Saints who I spoke with had similar experiences with learning about polygamy. It was instituted to support widows and was discontinued once the Utah population stabilized on the eve of statehood. As one LDS sister of my generation recalled "It was portrayed as a hardship for the men, who didn't want it. I was shocked when I found out that Joseph Smith was a polygamist. It never got brought up in church. Polygamy was a survival tactic, and that was all."[11]

With other branches of the restoration, Joseph Smith's practice of polygamy has not always been accepted as fact. Although the majority of restoration leaders have, over time, recognized the reality of polygamy in the early church, that acceptance has come gradually. One former RLDS member recalled the teaching that Mormon polygamy was an abomination started by Brigham Young. Another remembered it as a smear campaign from Utah. Similar to the RLDS attitude, one Bickertonite recalled learning that "polygamy was the crux of apostasy of the LDS church. The Mormons had contaminated the image of the Book of Mormon by adding polygamy

11. Interview with AF, September 10, 2017; Interview and personal correspondence with AP, September 11, 2017; Interview with GS, September 10, 2017; Interview with LBA, September 11, 2017; Interview with SA, September 9, 2017; Interview with TB, September 10, 2017; Interview with KH, September 10, 2017.

to their doctrine." In more recent times many of his fellow Bickertonites have come to accept that Smith was a polygamist, but officially the leadership of the church has little interest in engaging in that argument anymore.[12]

Perhaps not surprising is the attitude of those in the Raelian Movement. Practicing a form of spiritual marriage that links any number of men and women together, Raelians are unaffected by Smith's polygamy. As one member explained, "Joseph Smith was a hedonist, but so are we. We are very open about sexuality. Joseph Smith was killed because his sexual activities upset the people of his time, but we agree with the ideas of polygamy."[13]

What does all of this mean for the memory of modern-day polygamists? That depends very much on which branch of the restoration you belong to as well as your generation. Outside of the LDS world, most restorationists spend very little time dwelling on the polygamists. It just is not a part of their identity or memory any longer. While my generation of LDS was raised with a great many myths about the practice, this was not the case for earlier Mormons. My father grew up in Provo with two polygamist families in his neighborhood. As he remembered it, "we treated the kids fine and didn't ostracize them. . . The kids came to church and the parents would sit quietly in the back and not take the sacrament. It didn't strike us as that strange."[14]

For those of my generation who grew up outside of the so-called "Zion Curtain" it was easy to condemn the modern polygamists. If the practice was only instituted to care for widows, then those who followed it in modern times were sexual deviants who were damaging the reputation of the church and making things uncomfortable for us in history classes. As one LDS sister in Texas pointed out, "Modern polygamists are talked about it the darkest of terms. They only broke off to do horrible things." In addition to this, stories abound about FLDS coming into towns near Colorado City driving Cadillacs and paying for groceries with food stamps.[15]

While Ervil LeBaron and Warren Jeffs seem to support such broad stroke assessments, polygamists who reject child marriage and welfare fraud have struggled with their public image. Some of these groups have attempted to mainstream themselves into the larger society of the West. A few LDS mentioned how their current ideas about polygamists are shaped less by past memories and more by their experiences hiring young polygamist men and women as hardworking construction workers and house cleaners. The greatest strides to reform the modern memory of polygamy, however, have been made by the Kody Brown family of the Apostolic United Brethren. Hundreds of thousands of Americans tune in weekly to The Learning

12. Interview with DJ, August 27, 2017; Interview with NS, August 18, 2017; DS Interview.

13. HH Interview.

14. Interview with Richard Van Wagenen, September 9, 2017.

15. Interview; Interview with WR, September 10, 2017.

Channel to watch Kody, his four wives, and eighteen children on the reality television program *Sister Wives*. As one LDS woman in California observed "I only heard about the people living on the compounds. It wasn't until *Sister Wives* that I learned they were normal people. Before that I thought that they were really cultish, wearing prairie dresses and high hair." A Utah Mormon echoed that sentiment stating "Then there's the Kody Browns who are pretty good guys who don't try to bring bad publicity on the church. He seems like a genuine, nice dude." Having known Kody Brown since we were missionaries in Texas over thirty years ago, I can attest to the fact that he is, in fact, a nice dude.[16]

In preparing for this talk, I met with Kody and some of his friends and family twice over the summer: one evening for dinner in Utah and another time in his home in Las Vegas. It was here that I learned that the differences between polygamists, while less obvious to me and other outsiders, were clearly demarcated between the groups. History and folktales combined to create a collective memory that promoted loyalty to their group and safety from the threats of outsiders. The 1977 assassination of AUB founder Rulon Allred by followers of Ervil LaBaron highlighted the very mortal danger that members faced from competing sects. Allred's granddaughter, Christine, is Kody Brown's third wife. I sat down with her to better understand the ways in which the AUB uses memory to protect its members from the LDS and FLDS churches. In the wake of her grandfather's murder, Christine and the youth of her generation were raised "to think that all other polygamist groups were bad." Key to this was the practice of the FLDS kidnapping AUB women as brides. Christine recalled that "they would come in, take our girls, marry them, and take them out of the community. We always felt bad for those girls." To protect their teenagers, the youth had to present recommends at church dances to ensure that FLDS boys were kept away. According to stories told by Christine's family, in the 1950s her aunt was kidnapped by FLDS who forced her into marriage against her will. In a time when the police could and did arrest the men of the church, polygamists did not involve law enforcement. Therefore, it was particularly important that children be taught the dangers of people outside the Order. Frequent evoking of FLDS kidnappings in the 1950s and 60s, along with murder in the 1970s, created a memory which reinforced group cohesion and defensiveness in the 1980s and beyond. As a testament of this, a teenager visiting the Brown family told me about an FLDS acquaintance who befriended an AUB woman and was chased off by church leadership before he could "marry one of our girls and take her away."[17]

The AUB also has many misgivings about the LDS. Maintenance of group boundaries was particularly important for those members who integrated into the

---

16. Interview with RV, September 9, 2017; TB Interview; WR Interview; KH Interview; Kody Brown and I served in the Texas San Antonio Mission 1986–88.

17. Interview with Christine Allred Brown, July 6, 2017; Interview with MT, July 6, 2017.

larger Mormon culture around them. Christine, for example, grew up in Taylorsville, Utah, and attended public school. Her parents sought to protect the family by telling her and her siblings to pretend to be Mormon. Now in her forties, she has still never attended an actual LDS church service. Nonetheless she became adept at the ruse. Still, she avoided close friendships with Mormons because she feared their questions, and "questions get fathers arrested." As she explained, the LDS were "not the enemy, but are scary to us. They are mean to us. We are not invited in their club." Supporting her claim is the fact that I spent the better part of a month arguing via Internet, email, and telephone for her and Kody to be invited to our last mission reunion. Oddly, the most outspoken critic of their attendance cornered them at the reunion and asked to have her photo taken with them. She then proceeded to spend twenty minutes discussing the details of the last season of their show.[18]

Kody's adult children are not married polygamously, but the lessons they have learned growing up hiding in plain sight in Utah have shaped their views of the LDS church. When Kody's nineteen-year-old daughter fell in love with a Mormon man, she attempted to convert. Because of her membership in the AUB, the local high council required her to meet with them to approve her baptism. She left the meeting demoralized as most of the questions centered not on her newfound faith, but rather her father's romantic relationships with his wives. They ultimately rejected her request for baptism, and the church lost not only her, but her husband. Such experiences become the building blocks of tomorrow's collective memories. Indeed, Kody's oldest son voiced what several of the children believed when he lamented that Mormons claim to be "all about family but they make you denounce your own gay and polygamist relatives." He discussed attending church services with his Mormon cousins and proudly knowing more church history and doctrine than the LDS kids in Sunday school class. He smiled, "if they knew I was a polygamist they would have thrown me out." For the younger members of the AUB, their fear of the LDS is being replaced by their focus on perceived Mormon hypocrisy. Once again, collective memory evolves to fit the needs and values of the present.[19]

As previously mentioned, the RLDS rivaled for generations with the polygamous Brighamites. This created a unique collective memory that survives among members of the Community of Christ and restoration branches to this day. One major theme of RLDS memory was the physical violence and danger inherent in nineteenth-century LDS society. One popular story that came up with every person I spoke to who was raised RLDS dealt with escape from the wagon trains headed west or from the Mormon settlements in the Utah Territory. As one man of my generation put it, "our ancestors fled from Utah with flour sacks around their wagon

18. Brown Interview.

19. Interview with MB, July 6, 2017; Interview with HB, July 6, 2017.

wheels to escape from the Avenging Angels in the dead of night." Another member of the Community of Christ further explained that "though you never find this written down contemporaneously, this has become the universal RLDS escape experience." I heard variations of the story multiple times. Reports of Mormon violence circulated around the United States during the nineteenth century. While some accounts were clear exaggerations, others, like the Mountain Meadow Massacre, point to very real concerns for those people who threatened the status quo in the Great Basin kingdom. More importantly, it demarcated the theocratic and militaristic Mountain Saints from the peace-loving reorganization in the Midwest.[20]

Another story that commonly circulated around the RLDS had to do with the LDS treatment of Emma Smith. One former member of the RLDS church who was raised in the 1950s stated that "I always heard that the Mormons were pretty down on Emma. Emma was a real heroine for us and we couldn't understand why she wasn't for the Mormons, but there has been a switch in view." The recollections of the Latter-day Saints I interviewed support this contention. One Mormon who was raised in the 1960s recounted that in her ward "Emma was the bad guy, and what made the RLDS bad was they chose to follow her as opposed to a male priesthood member. She was to blame for us losing their family." While I only have the vaguest of recollections of Emma's bad reputation, I clearly recall her rehabilitation. About twenty-five years ago I began hearing accounts that Joseph Smith claimed he would go to the depths of Hell to save his first wife. Somehow Emma's apostasy paled in comparison to his perceived devotion to her. Todd Compton's 1997 book *In Sacred Loneliness: The Plural Wives of Joseph Smith* also influenced memory as it moved surreptitiously through the Mormon pews. Even my mother, who has yet to finish reading the Book of Mormon, read Compton's book and was changed by its content. One LDS interview captured the evolving memory of Mormonism's newfound "elect lady." According to this Latter-day Saint, "Emma didn't want to come west so they left her. I think she remarried. Her new husband had a child with another woman, and Emma hired that woman to work in their home. That was an incredibly Christian thing to do." A number of official and unofficial LDS films of the last two decades have recast Emma as a devoted wife and stalwart Latter-day Saint. The new Mormon memory has finally and belatedly fallen in Mrs. Smith's favor.[21]

As the wealth of the LDS church grew during the latter half of the twentieth century, many believed that the outward manifestation of success was evidence of God's pleasure with his Utah saints. Certainly for those of us who witnessed our transformation from a rural sect in the Rocky Mountains to a multinational corporation, the evolution was as impressive as it was troubling. I heard many a late-night

---

20. AS Interview; DH Interview; NS Interview; RR email, September 8, 2017.

21. AS Interview; AP Interview and correspondence; Todd M. Compton, *In Sacred Loneliness: The Plural Wives of Joseph Smith* (Salt Lake City: Signature, 1997); RV Interview.

missionary discussion interpreting our financial triumphs as the beginning of our world spiritual domination. Ironically, those things that became a point of pride to us, became the symbols of Mormon excesses and fanaticism in the eyes of the RLDS, their theological successors, and other branches of the restoration. A few of these trappings emerged in interviews with many of my informants. These include the corporate structure of the church, the food storage program, and obedience to the Word of Wisdom.

Tithing makes the Mormon corporate world go around. In the 1960s, the church produced a film titled *The Windows of Heaven* which promoted an apocryphal tale in which president Lorenzo Snow promised the Saints of Southern Utah that God would end a destructive drought if they would pay tithing. The film supported a campaign to promote a 10 percent tithe on member's gross earnings. The program worked, and ward coffers filled with money which eventually worked its way to Salt Lake City. While we have held that up as a token of our obedience, others within the restoration have taken pity on the heavily taxed Mormons. One member of an independent Restoration Branch remembered his days in the RLDS church when people had compassion for the "poor Mormon families scrimping to pay the 10% even though they had barely enough to live." Another recounted the tale of an impoverished Mormon who was refused help from his church because he was not a full tithe-payer. Stories also circulated that the LDS were being surreptitiously supported by Coca Cola and Marriott Hotel money. As one man observed, "Wow, that's quite an organization and corporation. Still, control can be taken too far."[22]

While Mormons took great pride in their devotion and sacrifice, their cousins saw their unquestioning commitment as a warning sign of fanaticism. As one former member of the RLDS church recalled, "there was a strictness of Mormonism in towing the line. We felt that was a little too strong." A Bickertonite agreed, stating that Mormons did things that "were so off the wall" that they did not make sense. He continued noting that "we didn't make fun, but we teased them a bit." In spite of good natured joking, the Bickertonites noted a more sinister side to LDS devotion as they laid blame for the Mountain Meadow Massacre on the fanatical Danites of Utah. Appropriate levels of piety remain a point of contention within the LDS culture today. Indeed, the online Mormon Bloggernacle is filled with dozens of web communities that continue to debate the finer points of LDS devotion and culture.[23]

One area of seemingly benign Mormon fanaticism is the Word of Wisdom. I remember as a child thumbing through my grandmother's scrapbook. Featured prominently was a photo of my great-grandparents standing beside their car in 1947. My

22. Church of Jesus Christ of Latter-day Saints, *Windows of Heaven*, Motion Picture, Directed by Wetzel O. Whitaker, 1963; for the latest work on the LDS Church's finances see D. Michael Quinn, *The Mormon Hierarchy: Wealth and Corporate Power* (Salt Lake City: Signature, 2017); NS Interview; AS Interview.

23. AS Interview, DS Interview.

great-grandmother was in her usual ranching clothes, while my great-grandfather casually dangled a cigarette from his fingers. The image was labeled "My parents coming home from the temple after being sealed." I asked my grandmother about her dad's cigarette smoking so close to the most sacred of Mormon ordinances. She laughed and told me that it was different back then with the Word of Wisdom. Certainly there seemed to be a pervasive casualness across the board when it came to Joseph Smith's health code. After all, he declared it more of a suggestion than a commandment. In the early-to-mid twentieth century, however, the LDS began to take a more hardline approach. As the Mormons became distinctive and pulled away from the pack, the Word of Wisdom became fodder for collective memory.[24]

Twenty years ago I moved into a small LDS branch in the Texas town of Port Isabel while I attended graduate school. By complete coincidence I was back in my old mission area on the US-Mexico border. When I arrived, the congregation was in disarray. Apparently a heated debate had just broken out in the Relief Society over whether or not green papayas violated the Word of Wisdom's admonishment to eat "fruit in the season thereof." Everyone had gotten very emotional about the unripe fruit fight, and several families were no longer speaking to each other. My relationship with the church was already strained so I decided to seek out some alternative spirituality. This eventually led me back to that original RLDS church in Los Fresnos. Nine years later I walked through the same door I had pounded on as a missionary. After the services I was offered coffee and donuts. Until "papaya-gate" blew over, I had found a new home.[25]

While a lifestyle of eating fruits and vegetables, along with the avoidance of hard alcohol and tobacco is widely accepted as ideal, many health professionals question the prohibition on coffee and tea. This has left a gap which separates the LDS from the other branches of the restoration and provides room for a little humor on both sides. Outside of the LDS church, most restorationists marvel at the Mormon devotion to the health code. One man who grew up RLDS joked that while some of the old-timers abstained, coffee was an "unofficial sacrament" in the church. One Bickertonite remembered that the fuss about coffee was a funny recurring joke among his people. A Strangite brother admired LDS devotion, but noted that the Mormons really are fanatics about it. A member of the Hedrickites stated that it was a good idea, but that Joseph Smith was already a fallen prophet by the time he wrote the Word of Wisdom, therefore, it was not binding. A member of the AUB recalled

24. Thomas G. Alexander, "The Word of Wisdom: From Principle to Requirement," *Dialogue: A Journal of Mormon Thought* 14, no. 3 (1981): 78–88.

25. Church of Jesus Christ of Latter-day Saints, *The Doctrine and Covenants of the Church of Jesus Christ of Latter-Day Saints* (Salt Lake City: Church of Jesus Christ of Latter-Day Saints, 1989), section 89.

with some levity an LDS peer warning her about the evils of coffee, stating that "hot drinks burn you from the inside."[26]

Mormons have certainly had their laughs about the Word of Wisdom too. Levels of adherence also demarcate boundaries between the so-called "Peter Priesthoods" and the "Jack Mormons." My high councilman grandfather was known to rush out the back door with his coffee so his grandchildren wouldn't witness his moral failing. Bring up the topic of "Word of Wisdom fanaticism" and you will get a lot of chuckles and tales about devotion gone wrong. My father liked to recount the story of one of his high school peers who got pregnant, but assured her bishop that she had not once broken the Word of Wisdom. He also recalled that his parent's generation was the last to accept smoking elders and bishops. The drinking of caffeinated sodas became the battleground of my childhood, and several of my respondents laughed at how seriously they took that fight before becoming more invigorated adults. One convert to caffeinated Coca Cola chuckled that it was his only alternative as his grandmother "drank coffee, and she was mean so I associate the smell of coffee with bad grandmas."[27]

Humor has always been a component of memory. Jokes are a way to talk about serious issues while defusing the deep emotions attached to them. A young member of the AUB recounted to me the old riddle of "Why do you need to take two Mormons with you when you fish? The answer: if you bring only one, he'll drink all your beer." Alan Smith, who was raised RLDS, has devoted years collecting and publishing the humor of his people. I spent a couple of hours laughing over his book *Our Heritage of Humor* which includes nineteenth-century jokes about the LDS. Let me share a couple of his gems.[28]

The following story comes from the *True Latter Day Saints Herald* on July 1, 1871:

"What have you got that's good?" said a hungry traveler, as he seated himself at a dinner table in Salt Lake City.
"Oh, we've got roast beef, corn beef, roast mutton, boiled and fried ham, and broiled curlew!"
"What is curlew?" said the stranger.
"Curlew! Why curlew is a bird, something like a snipe."
"Could it fly?"
"Yes."
"Did it have wings?"
"Yes."

26. Interview; DS Interview; WS Interview; HS Interview; CB Interview.

27. Richard Van Wagenen Interview; TB Interview.

28. MT Interview; H. Alan Smith, *Our Heritage of Humor* (Independence, MO: Herald House, 1982).

"Then I don't want any curlew. Anything that had wings and could fly, and didn't leave this country, I don't want for dinner."[29]

Another humorous musing is from an 1868 letter that an RLDS missionary wrote to the *True Latter Day Saints Herald*: "My reasons for staying in Utah are chiefly these: 1. If our mission is to the Lost Sheep of the House of Israel, Utah is as likely a place to meet them as any. 2. If blessed be the Elders when they are persecuted, and have all manner of evil spoken against them falsely, Utah is a convenient a place to them as any other. 3. If Hell is to be prevailed against in the gate, Utah is the chief place of attack."[30]

Humor can be a two-way street, and I remember a joke told to me as an adult that fired back at our reorganized cousins. "The secretary for the prophet of the RLDS church ran into his office panting. 'Sir, I have good news, and I have bad news.' 'Well, out with it,' President Smith replied. 'The good news is that I have the Savior on the phone. The bad news is he is calling from Salt Lake City.'" I have subsequently heard variations of this joke told at the expense of both the Pope and Billy Graham. While intended to be a harmless jest, it nonetheless hits at the heart of LDS memory and the need to confirm the correctness of their path. Without a doubt, the LDS have their fair share of collective memories about the RLDS and other denominations. I recall back in my graduate school days in Texas hearing a young LDS missionary telling a group of people in the church foyer that the RLDS church had abandoned the Book of Mormon in order to become accepted as a Protestant denomination. They also gave women the priesthood because they had run out of male descendants of Joseph Smith to fill the role of prophet. He further claimed that the church was about to go broke, and because we had loaned them so much money, they would have to give us back the Kirtland Temple. As someone who studies memory, I listened to his entire tale before shutting him down and setting the record straight. Nevertheless, this missionary, in one fell swoop, addressed all of the themes of collective memory that I documented with my LDS informants.

Many of my Mormon subjects admitted to being particularly ashamed of their childhood attitudes toward the RLDS when visiting our shared history sites. One sister recalled the condescension that she witnessed in Nauvoo. She admitted that while taking tours, the RLDS guides "always seemed anxious when the LDS groups come in. For us there was always an assumption that anything they said could be incorrect because they are RLDS. I remember people looking at their artifacts and saying these things should really belong to us." Another remembered visiting Independence and stated that with "knowing smiles and eye rolls at each other. . . . we were the kind of tourists who felt smug about our knowing the real story that was

---

29. Alan Smith, Personal correspondence with the author.

30. Smith Correspondence.

butchered by the RLDS guides." Visitor feedback cards left at church history sites show the unfortunate persistence of these attitudes. Two recent cards scrawled in adolescent script read "I wish the temple belonged to the true church," and "Give us back our land / the property for which the temple is on." Tom Kimball, a Mormon volunteer at the Community of Christ's Kirtland Temple reported a group of Latter-day Saint youth standing out front of the building chanting "Give it back! Give it back! Give it back!" Fortunately, such behavior seems to be the exception rather than the rule these days. Still, it bears witness that our persistent need for exclusive correctness and historical entitlement have not quite left our collective consciousness. It also suggests a tendency for youth to unquestioningly accept collective memory as fact.[31]

Such outdated relics of recollection do very little good in the present. Many people hold to their negative group memories for tradition's sake, not realizing the emotional and spiritual damage it can do. Since collective memory is often ingrained in childhood, it can also be extremely difficult to extricate from one's sense of self and understanding of reality. Education can do wonders for the process, but deconstructing collective memory is a complex task. My own experiences with challenging my cultural myths go back to Brigham Young University which I attended immediately following my mission. Living in Utah for the first time in my life, I heard much of the folklore and collective memories that shaped our views of those outside our faith. It was also in Provo where I began to arm myself with the knowledge to challenge these notions. A few of my LDS informants specifically mentioned their time at BYU as being critical to their journey to a fuller understanding of beliefs outside of our faith, particularly those of the other branches of the restoration. That was certainly my case.[32]

For me it began in the early 1990s, when Ronald Romig came to BYU to present his findings about the disputed Joseph Smith daguerreotype. It was a fascinating program that combined history and art with the physical sciences. It was the first time I ever recall taking an interest in Mormon history. Approaching the stage after the presentation, it was also the first time I ever met a member of the Reorganized Church of Jesus Christ of Latter Day Saints. Aside from his honor-code-violating mustache, Ron seemed like a pretty normal guy, not quite the Emma-worshipping apostate that old lore would have had me believe. It was an ecumenical moment that began my journey into Mormon history.

While this was all new to me, it was far from the first time that the LDS and the RLDS had come together in the spirit of peace and kinship. In 1951, RLDS president Israel A. Smith journeyed to Salt Lake City to attend the funeral of his second cous-

31. Interview with ARM, September 10, 2017; AP Interview and correspondence; Interview with Tom Kimball, July 11, 2017.

32. Interview with SN, September 10, 2017; ARM Interview; WR Interview.

in, LDS president George Albert Smith. He stayed on a few extra days to participate in the semiannual conference of the church held in the historic tabernacle. As part of the business proceedings of the service, David O. McKay was sustained as the new prophet, seer, and revelator for the church. When the congregation was asked for a sustaining vote, President Smith raised his hand in support. Many of the Mormons who witnessed this magnanimous gesture spread the word that the RLDS had just acquiesced to the LDS church. After taking considerable criticism from his own membership and receiving word that missionaries were attempting to use this as a tool to bring Midwestern saints back into the fold, Smith wrote a gently worded request to McKay to rein in his people. The embarrassed Mormon prophet sent his immediate apologies and assurances that he would put an end to such rumors.[33]

While geographic isolation and slow communication hampered past attempts at goodwill, our modern age has helped narrow these gaps significantly. Historians have taken the lead over the last thirty years by publishing books and articles that have challenged former interpretations of our past. Leonard Arrington, Richard P. Howard, and many of the people here tonight have played integral roles in breaking down prejudices and constructing new collective memories. Academic conferences such as those held by the John Whitmer Historical Association and the Mormon History Association have brought together restorationists of all stripes. RLDS professor, Danny Jorgenson, explained to me that over the last several years the JWHA and MHA "began cross-fertilizing. Scholars were interacting and finding that they liked each other." Even the polygamists are overcoming their self-imposed exile, discovering common ground, and attending conferences related to the restoration. Who knows? Perhaps we may even see the day when the Raelians may stop in for a visit while they await Joseph Smith's return to Earth.[34]

Similar to the role of our common history, our shared sacred spaces also bring us together. Our temples and temple lots, our visitor centers and sacred groves, our places of sorrow and martyrdom, if approached with humility and an open heart, offer opportunities to forge new collective memories for the rising generation. Ron Romig recounted to me his experiences sharing the Kirtland Temple with the diverse believers of the restoration and the tears that flow as they join together to sing the hymns of our fathers and mothers. Having attended one such gathering at the 2003 Mormon History Association in Kirtland, I can attest that he spoke the truth. Ron, his family, and other members of the Community of Christ led a diverse group of restorationists in singing our sacred songs in that hallowed building. As a long-fallen "saint" I was surprised to feel long-dormant spiritual stirrings within my own heart as we transcended our pasts to experience the deep joy of our shared roots. When I

---

33. Smith's correspondence regarding the affair is held in the Community of Christ archives. Typescripts were provided in the RR email.

34. Interview with Danny Jorgensen, August 27, 2017.

found out that there would be a historic hymn fest this Sunday, I extended my trip so I would not miss this unique experience.[35]

In conclusion, I want to point out that the wonderful thing about collective memory is that it is ultimately the servant of the present, not the past. Its dynamic properties allow for, and even encourage, evolution. I have no expectations that we will ever overcome our many doctrinal differences. I am content to let the theologians and fanatics worry about that. As historians, however, we are in a unique place to help shape the memories of the future. Through our books, articles, museum exhibits, historic tours, and lectures, we can correct the errors of the past and make our memories relevant for future generations. With humor, humility, and, no doubt, some hymns, I suspect we will yet see Richard Howard's dream of transforming "walls to windows."[36]

DR. MICHAEL SCOTT VAN WAGENEN, a graduate of the University of Utah, is associate professor and public history coordinator at Georgia Southern University. He is the author of the award-winning, *Library Journal* best seller *Remembering the Forgotten War: The Enduring Legacies of the U.S.-Mexican War* (University of Massachusetts, 2012), *The Texas Republic and the Mormon Kingdom of God* (Texas A&M, 2002), as well as several articles, book chapters, and encyclopedia entries. He is also co-editor with W. Paul Reeve of *Between Pulpit and Pew: The Supernatural World in Mormon History and Folklore* (Utah State University, 2011). In addition to his academic writing, he has written, produced, directed, and/or edited over 20 documentary films.

---

35. Ronald Romig, email message to the author, September 8, 2017.

36. Richard P. Howard, "The Mormon-RLDS Boundary, 1852–1991: Walls to Windows," *Journal of Mormon History* 18, no. 1 (Spring 1992): 1–18.

Anointed Queens and Priestesses: Alpheus Cutler's Plural Wives[1]

Danny L. Jorgensen and Andrew Leary

A T Nauvoo, Illinois, in the early 1840s the founding Latter-day Saint prophet, Joseph Smith Jr., began covertly introducing a highly selective collection of men and women—the "Anointed Quorum"—to an emergent theology and accompanying rites that eventually would become associated centrally with the Mormon temple and salvation.[2] This radically innovative theology re-envisioned deity and the cosmos, unifying earthly existence with the glories of the celestial world, and linked the living and the dead as well as extended marriage and kinship relations eternally.[3] In so doing, it specifically sanctioned polygamy, a multiplicity of spouses; or, technically polygyny, the marriage of a man to more than one

---

1. This essay is based on a paper presented at the Mormon History Association Annual Meetings, St. Louis, Missouri, June 2, 2017. The authors appreciate the comments of Lawrence Foster and the anonymous reviewers of this journal on this paper.

2. See Andrew F. Ehat, "Joseph Smith's Introduction of Temple Ordinances and the 1844 Succession Question" (master's thesis, Brigham Young University, 1982); Lisle G. Brown, "The Ordinances of Godliness: A Paradigm of Mormon Sacerdotal Ceremonies," *Research Report* 1 (November/December 1989): 1–15; Lisle G. Brown, "Temple Ordinances as Administered in Nauvoo, Illinois, 1840–1846," *Research Report* 1 (March/April 1990): 1–21; David John Buerger, *The Mysteries of Godliness: A History of Mormon Temple Worship* (San Francisco: Smith Research Associates, 1994); D. Michael Quinn, *The Mormon Hierarchy: Origins of Power* (Salt Lake City: Signature Books, 1994), especially 105–41; Devery S. Anderson and Gary James Bergera, eds., *Joseph Smith's Quorum of the Anointed 1842–1845: A Commentary History* (Salt Lake City: Signature Books, 2005); Richard Lyman Bushman, with the assistance of Jed Woodworth, *Joseph Smith: Rough Stone Rolling, A Cultural Biography of Mormonism's Founder* (New York: Alfred A. Knopf, 2005), especially 195–214, 305–21, 417–500; and Laurel Thatcher Ulrich, *A House Full of Females: Plural Marriage and Women's Rights in Early Mormonism, 1835–1870* (New York: Alfred A. Knopf, 2017), 108–34

3. This synthetic theology drew heavily on Renaissance hermetic, filtered through European-American folklore and freemasonry, combined with a reconciliation of the Old and New Testaments of the Christian Bible. See, for example, Richard L. Bushman, *Joseph Smith and the Beginnings of Mormonism* (Urbana: University of Illinois Press, 1984), especially 179–88; Bushman, *Joseph Smith*, especially 418–25, and 436–58; Michael W. Homer, *Joseph's Temple: The Dynamic Relationship between Freemasonry and Mormonism* (Salt Lake City: University of Utah Press, 2014); and Clyde R. Forsberg Jr., *Equal Rites: The Book of Mormon, Masonry, Gender, and American Culture* (New York: Columbia University Press, 2003).

woman, based loosely on Old Testament practices.[4] The new teachings and rituals thereby legitimated the recent plural marriages of Joseph Smith and a few associates religiously—although not as legally recognized unions.[5] Yet, their prophet's 1844 death left those committed to these novel doctrines and rituals to work on how they would be enacted practically in everyday life.[6] Sociologist Thomas F. O'Dea con-

---

4. *The Doctrine and Covenants of The Church of Jesus Christ of Latter-day Saints: Containing Revelations Given to Joseph Smith, the Prophet with Some Additions by His Successors in the Presidency of the Church* (Salt Lake City: The Church of Jesus Christ of Latter-day Saints, 2013), section 132 (for the historical text see "Revelation 12 July 1843," Joseph Smith Papers, http://www.josephsmithpapers.org/paper-summary/revelation-12-july-1843-dc-132/1#full-transcript). Mormon polygamy specifically was envisioned as a revival of Old Testament practices, notwithstanding little scriptural authorization, see, for example, Isaiah Gafni, "The Institution of Marriage in Rabbinic Times," in *The Jewish Family: Metaphor and Memory*, ed. David Kraemer (New York: Oxford University Press, 1989), 13–30; and Michael David Coogan, *God and Sex: What the Bible Really Says* (New York: Twelve, 2010). For technical scholarly discussions of these marriage terminologies see, for example, Robin Fox, *Kinship and Marriage: An Anthropological Perspective* (Baltimore: Penguin, 1967); Jack Goody, *Production and Reproduction: A Comparative Study of the Domestic Domain* (Cambridge: Cambridge University Press, 1976); Jack Goody, "Polygyny, Economy and the Role of Women," in *The Character of Kinship*, ed. Jack Goody (Cambridge: Cambridge University Press, 1973), 175–90; Douglas White and Michael Burton, "Causes of Polygyny: Ecology, Economy, Kinship, and Warfare," *American Anthropologist* 90, no. 4 (December 1988): 871–87; and Miriam Koktvedgaard Zeitzen, *Polygamy: A Cross-Cultural Analysis* (Oxford: Berg Publishing, 2008). On Mormon polygamy specifically see Danel Backman and Ronald K. Esplin, "Plural Marriage," in Daniel H. Ludlow, ed., *Encyclopedia of Mormonism* (New York: Macmillan, 1992), 1091–95.

5. *The Doctrine and Covenants of The Church of Jesus Christ of Latter-day Saints*, section 132. For consequential studies of the origin of Latter-day Saint plural marriage see, for example, Fawn M. Brodie, *No Man Knows My History: The Life of Joseph Smith* (New York: Alfred A. Knopf, 1945); Kimball Young, *Isn't One Wife Enough?* (New York, Henry Holt and Company, 1954); Stanley S. Ivins, "Notes on Mormon Polygamy," *Western Humanities Review* 10 (Summer 1956): 229–39; Danel W. Backman, "A Study of the Mormon Practice of Plural Marriage before the Death of Joseph Smith" (master's thesis, Purdue University, 1975); Lawrence Foster, *Religion and Sexuality: Three American Communal Experiments of the Nineteenth Century* (New York: Oxford University Press, 1981); Richard S. Van Wagoner, *Mormon Polygamy: A History* (Salt Lake City: Signature Books, 1986); Jessie L. Embry, *Mormon Polygamous Families: Life in the Principle* (Salt Lake City: University of Utah Press, 1987); B. Carmon Hardy, *Solemn Covenant: The Mormon Polygamous Passage* (Urbana: University of Illinois Press, 1992); Todd Compton, *In Sacred Loneliness: The Plural Wives of Joseph Smith* (Salt Lake City: Signature Books, 1997); Kathryn M. Daynes, *More Wives Than One: Transformation of the Mormon Marriage System, 1840–1910* (Urbana: University of Illinois Press, 2001); George D. Smith, *Nauvoo Polygamy: "…but we called it celestial marriage"* (Salt Lake City: Signature Books, 2008); Merina Smith, *Revelation, Resistance, and Mormon Polygamy: The Introduction and Implementation of the Principle, 1830–1853* (Logan: Utah State University Press, 2013); and Christine Talbot, *A Foreign Kingdom: Mormons and Polygamy in American Political Culture, 1852–1890* (Urbana: University of Illinois Press, 2013). Also see Brian C. Hales, with the assistance of Don Bradley, *Joseph Smith's Polygamy: History, Volumes 1 and 2* (Salt Lake City: Greg Kofford Books, 2013); and Newell G. Bringhurst and Craig L. Fosters, eds., *The Persistence of Polygamy: Joseph Smith and the Origins of Mormon Polygamy* (Independence, MO: John Whitmer Books, 2010).

6. Thomas F. O'Dea, *The Mormons* (Chicago: University of Chicago Press, 1957), 247. This study was based in part on a Harvard Laboratory of Social Relations project, "The Comparative Study of Values in Five Cultures" in northern New Mexico in which O'Dea focused on Mormon life, resulting in his 1953 doctoral dissertation. He, furthermore, engaged in a participant observational methodology while residing in Utah in the 1950s, including six months in a rural village. Extensive notes as well as interviews deriving from this study are available in the Thomas F. O'Dea Papers, L. Tom Perry Special Collections, Harold B. Lee Library, Brigham Young University, Provo, Utah, hereafter cited as L. Tom Perry Special Collections. "Whatever astigmatisms this book may reveal," he asserted, "cannot be attributed to a lack of firsthand acquaintance, for I have tried to supplement the necessary

cluded that, "On the whole, no stable patterns of polygamous behavior with regard
to status among wives, rules of residency, priority of children, and the like had time
to form before the federal offensive drove the practice underground" (in the 1890s).[7]
In the Anointed Quorum men and women—included for the first time in a priesthood organization—received a "first anointing" (or "endowment"), and the marriage
of a husband and wife or wives could be "sealed" eternally. Some of the anointed
also underwent the ultimate ordinance, the "fullness of the priesthood" (or "second
anointing"), extending to them the exclusive "keys" to priestly authority and promises
of exaltation to a husband as a "king and priest" and to his wife or wives as a "queen
and priestess" eternally. Alpheus Cutler (1784–1864) and Lois Lathrop (1788–1878),
the woman he married in 1808, were among the earliest initiates of the Anointed
Quorum, and within the next few years six more women would be anointed as wives
with Alpheus.[8]

   We report on what little is known about Alpheus Cutler's wives—Lois Lathrop
and the six additional women married to him at Nauvoo in 1845 and 1846. All of
Cutler's plural wives have been identified openly since at least 1979; yet, with one exception, there has been little previous effort to research and narrate their lives.[9] Inves-
tigating these plural relationships entails many of the daunting complexities of other

---

library research with as much living experience as possible" (vii). In addition to his own firsthand observations
on Mormon plural marriage, O'Dea cites the research found in Kimball Young's *Isn't One Wife Enough?* Also
see Cardell K. Jacobson, John P. Hoffmann, and Tim B. Heaton, eds., *Revisiting Thomas F. O'Dea's The Mormons:
Contemporary Perspectives* (Salt Lake City: University of Utah Press, 2008). Another sociologist Nels Anderson,
Desert Saints: The Mormon Frontier in Utah (Chicago: University of Chicago Press, 1942), likewise opined that:
"Had there been no persecution, polygamy in Deseret would have perished of its own disabilities" (quoted from
Phoenix Books edition, xxxxii). Anderson, unlike O'Dea, joined the LDS church in 1909 and he still regarded
himself "as a Mormon," in 1966 (xxi–xxiii). His work, like O'Dea's, is based on a variety of social scientific meth-
ods of research, including participant observation over many years.

7. This observation is based on a technical sociological concept of "social institutions" involving a complex process
whereby social norms governing social interactions, such as marriage, are formulated, used to modify existing
norms, and adapted to form stable, recurrent, and obligatory patterns of human conduct. Subsequent studies of Latter-day Saint polygyny, such as Embry's *Mormon Polygamous Families* and those discussed by way of
conclusion here, confirm that this daring experiment in an alternative form of marriage and family never achieve
anything more than exceedingly rudimentary institutionalization.

8. On Alpheus Cutler see Rupert J. Fletcher and Daisy Whiting Fletcher, *Alpheus Cutler and the Church of Jesus
Christ* (Independence, MO: The Church of Jesus Christ, 1974, privately published); Danny L. Jorgensen, "The
Old Fox: Alpheus Cutler," in *Differing Visions: Dissenters in Mormon History*, ed. Roger D. Launius and Linda
Thatcher (Champaign: University of Illinois Press, 1994), 312–58; and Biloine Whiting Young, *Obscure Believers:
The Mormon Schism of Alpheus Cutler* (St. Paul, MN: Pogo Press, 2002). The contemporary Cutlerites dispute
that Alpheus ever engaged in plural marriage.

9. The first public disclosure of Cutler's additional wives, based on Nauvoo Temple records, is found in the family
history of Clare B. Christensen, *Before and After Mt. Pisgah* (Salt Lake City, published by author, 1979), 175–76.
On Luana Hart Beebe, Cutler's first plural wife and the ex-wife of the famous bad-boy Orrin Porter Rockwell,
see Harold Schindler, *Orrin Porter Rockwell: Man of God, Son of Thunder* (Salt Lake City: University of Utah
Press, 1966), as well as Danny L. Jorgensen and Andrew Leary, "Luana Hart Beebe (1814–1897): A Biographical
Sketch of a Remarkable Early Latter-day Saint," *Journal of Mormon History* 42, no. 3 (July 2016): 120–54.

scholarly efforts to illuminate the origin, implementation, and development of early Latter-day Saint polygamy. This includes the secrecy and denials surrounding these religious-but-not-civil-marriages, even within Mormon society. It further involves other significant departures from typical American marital and family patterns, such as the rationale for entering the relationship, consent and agreement among partners, age differences, living arrangements, spousal and family roles, acknowledgement of paternity, inheritance, and the duration of the relationship (including unofficial dissolutions and divorces) among other anomalies. Moreover, the introduction of plural marriage produced severe social conflicts and cleavages among the early Latter-day Saints involving ongoing affirmations and denials of these relationships and their religious justification.[10] None of Cutler's plural partners left much documentation of their lives; yet, in spite of all of these difficulties and obstacles, it is possible to pull together fragments of their existence from surviving records.

The obscurity of Cutler's plural wives and the lack of even rudimentary information about most of them have hindered scholarly efforts to interpret their relationship with Alpheus Cutler and any residual importance of plural marriage for his subsequent religious organization.[11] Presenting what may be ascertained about these women alleviates much of this difficulty. It also provides fresh data for further considering the origins and early development of Latter-day Saint polygamy. Massive scholarly attention has focused on Joseph Smith's introduction and practice of

---

10. While there is little disagreement today among scholars that Joseph Smith Jr. authored and practiced plural marriage (polygamy) as a part of an emergent Nauvoo Temple theology, this matter and its far-reaching consequences have been debated and disputed from the beginning by rival Latter Day Saint collectivities and organizations. The Church of Jesus Christ of Latter-day Saints (LDS) initially championed the practice, then begrudgingly ended it—resulting in schism and its continued practice by rival sects—while tending to distance itself from the matter today. The Reorganized Church of Jesus Christ of Latter Day Saints (RLDS) included some of the original opponents of Joseph Smith's novel doctrines, particularly plural marriage, and under the leadership of Joseph Smith III, they rejected plural marriage and denied that it was originated by Joseph Smith. The RLDS, now known as Community of Christ, generally acknowledges the veracity of contemporary scholarship on this matter, although some members as well as most of those forming conservative RLDS schismatic groups continue the traditional denials. The founding Cutlerite generation, many of them eyewitnesses to the emergence and development of plural marriage and its practice by friends and family, rejected the practice, and subsequent generations gradually embraced the RLDS stance on the matter. The contemporary Cutlerites adamantly deny that Alpheus Cutler participated in plural marriage.

11. Christensen, *Before and After Mt. Pisgah*, 183, in very briefly reviewing Cutler's plural marriages, concluded that: "Confronted with problems from the law, Alpheus decided to put away his plural wives." He further noted that: "Not knowing what else to do, at least two of the wives although disowned, continued to live as part of the community." This view of Cutler, grounded in a Utah Mormonism perspective, greatly influenced subsequent scholarship. Jorgensen, "The Old Fox," 162–70, for instance, accepted Christensen's conclusions and incorporated them into his interpretation of Cutler and the Cutlerites. Taking Christensen's viewpoint as a point of departure, Young, *Obscure Believers*, 195–98, speculated about Cutler's repudiation of his plural wives; and Christopher James Blythe, "'The Highest Class of Adulterers and Whoremongers': Plural Marriage, the Church of Jesus Christ (Cutlerite), and the Construction of Memory," *Dialogue: A Journal of Mormon Thought* 26, no. 2 (Summer 2013): 1–39; and Christopher James Blythe, "The Church in the Days of Alpheus Cutler: New Insights into Nineteenth-century Ecclesiology," *John Whitmer Historical Association Journal* 29 (2009): 73–93.

plural marriage and the continuation of this unique form of marriage among the Utah Mormons; yet, there has been much less concerted scholarly consideration of this highly controversial early Latter-day Saint form of marriage and family by other leaders and groups, especially before 1852.[12] This is unfortunate since alternative cases of very early Latter-day Saint polygamy offer a consequential basis for comparative analysis and interpretation as well as providing a more complete portrait of important features of this historical situation and related events.

Alpheus Cutler and the Latter Day Saints

Alpheus Cutler joined the newly founded Latter Day Saint religion in 1833 at forty-one years of age along with his wife, Lois, and eventually all ten of their surviving children (Thaddeus, Lois Huntington, Louisa, Sally Maria, William, Benjamin, Clarissa, Emily, Edwin, and Betsy).[13] The Cutlers gathered to Kirtland, Ohio, subsequently moving with others of the faith to Far West, Missouri, and then to Nauvoo, Illinois.[14] The Cutlers, like most of the early Mormons, were tested by these events in conjunction with their participation in a socially unpopular new religion, involving the regular loss of friends and family—as with the death of their youngest child, eleven-year-old Betsy, in 1843. At Nauvoo Alpheus became a part of the uppermost Mormon leadership as a member of the three-person Temple Building Commit-

---

12. Merina Smith, *Revelation, Resistance, and Mormon Polygamy* focuses on this early period but adds little new to the discussion. For studies of polygamy among other Latter-day Saint leaders and groups see Melvin C. Johnson, *Polygamy on the Pedernales: Lyman Wight's Mormon Villages in Antebellum Texas, 1845–1858* (Logan: Utah State University Press, 2006); Vickie Cleverley Speek, "Marriage and Family Relationships among the Strangites, 1844–1856," in *The Persistence of Polygamy: From Joseph Smith's Martyrdom to the First Manifesto, 1844–1890,* ed. Newell G. Bringhurst and Craig L. Foster (Independence, MO: John Whitmer Books, 2013), 148–67; Christopher Blythe, "'Nearly All of the Factions': The Polygamous Passages of William Smith, Lyman Wight, and Alpheus Cutler," in Bringhurst and Foster, *The Persistence of Polygamy,* 168–201; and Lewis M. Weigand, "Nineteenth-Century Polygamists Who Became RLDS," in Bringhurst and Foster, *The Persistence of Polygamy,* 244–62.

13. In addition to the works cited above on Cutler, see Alpheus Cutler, file 8582, Land and Records Office, Nauvoo, Illinois, Church of Jesus Christ of Latter-day Saints; and "Cutler, Alpheus," Joseph Smith Papers, http://www.josephsmithpapers.org/person/alpheus-cutler. The Cutler children were: Thaddeus (1809–96), Lois Huntington (1811–80), Libbeus (1814–19), Louisa Elizabeth (1816–54), Sally (Sara) Ann or Sally (Mavea) Maria (1818–90), William Lathrop (1821–51), Benjamin Franklin (1823–66), Clarissa "Crissy" (1824–51), Emily Trask (1827/28–51/2), Edwin H. (1829–37), Betsy A. (1832–43), and Phineas (unknown). For a description of the Cutlers conversions see Emma Whiting Anderson, "Others, with the Church in an Early Day," *Autumn Leaves* 2 (1889): 494–96; and Inez Smith Davis, *The Story of the Church: A history of the Church of Jesus Christ of Latter Day Saints, and of its legal successor, the Reorganized Church of Jesus Christ of Latter Day Saints* (Independence, MO: Herald Publishing House, 1938), 141–42.

14. Emma (Whiting) Anderson, "An Incident of the Past," *Autumn Leaves* 8 (July 1895): 315–16; Fletcher and Fletcher, *Alpheus Cutler,* 9–46; and Jorgensen, "The Old Fox," 312–58.

tee, one of the governing Nauvoo Stake High Council, and an early initiate of the Anointed Quorum as well as a senior member of the Council of Fifty.[15]

Alpheus and Lois Cutler were endowed as Anointed Quorum members in October 1843, their marriage was sealed in the quorum that November, and they were among the first of this collection of only twenty men and sixteen wives to receive the highest priesthood ordinance, the second anointing, in late 1843 (notably ahead of all of the apostles and their wives).[16] Alpheus, like about half of the anointed, did not marry additional women until after the death of the Mormon prophet in 1844.[17] It therefore does not appear that he was especially eager to acquire additional wives. However, during the subsequently intense and bitter struggle for control of the fractured Nauvoo Mormon organization, taking plural wives became an important test of loyalty to the leadership of the remaining apostles and others, like Alpheus, committed to the continuation of the emergent temple rites and theology.[18]

---

15. Matthew J. Grow, Ronald K. Esplin, Mark Ashurst-McGee, Gerrit J. Dirkmaat, and Jeffrey D. Mahas, eds., *Joseph Smith Papers, Administrative Records, Volume 1: Council of Fifty Minutes, March 1844–January 1846,* vol. 1 of the Administrative Record series of The Joseph Smith Papers, Ronald K. Esplin, Matthew J. Grow, and Matthew C. Godfrey, general eds. (Salt Lake City: Church Historian's Press, 2016); Michael Quinn, *The Mormon Hierarchy: Origins of Power* (Salt Lake City, Signature Books, 1994), 105–85, 203–9; Anderson and Bergera, *Joseph Smith's Quorum of the Anointed;* Jedediah S. Rogers, ed., *The Council of Fifty: A Documentary History* (Salt Lake City: Signature Books, 2014), especially xxxix; Jorgensen, "The Old Fox," 161–63; Danny L. Jorgensen, "Building the Kingdom of God," *Kansas History* 15, no. 3 (1992): 192–209; Danny L. Jorgensen, "Conflict in the Camps of Israel: The Emergence of the 1853 Cutlerite Schism," *Journal of Mormon History* 21, no. 1 (Spring 1995): 24–62; Christopher James Blythe, "The Council of Fifty Minutes and Latter Day Saint Studies on Succession," *John Whitmer Historical Association Journal* 37 (Spring/Summer 2017): 83–94; and Christopher James Blythe, "The Church and the Kingdom of God: Ecclesiastical Interpretations of the Council of Fifty," *Journal of Mormon History* 43, no. 2 (April 2017): 100–130. The anointed and fifty were ranked by seniority, making Cutler one of the top-ranked Nauvoo Mormon leaders and equal in priesthood authority even to the apostles. Also see "John Alpheus Cutler," FamilySearch, https://familysearch.org/photos/artifacts/1318370. While family genealogists and some LDS records often add "John" to this name there is no indication it is anything more than an often repeated mistake

16. David John Buerger, "'The Fulness of the Priesthood': The Second Anointing in Latter-day Saint Theology and Practice," *Dialogue: A Journal of Mormon Thought* 16, no. 1 (Spring 1983): 10–44; Anderson and Bergera, *Joseph Smith's Quorum of the Anointed,* xxix–xxxvi, xxxix, 29–36, 185–220; and Gary James Bergera, "Identifying the Earliest Mormon Polygamists, 1841–44," *Dialogue: A Journal of Mormon Thought* 38, no. 3 (Fall 2005): 55.

17. Anderson and Bergera, *Joseph Smith's Quorum of the Anointed,* xxxv–xxxvi, calculate that a little more than half of the anointed men who received the second anointing were polygamists before 1845. They quote Michael Quinn's "Latter-day Saint Prayer Circles," *BYU Studies* 19, no. 1 (Fall 1978): 79–105, supporting contention that plural marriage only was "an appendage" to the quorum even for its fully anointed members (88). Plural marriage, moreover, was not restricted to the anointed since it already had spread somewhat eclectically to other friends and associates of the Latter-day Saint prophet. Also see Kathryn M. Daynes, "Mormon Polygamy: Belief and Practice in Nauvoo," in *Kingdom on the Mississippi Revisited: Nauvoo in Mormon History,* ed. Roger D. Launius and John E. Hallwas (Urbana: University of Illinois Press, 1996), 135–40.

18. During the 1844 trial of Sidney Rigdon at Nauvoo, Brigham Young cast the central issue of leadership in terms of those favoring or not favoring "Joseph's measures," referring generally to the emergent temple theology and ordinances, and more specifically in code to eternal (plural) marriage, see *Times and Seasons* 5, no. 15 (September 1844): 647; *Latter-day Saints' Millennial Star* 5, no. 7 (December 1844): 100; and Matthew S. Moore,

Cutler, at sixty-one years of age, demonstrated his unqualified commitment to "Joseph's measures" with a marriage sealing to thirty-one-year-old Luana Hart Beebe Rockwell on August 9, 1845, in a private temple ceremony performed by apostle Heber C. Kimball—Alpheus's son-in-law and counselor to the head apostle Brigham Young.[19] About six months later, on February 3, 1846, he was married to five additional women in the Nauvoo Temple.[20] These wives, all widowed women, were: seventy-five-year-old Margaret Kerr (or Carr) McCall; her sister, sixty-six-year-old Abigail Kerr Andrews; Disey Caroline McCall Allen, Margaret's forty-four-year-old daughter; fifty-two-year-old Sally (Sarah) Cox (Smith) Hutchings; and twenty-four-year-old Henrietta Clarinda Miller Cutler. During this period of accelerating plural marriage activity, Alpheus Cutler was one of the top wife-takers among about fifteen of the most influential Latter-day Saint leaders.[21] It nevertheless is significant

---

"'Joseph's Measures': The Continuation of Esoterica by Schismatic Members of the Council of Fifty," *Journal of Mormon History* 25, no. 2 (Fall 1999): 70–100.

19. Stanley B. Kimball, ed., *On the Potter's Wheel: The Diaries of Heber C. Kimball* (Salt Lake City: Signature Books, 1987), 133; Stanley B. Kimball, *Heber C. Kimball: Mormon Patriarch and Pioneer* (Urbana: University of Illinois Press, 1981), 122, 308. Kimball married two Cutler daughters, Clarissa (1824–52) on February 29, 1845, and Emily (1828–52), in December 1845. Also see Quinn, *The Mormon Hierarchy*, 143–55; and Danny L. Jorgensen, "Early Mormon Marriage, Family, and Networks of Kinship: Begets and Horizontal Genealogy of the Later Cutlerites at Nauvoo," *John Whitmer Historical Association Journal* 34, no. 1 (Spring/Summer, 2014): 127–50. In identifying Luana and all of Cutler's other plural wives we have as a matter of consistency identified them by all variations of their names; although it seems likely in the case of Luana that she did not use the name Rockwell after her divorce, even if others sometimes did identify her by that name.

20. Devery S. Anderson and Gary James Bergera, eds., *The Nauvoo Endowment Companies, 1845–1846: A Documentary History* (Salt Lake City: Signature Books, 2005), 565–83; and Anderson and Bergera, *Joseph Smith's Quorum of the Anointed*, 220. Also see Bergera, "Identifying the Earliest Mormon Polygamists, 1841–44," 1–74, for a useful discussion of the technical meanings of marriage terminologies like sealing, eternal, celestial, and so on. He notes that: "The second anointing was the highest ordinance in Smith's temple-related theology during which wives were anointed as queens and priestesses to their husbands, and husbands as kings and priests to God; the second anointing thus functioned as a defacto 'marriage' sealing" (10). In addition to Lois and Luana, all five of these women received the second anointing with Alpheus and therefore were understood to be married and eternally sealed to him. However, while all of the other wives also were "sealed" to Alpheus in a separate marriage rite, Abigail and Sally, for unknown reasons, do not seem to have undergone this separate eternal marriage sealing. Sally apparently was sealed to her first husband, Elias, according to Anderson and Bergera, *The Nauvoo Endowment Companies* record (580). This "sealings for the living," however, was an impossibility since Elias Hutching was deceased. We find no record of an independent marriage sealing of Abigail and Alpheus, or of Abigail being sealed to her first husband. These anomalies raise perplexing issues about how the participants understood these marriages, practically and theologically.

21. George D. Smith, "Nauvoo Roots of Mormon Polygamy, 1841–46: A Preliminary Demographic Report," *Dialogue: A Journal of Mormon Thought* 27, no. 1 (Spring 1994): 1–72. Alpheus Cutler and Newel K. Whitney, both with six new wives, only ranked behind Willard Richards and John Smith with seven wives, John Taylor and Samuel Brent with eight, Brigham Young with twenty-one, and Heber C. Kimball with twenty-four wives. Hales, *Joseph Smith's Polygamy*, 1:3, 2:165, estimates that only about 79 Latter-day Saints (29 men and 50 women) were polygamous when Smith died in June 1844, while this had increased to at least 717 (196 men and 521 women) by late 1847. The increase in plural marriage activity following Smith's death served the purposes of testing the commitment of the faithful, extended plural marriage to a larger collection of followers, and designating a male authority responsible for unmarried (single, divorced, and widowed) women and any dependent offspring. Some of these marriages may have been inspired and legitimated by the biblical idea of Levirate marriage, understood

that all of these women were widows, and all but two of them were within fourteen years of his age. Alpheus and Lois worked continuously alongside the rest of the anointed leadership, moreover, in providing the Latter-day Saints with a full complement of temple ordinances before departing Nauvoo. This further confirms their unambiguous and most solemn commitment to these theological and ritual innovations, including plural and celestial marriage.[22]

These drastic marital innovations required a substantial cognitive adjustment for this first generation of Latter-day Saint polygamists.[23] "The new marriage and family forms," sociologist Thomas O'Dea emphasized, "demanded attitudes toward and relations between husbands and wives for which the background of the people had ill prepared them, and as a result the new institution went against the grain for many."[24] Lois Cutler was a fifty-seven-year-old grandmother when her husband of thirty-seven years began taking plural wives.[25] Two of these additional wives were somewhat older than Lois, one was only a little younger, one was only eight years older than her oldest child, and the ages of the two youngest wives fell within the age range of her children. Lois may not have felt threatened by the two older wives; although from the standpoint of American monogamy any additional wife usually was morally problematic.[26] It would be surprising if Lois was not at least somewhat

literally and/or metaphorically. But we have not encountered any such explicit rationale for this in the Cutler case, further underscoring the informal, uninstitutionalized character of this emergent form of Latter-day Saint marriage.

22. Anderson and Bergera, *Joseph Smith's Quorum of the Anointed*, especially xxix–xxxix, 29–39, 88–220; and Anderson and Bergera, *The Nauvoo Endowment Companies*, xii, xl, 4–10, 29, 91–114, 138, 198–232, 315, 415–16, 562, 579. During the week of Monday, December 29, 1845, to Saturday, January 3, 1846, Lois assisted the washings and anointing of about one hundred women, including her daughters, Luana (her sister wife), and four of the other women who shortly would be married to her husband polygamously.

23. Robert Bruce Flanders, *Nauvoo: Kingdom on the Mississippi* (Urbana: University of Illinois Press, 1965), especially 306–41, observes that for some Latter-day Saints plural marriage and related innovation were too much, resulting in opposition to Smith, schism, and departures from this religion. Lawrence Foster, *Religion and Sexuality*, 146–80, notices that even many of the Saints who remained and eventually accepted plural marriage found it difficult to accept initially; and, on this point, also see Stephanie Smith Goodson, "Plural Wives," in *Mormon Sisters: Women in Early Utah*, ed. Claudia L. Bushman (Salt Lake City: Olympus Publishing Company, 1976), 89–111. Thomas F. O'Dea, *The Mormons* (Chicago: University of Chicago Press, 1957), 245–49, discusses plural marriage under the general heading of "sources of strain and conflict."

24. O'Dea, *The Mormons*, 245.

25. Lois Lathrop, the daughter of Samuel (1760–1821) and Lois Huntington (1759–1846) Lathrop, was born at Lebanon, New Hampshire, on September 24, 1788. See Fletcher and Fletcher, *Alpheus Cutler*, 10; Jorgensen, "The Old Fox," 159–60; and "Anderson Clan," http://anderson-clan.com/buckley_sally_anderson.html.

26. Paula Kelly Harline, *The Polygamous Wives Writing Club: From the Diaries of Mormon Pioneer Women* (New York: Oxford University Press, 2014), 4, notices that: "Mormons were trying to integrate polygamy into a culture that was overwhelmingly monogamous in practice and underlying attitude. Thus, in general wives never felt comfortable with polygamy because, despite their efforts to convince themselves otherwise, there still seemed something adulterous about it."

uneasy from a monogamous standpoint about sharing her husband with considerably younger women, especially the two wives as young as her own daughters.

Lois Cutler—like Margaret, Abigail, and Disey but not Sally or Henrietta—was a member of the Relief Society, and it therefore seems likely that they knew and interacted with one another prior to these plural marriages.[27] Whether or not this made sharing her husband with these women more or less difficult is unknown. While Lois lived to be almost ninety years of age, no record—written or oral—has survived to indicate her thoughts or feelings about participating in such a radical experiment in marriage and family.[28] Under these circumstances some Mormon women rejected plural marriage and the Latter-day Saint religion entirely; others—like Emma Smith, first wife of the Mormon prophet himself—accepted the new teachings and practices under duress and more or less loud protest; and still others were more accepting and more readily embraced it.[29] Lois's actions suggest that at the very least she acquiesced to plural marriage; and, her active participation as one of the anointed in assisting other women with endowments and sealings as well as the plural marriages of her two youngest daughters indicate considerable acceptance of this new theology, including polygamy, at least under some circumstances.

With the Mormon exodus from Illinois, Father Cutler—as he often was referred to respectfully—captained the third company of the "Camps of Israel" across Iowa.[30]

---

27. See The First Fifty Years of Relief Society, https://www.churchhistorianspress.org/the-first-fifty-years-of-relief-society/part-1/1-2/1-2-8; and Nauvoo Relief Society Minute Book, 1841–1846, entry of May 12, 1842. Sally and Henrietta may not have resided at Nauvoo long enough to have become members of the Relief Society.

28. Lois, some of her adult children, and their families trekked to western Minnesota in 1865 with the remaining Iowa Cutlerites, and other family members later joined them. In 1868 these families moved from the Cutlerite settlement at Clitherall, Otter Tail County, about sixty miles north to Oak Lake in Becker County, partly over disagreements with their fellow religionists. Lois and most of these relatives who were not already members of the Reorganized Church of Jesus Christ of Latter Day Saints (RLDS) subsequently joined them in 1875, like most of the other Cutlerites over several successive generations. Lois died March 23, 1878, and was buried in the Oakwood Cemetery, Audubon, Becker County, Minnesota. Interestingly, members of the Cutler families were among those denying the origination of plural marriage by Joseph Smith and any involvement of Alpheus Cutler, like the RLDS generally; although Lois obviously knew differently as did Luana who resided among the Minnesota Cutlerites with her adult son, Jacob, by Alpheus. See Harvey B. Black, *Early Members of the Reorganized Church of Jesus Christ of Latter Day Saints* (Provo, UT: Infobases, 1996), 2:415; Alvin H. Wilcox, *A Pioneer History of Becker County Minnesota* (St. Paul, MN: Pioneer Press Company, 1907), 331–32; *The History of the Reorganized Church of Jesus Christ of Latter Day Saints*, 8 vols. (Independence, MO: Herald House, 1967), 4:219; Lois Cutler obituary, *Saints' Herald* 25, no. 10 (May 15, 1878): 159; and "Anderson Clan."

29. Kahlile Mehr, "Women's Response to Plural Marriage," *Dialogue: A Journal of Mormon Thought* 18 (Fall 1985): 84–97; also see Linda King Newell and Valeen Tippetts Avery, *Mormon Enigma: Emma Hale Smith, Prophet's Wife, "Elect Lady," Polygamy's Foe* (Garden City, NY: Doubleday and Company, 1984), especially 95–156, for an excellent discussion of Emma Smith's ambiguous reactions to the introduction of polygamy.

30. Smith, *History of the Church*, 481; Rogers, *The Council of Fifty*, 113–19; Grow et al., *Council of Fifty, Minutes*, 481, 546; and Richard E. Bennett, "'And Should We Die': sickness and Death at Winter Quarters," in *Mormons at the Missouri, Winter Quarters, 1846–1852:* (Norman: University of Oklahoma Press, 1987). The companies of Cutler and Cahoon traveled together. They had worked closely as members of the Nauvoo Building Committee, and Cahoon ranked sixth in the 1844 Council of Fifty, the body responsible for the migration. See Quinn, *The*

By September 1845 he (along with captains Brent, Morley, and Cahoon) already had selected the one hundred families composing his company, and this list was presented to the Council of Fifty clerk. In January 1846, in addition to these families, Cutler's company included ninety-one horses, sixty-eight yoke of oxen, sixty-two wagons, nine buggies, and one hundred fifty-eight cows. This robust party, invigorated further when combined with the company of Reynolds Cahoon, departed the Mississippi River on March 14, arrived at the Missouri about the middle of June, and by early August 1846, began crossing the river.[31] Cutler presided as president of the high council over all of the Mormon encampments along the Missouri River until the spring of 1848 when the Saints either continued west or moved to the east side of the river. Following the return of the apostles from the intermountain west in December 1847, he received approval from the re-constituted Mormon leadership to establish an Indian mission in present-day Kansas.[32] After founding a mission settlement on Delaware lands, Cutler assumed leadership of a branch (congregation) at Silver Creek, Iowa, and over about the next four years he periodically traveled back and forth between these two locations.[33]

Cutler and the Silver Creek Saints became entangled in a protracted dispute with the Iowa High Council at this time over Alpheus's roles and the Indian ministries.[34] When the high council was unable to secure Cutler's subordination and immediate relocation to the west, he was disfellowshipped and then excommunicated in 1851. A year or so later Alpheus and some members of the Silver Creek Branch founded a southwestern Iowa village they named "Manti," where they established an

---

Mormon Hierarchy, 522; Jorgensen, "Conflict in the Camps of Israel," 31; and "Cahoon, Reynolds," Joseph Smith Papers, http://www.josephsmithpapers.org/person/reynolds-cahoon.

31. Alpheus Cutler and Reynolds Cahoon to Brigham Young and the Council of the Twelve from Upper Camp of Israel, June 12, 1846, Church History Library, The Church of Jesus Christ of Latter-day Saints, Salt Lake City, Utah, hereafter cited as Church History Library; Eldon J. Watson, ed., *Manuscript History of Brigham Young, 1846–1847* (Ann Arbor: University of Michigan Press, 1971), 297–98; William Farrington Cahoon, 1813–1897, "Autobiography" in *Reynolds Cahoon and His Stalwart Sons,* ed. Stella Shurtleff and Brent Farrington Cahoon (Salt Lake City: Paragon Press, 1960); and Juanita Brooks, ed., *On the Mormon Frontier: The Diary of Hosea Stout, 1844–1889* (Salt Lake City: University of Utah Press, 2009, originally published 1964), 182.

32. Jorgensen, "Building the Kingdom of God," 192–209; and Richard E. Bennett, "Lamanism, Lymanism, and Cornfields," *Journal of Mormon History* 13 (1986/87): 45–59.

33. The mission was located along the Grasshopper (later Delaware) River a few miles north of the confluence with the Kaw (now Kansas) River about twenty miles northeast of present-day Topeka, Kansas, just south of the present-day location of the Perry Lake dam. This site in present-day Kentucky Township, Jefferson County, Kansas, was known as Mormon Mills, then Indian Mills, and later Thompsonville. Lewis Denna, another Council of Fifty member and a Native American, with his spouse resided here continuously while other Cutler followers served at the mission for more or less extended periods of time. For a description of Silver Creek see Danny L. Jorgensen, "Cutler's Camp at the Big Grove on Silver Creek: A Mormon Settlement in Iowa, 1847–1853," *Nauvoo Journal* 9, no. 2 (Fall 1997): 39–51. The branch sometimes was referred to by all of these labels: Cutler's Camp, Big Grove, and/or Silver Creek. The Saints here were located along Silver Creek from immediately north of present-day Malvern to about three-to-five miles upstream to the north.

34. Jorgensen, "Conflict in the Camps of Israel," 46–56.

independent organization, the Church of Jesus Christ (Cutlerite), in 1853.[35] Other dissenting and unaffiliated Latter Day Saints in the area participated in this organization, although it was challenged seriously by the "new organization," eventuating in the Reorganized Church of Jesus Christ of Latter Day Saints (RLDS), headed by Joseph Smith III after 1860. Following Cutler's death in 1864, about one hundred remaining "Cutlerites," as they were known best, relocated to western Minnesota.[36] Today, a few faithful members compose a branch at Independence, Missouri, but there are no Cutlerites left in Minnesota or anywhere else.[37]

Luana Hart Beebe Rockwell

Luana was born October 3, 1814, at Lebanon, Madison County, New York, to Isaac and Olive Soule Beebe, a family of early Mormon converts.[38] The Beebes moved to the Zion-inspired consolidation of Mormons at Independence, Missouri, in 1831, where Luana married eighteen-year-old Orrin Porter Rockwell of considerable subsequent notoriety.[39] Their relationship was marked by the tumultuous Mormon events of this period and especially Porter's growing attachment to guarding his prophet. Luana birthed five Rockwell children (Emily, Caroline, Orrin, Sarah,

35. Danny L. Jorgensen, "The Fiery Darts of the Adversary: An Interpretation of Early Cutlerism," *John Whitmer Historical Association Journal* 10 (1990): 67–83; and Danny L. Jorgensen, "The Cutlerites of Southwestern Iowa: A Latter-day Saint Schism, 1846–1865," *The Annals of Iowa* 58, no. 2 (Spring 1999): 131–61. Also see Danny L. Jorgensen, "The Scattered Saints of Southwestern Iowa: Cutlerite-Josephite Conflict and Rivalry, 1855–1865," *John Whitmer Historical Association Journal* 13 (1993): 80–97; and Danny L. Jorgensen, "Mormontown: Collective Memory of a Cutlerite Colony in Iowa," *John Whitmer Historical Association Journal* 35, no. 1 (Spring/Summer 2015): 163–83.

36. Michael S. Riggs, "The Cutlerite Migration to Minnesota: An Epic Perilous Journey into Diaspora," in *Scattering of the Saints: Schism Within Mormonism*, ed. Newell G. Bringhurst and John C. Hamer (Independence, MO: John Whitmer Books, 2007), 177–89. Only about half of the Cutlerites went to Minnesota while almost all of those remaining in Iowa joined the Reorganized Church of Jesus Christ of Latter Day Saints or dropped out of this religion entirely.

37. Danny L. Jorgensen, "Back to Zion: The Emergence of the Church of Jesus Christ (Cutlerite) and Its Return to Independence, Missouri," in Bringhurst and Hamer, *Scattering of the Saints*, 161–76.

38. Jorgensen and Leary, "Luana Hart Beebe," 120–54. Although the Beebees and Cutlers both resided in western New York at about the same time, there is no indication that these families knew one another at the time.

39. Hyrum Smith's blessing on Luana Rockwell, January 22, 1843, Nauvoo, Illinois, Patriarchal Blessing Book, 4:373, Church History Library; "Luana Hart Beebe," Susan Easton Black, comp., *Membership of The Church of Jesus Christ of Latter-day Saints, 1830–1848*, 50 vols. (Provo, UT: Brigham Young University, Religious Studies Center, 1989); "Luana Hart Baldwin," Susan Easton Black, *Early Members of the Reorganized Church of Jesus Christ of Latter Day Saints*, 6 vols. (Provo, UT: Brigham Young University, 1996); Isaac Beebe, United States Census 1820, Chardon, Geauga, Ohio, page 101A, roll M33_91, image 117; "Isaac Beebe," Black, *Membership*; Thomas Bullock, comp., "A List of Saints in Jackson County," Church History Library, as cited by Schindler, *Orrin Porter Rockwell*, 8 (Schindler gives the date of February 2 for this marriage); Scott H. Faulring, "Early Marriages Performed by the Latter-day Saint Elders in Jackson County, Missouri, 1832–1834," *Mormon Historical Studies* 2, no. 2 (Fall 2001): 197–210, especially 199nn6–11. Contrary to Faulring's account, Luana's mother did not accompany them to Missouri unless the 1830 date of her death is mistaken.

and Joseph), before formally divorcing Porter in June 1845, unwilling to endure his lengthy absences, lack of support, and womanizing.[40]

It would be surprising if Alpheus and Luana had not become at least acquainted a year or more before their August 1845 marriage. According to a much later, second-hand account, Luana said that "she had been a poor girl without relatives to care for her and Cutler told her if she would be sealed to him he would support her."[41] Luana had Beebe Mormon relatives, but she was a divorcee with four dependent children during a period of severe crisis in Nauvoo Mormonism. Having the emotional and economic support of a stable husband no doubt was appealing to her. It appears likely that Lois had consented (or at least acquiesced) to the relationship since in January 1846 she attended Luana in receiving the Nauvoo Temple endowment, and a little more than a week later Luana accompanied Alpheus and Lois to the temple for a re-enactment of their marriage sealings, the second anointing, and apparently the sealing of the four surviving Rockwell children to Alpheus.[42] Notwithstanding all of the complications of sharing a husband in a not yet institutionalized arrangement, this plural relationship offered certain rights and obligations, even if they were not sanctioned legally. This entailed the implicit prestige of marriage to a prominent, mature, economically and psychologically steady Mormon leader. Luana, unlike Lois, entered the marriage with the understanding that she would be sharing a husband, and knowing that expectations for her roles as wife and mother were limited by a first wife and perhaps eventually still other wives. Very significantly she received the promise of eternal salvation with her children as a queen and priestess—one of God's anointed—in the celestial world. Luana and her children accompanied Alpheus on the Iowa crossing while Lois remained at Nauvoo, most likely to attend two pregnant daughters, twenty-two-year-old Clarissa and nineteen-year-old Emily,

---

40. "Luana H. Bybee," Historical Pioneer Research Group, Early Latter-day Saints, A Mormon Pioneer Database, http://www.earlylds.com notes that: "Divorce granted 26 June 1845. Charge was non-support during previous five years, and named a Mrs. Hasis (may be Davis) as being a third party to the affair." Rockwell had a reputation for heavy drinking and while it is not mentioned, this also may have been a factor in this divorce.

41. This statement is from a letter by Iva Gould reporting on a conversation between Luana and Iva's father, Winfield Gould, as well as conversations between her parents and grandparents, the Francis Lewis Whitings, and Cutlerite folklore, quoted by Young, *Obscure Believers*, 197–98. Unfortunately, we have been unable to verify the existence of this letter based on the citation by Young; although we do not doubt its existence. It is consistent with the oral tradition on Alpheus Cutler and his followers. Also see Blythe, "The Highest Class of Adulterers and Whoremongers," 12.

42. Anderson and Bergera, *The Nauvoo Endowment Companies*, 278–80. Besides Lois the other Mormon women performing the washings were Thirza Cahoon, Olive Farr, Sarah D. Rich, Mercy R. Thompson, and Lydia Granger. Schindler, *Orrin Porter Rockwell*, says the Rockwell children were sealed to Cutler (145). If Porter objected to his children being sealed to Alpheus, we have found no record of it. Alpheus and Lois, as longstanding members of the anointed, previously had been anointed and sealed many times. See Anderson and Bergera, *Joseph Smith's Quorum of the Anointed*, xxix, xxxvi, xxxix, 35–36, 38–39, 194–95, 208–9, 211.

both plural wives of apostle Heber C. Kimball.[43] Luana's marriage to Alpheus clearly involved sexual relations, as evidenced by her conceiving around the middle of May and then delivering a son named Jacob Lorenzo Boyd at Winter Quarters on February 18, 1847.[44] They apparently felt it necessary to supply the baby with this alias surname, one constructed from Cutler's mother's maiden name. When Alpheus moved to Silver Creek in 1848, Luana and the children relocated about eighteen miles away to Farm Creek, next to her brother Calvin.[45] Luana's mortal marriage to Cutler was inexplicably terminated by no later than the summer of 1849 when she married Isaac Perry (1807–85) monogamously.[46] Later folklore holds that Cutler gave one of his plural wives "away to a man who wanted to marry her," surely referring to Luana.[47] This exceedingly derogatory depiction, along with the conclusion that Luana was, "with a single pronouncement, cast off," reflects highly partisan views of plural marriage and it fails to consider salient features of the situation.[48] The plural marriage was not legally sanctioned, and it therefore required no formal divorce. In a variety of other instances Mormon plural wives terminated these relationships without penalty.[49] Alpheus may have been relieved to be free of earthly obligations for Luana. She most likely took advantage of an opportunity to enact a conventional marriage while

---

43. Elizabeth Ann Whitney in a letter of May 10, 1846, from Garden Grove to Mrs. Thirza Cahoon at Nauvoo anticipated seeing her and Sister (Lois) Cutler soon, "The Papers of Reynolds Cahoon, 1831–1865," item 31, http://www.mormonism.com/Mormonism.pdf.

44. "Jacob Boyd," Early Members of the Reorganized Church of Jesus Christ of Latter Day Saints, Ancestry.com, goo.gl/yiRpLE; and "Jacob Lorenzo Boyd," Utah, Death and Military Death Certificates, 1904–1961, Ancestry.com, goo.gl/wFvEsI.

45. Baptized a Latter-day Saint in 1831 while living near Kirtland, Ohio, Calvin was ordained an elder, then moved to Jackson County, Missouri. He served a midwestern American mission in 1832 (and several other missions in later years), then was ordained a high priest by Oliver Cowdery, before enduring the Missouri conflicts, where he was a member of the Far West High Council. He then moved to Montrose, Lee County, Iowa Territory in 1839, where he likely knew Wheeler Baldwin. Calvin was excommunicated, perhaps as early as 1851, and eventually moved to Farm Creek where he presided over a Latter-day Saint branch that joined the Cutlerites and then the RLDS. He died July 12, 1861, at Farm Creek. See "Beebe, Calvin," Joseph Smith Papers, http://www.josephsmithpapers.org/ person/calvin-beebe; and Davis, *The Story of the Church*, 347–48. Another brother, Isaac Beebe Jr., was married to Phoebe Wilcox. He resided about thirty miles to the west at Kanesville (later Council Bluffs), and he also later joined the RLDS. Still another brother George also lived not too far way in Iowa.

46. "Luana Hart Beebe," Nauvoo Community Project, Brigham Young University, http://nauvoo.byu.edu/ ViewPerson.aspx?ID=3141; "Isaac Perry," Nauvoo Database, http://nauvoo.iath.virginia.edu/nauvoo_db/ person.php?id=3517, give January 28, 1849, as the date of this marriage. There is no record of what the participants understood regarding the earthly or eternal status of these marriages. Since there was no divorce, it is possible that Luana and Alpheus considered themselves to be married, in which case Luana's relationship with Issac Perry was polyandrous; and, in any case, by the logic of the related theology, it is likely that Luana and Alpheus considered themselves to be sealed (married) together eternally.

47. Young, *Obscure Believers*, 198.

48. Young, *Obscure Believers*, 57.

49. Backman and Esplin, "Plural Marriage," 1091–95; Daynes, *Transformation of the Mormon Marriage System*, 141–70; and Embry, *Mormon Polygamous Families*, 175–82.

ending a relationship that would have been exceedingly difficult to sustain at that time in Iowa (or most anywhere else in the United States).

Perry, like Luana, was an early Mormon convert from New York and was unattached, his wife and their children having left him at Nauvoo. Their marriage produced two daughters, Olive and Lydia Ann, although only Olive survived infancy.[50] In 1852 Isaac continued west to Utah, leaving Luana and the children in Iowa and ending their approximately three-year marriage.[51] Luana subsequently married sixty-five-year-old Wheeler Baldwin, a prominent early Mormon convert and a Cutlerite leader, and they lived at Manti.[52] The Baldwins, like growing numbers of Cutlerites, converted to RLDS in 1863. Luana left Wheeler in the early 1870s, however, apparently without formally divorcing him, and moved to Minnesota where she resided with Jacob, her son by Cutler, and his family among the relocated Cutlerites, including a married Rockwell daughter and Lois Cutler.[53] Then in 1892, Luana and the Boyds took a train to Utah, and she lived there with Rockwell children until her death on March 6, 1897.[54]

Margaret Kerr McCall, Abigail Kerr Andrews, and Disey Caroline McCall Allen

Margaret and Abigail Kerr were born in Mecklenburg County, North Carolina, on October 16, 1771, and April 10, 1780, respectively. Margaret married Alexander King McCall (1772–1833) in 1796, and they had nine children while living in North

---

50. "Olive Luana Perry," Descendants of Miller, Burris, Hill, Hall Family Tree, Ancestry.com, http://trees.ancestry.com/tree/4495604/person/24028789183. Mormons at this location were dispersed across the rural countryside along Farm Creek. Later congregations of Latter Day Saints (after 1859 affiliated with the RLDS) were housed at the present-day cross roads of US Highway 59 and Iowa H-12 (or Brothers Avenue), about four miles south of Macedonia and less than two miles east of Henderson. The Farm Creek Cemetery, dating from this period, is located on what is Cary Avenue today, immediately southeast of Henderson, among the corn fields along the creek. Also see "Lydia Ann Perry," AJR-FT10-21-14 Family Tree, Ancestry.com, http://trees.ancestry.com/ tree/74323436/person/42292517207.

51. Johnson, "The Perry Papers," especially 23, 26–31, 33–34, and 43–46; and John S. Higbee/James W. Bay Company (1852), Mormon Pioneer Overland Travel 1847–1868, The Church of Jesus Christ of Latter-day Saints, https://history.lds.org/overlandtravels/companyDetail?companyId=146/. Unfortunately, nothing more is known about the end of this marriage. Isaac joined family members in Springville and then, after being cut off from the LDS church, moved to California about 1854 and eventually to the state of Washington around 1860 where he died about 1885.

52. See "Baldwin, Wheeler," The Joseph Smith Papers, http://www.josephsmithpapers.org/person/wheeler-baldwin.

53. It is possible that Jacob never was told that Alpheus Cutler was his biological father; although, all considered, it would be surprising if he did not discover this information at some point. His death certificate, nevertheless, lists his father as "unknown," see Utah Death Certificates, 1904–1956, Salt Lake City, UT, certificate 65a, series 81448, http://www.wikitree.com/photo/jpg/Boyd-4411.

54. "Luana Hart Beebe Rockwell," Find A Grave, https://www.findagrave.com/memorial/18378459/roc.

Carolina and later Henry County, Tennessee, where Alexander died in 1833.[55] Abigail married John Andrews (1783–1835) in Giles County, Tennessee, around 1800; they produced four known children, and John died there in 1835.[56] Disey Caroline Kerr, Margaret's daughter, was born in Lincoln County, North Carolina, on October 26, 1802. She married Joseph Kerr Allen (1805–43) in 1833 while living in Tennessee, and they produced five known children before Joseph died at Nauvoo in 1843.[57]

Almost nothing is known about the Kerr family conversions to Mormonism. There is no evidence that members of the Kerr, McCall, or Andrews families, besides Margaret, Abigail, and their surviving children, became Latter-day Saints. They first appear in Mormon records at Nauvoo around 1840. These women, significantly, were members of the Relief Society, indicating that they were active and respectable Nauvoo Mormons and that they most likely knew as well as interacted with Lois Cutler. Under the circumstances it is possible that Lois suggested them as plural wives. Margaret, Abigail, and Disey received Nauvoo Temple endowments on December 31, 1845, all of them attended by Lois.[58] Existing information provides few clues as to possible reasons for these marriages beyond their status as widowed women and the eternal promises of the new theology. These women, unlike Luana, did not transverse Iowa with Alpheus Cutler or have any of their children sealed to him. Disey and three of her children (twelve-year-old Susan Emerette, seven-year-old Joseph Moroni, and five-year-old Emeline), accompanied by Margaret, went from Nauvoo to St. Louis where they were located among a sizeable body of Latter Day Saints in 1847. They then went by steamboat, the *Mandan*, from there to Kanesville (present-day Council Bluffs), arriving on May 9, 1848.[59] Abigail, her daughter Margaret Minerva, and son-in-law David Pinkney Rainey crossed Iowa with some of the first companies.[60] David joined the Mormon Battalion on June 16, 1846, leaving

55. These children were: John, 1797–1852; Dovey, 1798–1816; Mary, known as Polly, 1801–58; Disey Caroline, 1802–90; Rachel, 1804–85; Charlotte, 1807–43; Margaret Brown, 1811–85; and Joseph A., 1814–nd.

56. There is considerable confusion in various genealogies about the identity of this John Andrews, and these dates work best with what is known rather than several alternative identities. Their children were: Emeline, 1806–nd; Jane, 1814–before 1841; Joseph Albert W., 1810–43; and Margaret Minerva, 1816–57.

57. The children were: Susan Emerette, 1834–69; Joseph Moroni, 1839–80; James, 1840–nd; Margaret, 1840–44; and Emeline, 1841–1914.

58. Membership of The Church of Jesus Christ of Latter-day Saints, 1830–1848, Ancestry.com; Anderson and Bergera, *The Nauvoo Endowment Companies*, 244–51.

59. Sheri E. Slaughter, "Meet Me in St. Louie" An Index of Early Latter-day Saints Associated with St. Louis Missouri, *Nauvoo Journal* 10, no. 2 (Fall 1998): 49–108, especially 55, 84; also see Stanley, B. Kimball, "The Saints and St. Louis, 1831–1857: An Oasis of Tolerance and Security," *BYU Studies* 13, no. 4 (Summer 1973): 489–519; Journal History of the Church, vol. 24, January–June 1848, Church History Library; and Robert Glass Cleland and Juanita Brooks, eds., *A Mormon Chronicle: The Diaries of John D. Lee, 1848–1876* (San Marino, CA: The Huntington Library, 1955), 26.

60. "The Life Sketch of David Pinkney Rainey," MSS SC 1063, L. Tom Perry Special Collections. It is possible that they traveled with Cutler's company but this is unknown.

the women in a covered wagon at Winter Quarters where Alpheus Cutler presided over the settlement.

In 1850 Margaret (McCall) and Disey (Allen) were living at Silver Creek with the three Allen children (Susan, Joseph, and Emeline), four households away from the residence of Abigail (Andrews) and the Raineys.[61] Located immediately between them was the Cutler family, composed of Alpheus and Lois, daughters Clarissa and Emily along with their Kimball sons, Abraham and Isaac, and a more distant relative, eighteen-year-old Oscar Cutler.[62] It is likely that all of these families gathered to this Iowa location by no later than 1848 when the Mormons abandoned the camps west of the Missouri River; their patterns of residency are indicative of the continuation of marriage and family relationships. We have found no further record of Margaret or Abigail, in all probability indicating that they died within about the next five years. The status of their marriage to Alpheus and the exact character of these relationships remain unknown. The close proximity of these households nevertheless does not support the claim that these women were disowned and cast-off. Just the contrary, it seems highly likely that they sustained interdependent connections involving regularly recurrent (daily) interaction with Alpheus to the end of their lives. The presence of these women, taken to be "wives," surely was the cause of Cutler's legal difficulties with Iowa authorities over plural marriage in 1851.[63]

By 1856 Disey (Allen) and two children (Joseph and Emeline) had relocated to Kane township (what is today Council Bluffs), approximately sixty miles northwest of Cutlerite headquarters at Manti, in a household that included her widowed sister, Rachel Allen, and Rachel's thirteen-year-old son, Henry.[64] In 1860 Disey and Rachel still were living in this same vicinity, along with two of their children and a

---

61. United States Census 1850, District 21, Pottawattamie, Iowa, roll M432_188, page 146A, image 300; also see "Margaret Kerr McCall" and "Disey Caroline McCall Allen," Iowa, Pottawattamie County, Annotated Record of United States Census 1850, Ancestry.com.

62. This most likely is Oscar Fitsland Cutler (1833–83), the son of Perley Cutler (1798–1846), one of Alpheus's cousins, the son of Perley Cutler (1761–1842), a brother of Alpheus's father, Knight Cutler (1755–1830). See "Beach Cutler," Perry Exley Ancestry Family Tree, Ancestry.com, http://person.ancestry.com/tree/ 3047270/ person/-1782863082/facts; and "Parley (Perley) Cutler," Historical Pioneer Research Group, Early Latter-day Saints, A Mormon Pioneer Database, http://www.earlylds.com/getperson.php?personID=I117431& tree=Earlylds.

63. Christensen, *Before and After Mt. Pisgah*, 183, speculates that: "Confronted with problems from the law, Alpheus decided to put away his plural wives." Also see Daynes, *More Wives Than One*, 38, for a discussion of F. Walter Cox who also was party to these difficulties with Iowa authorities over plural wives.

64. "Disey C. Allen," Iowa State Census Collection, 1836–1925, Ancestry.com. Rachel McCall married William Allen (1807–nd) at Nauvoo on November 19, 1843, after the death of his first wife, Charlotte, Rachel's older sister in October 1843, according to Illinois records. See "William Allen," Illinois Marriages to 1850, Ancestry.com. Electronic transcription of marriage records held by the individual counties in Illinois. She assumed responsibility for raising Charlotte and William's approximately five children, along with perhaps one child resulting from this marriage. William apparently died between 1850 and 1856 in Iowa. It seems likely that William, the husband of Charlotte and Rachel McCall, and their sister Disey's husband, Joseph Kerr Allen, were related but the exact character of that relationship remains undetermined.

granddaughter.[65] Whatever happened between Alpheus and Disey, she clearly was autonomous and no longer an earthly plural wife. Furthermore, in describing a visit with Alpheus at Manti in the fall of 1863, Joseph Smith III reported finding a "...poor, helpless old man...too weak to talk, too bungling to even feed himself...."[66] Obviously then, by the early 1860s Cutler was unable to perform much of any husband role to his wives.

Disey, Rachel, and some of their children crossed the plains to Utah in 1862 with the Lewis Brunson Company, leaving on June 14 and arriving on August 29.[67] By 1870 Disey and Rachel had formed a household at Salt Lake City in Ward 7, a few blocks south of the temple, with some of their adult children and grandchildren; ten years later these aging sisters, now seventy-seven and seventy-five respectively, were living alone in Salt Lake.[68] Disey died on October 16, 1890, at the home of her daughter in Ogden, Utah, where she is interred in the city cemetery.[69]

Sally Cox Hutchings

Sally Cox was born February 26, 1794, at Bernards Township, Somerset, New Jersey, and married Elias Hutchings (1784–1845) at Avery, Huron, Ohio, on December 29, 1816.[70] They were parents of twelve children, although only five of them

---

65. Disey C. Allen, United States Census 1860, Crescent, Pottawattamie, Iowa, roll M653_338, page 81, image 380, Family History Library Film 803338. Besides Rachel's now eighteen-year-old son, Henry, the residents included Disey's twenty-five-year-old daughter Susan, now using the surname, Rogers, and her six-year-old daughter, Emeretta Rogers.

66. Richard P. Howard, ed., *The Memoirs of President Joseph Smith (1832–1914)* (Independence, MO: Herald Publishing, 1979), 98.

67. Nauvoo Community Project, Center for Family History and Genealogy, BYU, http://nauvoo.byu.edu/ViewCompany.aspx?ID=277; "Arrival of Captain Bronson's Company," *Deseret News*, September 3, 1862, 6. The Journal History, August 29, 1862, p. 3, confirms that Rachel was with this company.

68. Dessie (Disey) Allen, United States Census 1870, Salt Lake City Ward 7, Salt Lake, Utah Territory, roll M593_1611, page 585A, image 358504, Family History Library Film 553110. The children were thirty-year-old Joseph Allen, twenty-two-year-old Julia Allen, two-year-old May Allen, and sixteen-year-old George Allen; Disey C. Allen, United States Census 1880, Salt Lake City, Salt Lake, Utah, Enumeration District 043, roll 1337, page 51A, Family History Library Film 1255337.

69. "Daisey (Disey) Caroline Allen," Find A Grave. Also see *The Ogden Standard Examiner*, October 17, 1890, 4. She is listed as the spouse of Joseph Kerr Allen, and the surviving children included Emeline Eggleston (spouse Reuben Burgess Eggleston, and their children Charles M., Frank S., George E. Ida May, Joseph M., Mary A., Mary Julia, and Ruben Burgess Eggleston), Susan Emerette Snider (spouse, John Snider Jr, and their children Emeretta Victoria Owen, Rosalie Cummings, Frank Leslie Snider, and John Edgar Snider), and Joseph Moroni Allen (spouse Julia Hester Allen, and their children Joseph Milton Allen and May Snell).

70. "Sally Cox" (also see "Sarah Smith"), Membership of The Church of Jesus Christ of Latter-day Saints, 1830–1848, Ancestry.com, goo.gl/GFmcSy. Sally was the daughter of John and Amy Smith Cox, while Elias's parents were Asa and Abigail Stowell Hutchins. See "Elias Hutchings" and "Sally Cox," Family Central Family History Services, http://www.familycentral.net/index/family.cfm?ref1=6226:8243&ref2=6226:8244. Little more is known about their childhoods. Elias, as youthful frontier hunter and trapper, is credited widely with the discovery or re-discovery of Mammoth Cave in Kentucky, having tracked a wounded bear there about 1809. See,

survived into adulthood.[71] The Hutchings were among the first Ohio Mormon converts in November 1830.[72] Elias was ordained an elder in December 1834 while in Missouri with the Camp of Zion and was then appointed a seventy upon returning to Ohio in 1835.[73] They left Ohio in 1838, sojourning in Illinois and then Iowa because of the Mormons' 1839 expulsion from Missouri, during which time the three youngest children died of disease. The Hutchings finally arrived at Nauvoo in late 1844, where Elias died very suddenly on January 13, 1845.[74] How Sally coped with the deaths of three young daughters followed immediately by the death of her husband is unimaginable to us.

Sally, along with other immediate family, received a Nauvoo Temple endowment on January 12, 1846, preliminary to her February marriage and second anointing with Alpheus Cutler.[75] Almost nothing else is known about Sally's relationship with Alpheus. There is no indication that she ever cohabited with him, accompanied him west, or even lived near him. She probably resided with some of her five adult sons and crossed Iowa with them, although once there she, seemingly alone, belonged to the Blockhouse Branch at Kanesville (Pottawattamie County), Iowa, until 1849.[76] Sally continued west in the company of her son, Lyman Smith Hutchings, traveling

---

for example, Daniel Coit Gilman, Harry Thurston Peck, and Frank Moore Colby, eds., *The New International Encyclopaedia*, 17 vols. (New York: Dodd, Mead and Company, 1911), 12:766; also see the National Park Service's interpretation of this story, "Some say the bear chased Houchins," National Park Service, Mammoth Cave, National Park Kentucky, https://www.nps.gov/maca/learn/historyculture/history2.htm. The "Hutchins" surname eventually became "Hutchings," but both continued in common usage. Sally also sometimes went by "Sarah" and the "Smith" surname, perhaps resulting from being raised by her mother's family (see "Sally Smith," Pioneer Immigrants to Utah Territory, Ancestry.com).

71. "Elias Hutchings," Duffin Family Tree, Ancestry.com, http://person.ancestry.com/tree/102534822/person/120016828390/facts; and "Sally," Duffin Family Tree, Ancestry.com, http://person.ancestry.com/tree/102534822/person/120016828391/facts. These children were: Harvey, 1817–83; Shepherd Pierce, 1818–95; Matilda, 1819–19; Erwin, 1820–21; Elias, 1821–22; William Willard, 1823–1904; Joseph Stowell, 1825–1909; Samuel, 1826–26; Lyman Smith, 1828–89; Sally Lovina, 1830–39; Mary, 1833–39; and Martha, 1833–39. The three youngest children—Sally, Mary, and Martha—died within months of one another in 1839 in Iowa from canker while moving from Ohio to Missouri but what turned out to be Illinois instead.

72. "Elias Hutchings autobiography, circa 1842," MSS SC 2470, L. Tom Perry Special Collections. Multiple internet sites contain considerable biographical information about Elias Hutchings (also spelled Hutchins) and his family (see, for example, "Elias Hutchings" at http://nali2.tripod.com/elias.html). Also see "Elias Hutchings" and "Sally Cox," Membership of The Church of Jesus Christ of Latter-day Saints, 1830–1848, Ancestry.com.

73. See Roger D. Launius, *Zion's Camp: Expedition to Missouri, 1834* (Independence, MO: Herald Publishing House, 1984) for a sound summary of these events.

74. "Elias Hutchings," Find A Grave, https://www.findagrave.com/memorial/10367475/elias-hutchings.

75. Anderson and Bergera, *The Nauvoo Endowment Companies*, 402–10; "Sally Cox," Nauvoo Database, http://nauvoo.iath.virginia.edu/nauvoo_db/person.php?id=55428; and "Sally Cox," Membership of The Church of Jesus Christ of Latter-day Saints, 1830–1848, Ancestry.com.

76. Sally is listed as a member of this branch under both the Cox (286) and Hutchins (600) surnames, see Historical Pioneer Research Group, Early Latter-day Saints, A Mormon Pioneer Database, Blockhouse Branch, Pottawattamie, Iowa, USA, goo.gl/Nr5jfu. Surprisingly, her sons and their families are not listed among the membership.

with the Ezra T. Benson Company that departed Kanesville in July and arrived at the Salt Lake Valley in October 1849.[77] Her sons built her a small house in Salt Lake City's 17th Ward where she died in 1863.[78]

Henrietta Clarinda Miller Cutler

Cutler's youngest plural wife, Henrietta, was born November 16, 1821 (or 1822) at Alfred, Allegany, New York, to Peter and Elizabeth Miller, and she married Moses Cutler at Nauvoo on December 4, 1842.[79] He was born on November 4, 1820, at Grafton, Rensselaer, New York, to Mason (1799–1879) and Emeline Patience Sprague (1800–1870) Cutler. In spite of the surname, there does not appear to be any close kinship relationship to Alpheus. Moses Cutler's younger brother, Mason Jr. (1827–1908), and perhaps two of his sisters, Philinda Emily (1825–1901) and Caroline Eleanor (1838–86), also became Latter Day Saints.[80] Otherwise little is known about the conversion of the Miller or Mason Cutler families and their involvements in early Mormonism.

Moses and Henrietta Cutler moved to Nauvoo sometime in 1843, settling in the 5th Ward.[81] He died there about October 11, 1844, reportedly of diarrhea, shortly after the birth of twin daughters, Philinda and Clorinda, around April 11, 1844.[82] Philinda survived but Clorinda died sometime over about the next two years. In a

---

77. Journal History, Supplement after December 31, 1849, p. 12B; Ezra T. Benson Company (1849), Mormon Pioneer Overland Travel, 1847–1868, The Church of Jesus Christ of Latter-day Saints, https://history.lds.org/overlandtravel/companies/65/ezra-t-benson-company.

78. Sally Hutchins, United States Census 1850, Great Salt Lake, Utah Territory, roll M432_919, page 28B, image 60, where she is listed as residing between the families of her sons, William W. Hutchins and Shepherd Hutchings; and Sally Hutchings, United States Census 1860, Salt Lake, Utah Territory, roll m653_1313, page 15, image 19, Family History Library Film 805313, where she is residing next to the families of sons, Lyman F. Hutchings and William W. Hutchings; "Sarah Hutchins," Utah, Salt Lake County Death Records, 1849–1949, FamilySearch, https://familysearch.org/ark:/61903/1:1:NQH2-4PT; and "Sarah or Sally Smith or Cutler," Find A Grave, https://www.findagrave.com/memorial/59886905.

79. The most accurate single source on Henrietta is Corinne Roylance Allen, "Henrietta Clorinda Miller and Moses Cutler," FamilySearch, https://familysearch.org/photos/artifacts/9978213. Also see "Henrietta Clarinda Miller," Historical Pioneer Research Group, Early Latter-day Saints, A Mormon Pioneer Database; "Henrietta Clarinda Miller," Membership of The Church of Jesus Christ of Latter-day Saints, 1830–1848, Ancestry.com; "Henrietta Clarinda Miller," Kteich.GED Family Tree, Ancestry.com, http://person.ancestry.com/tree/58320448/person/200022624120/facts; and "Moses Cutler," Nauvoo Community Project, Center for Family History and Genealogy, BYU, http://nauvoo.byu.edu/ViewPerson.aspx?ID=27082.

80. Mason Cutler Jr., served a mission in Michigan before relocating to Utah, see "Mason Cutler, Pioneer, Buried at Rigby," *Deseret Evening News*, September 26, 1908.

81. Patriarchal Blessing of Henrietta Cutler by John Smith, March 15, 1845, Nauvoo, Ill, Patriarchal Blessing Book, vol. 9, page 31, no. 99, Church History Library.

82. Fred E. Woods, "Nauvoo Cemetery Record of William D. Huntington, Nauvoo Sexton," *Mormon Historical Studies* 3, no. 1 (Spring 2002): 131–63; *Nauvoo Neighbor*, October 16, 1844, http://boap.org/LDS/Nauvoo-Neighbor/1844/10-16-1844.pdf; and "Moses Cutler," Find A Grave, https://www.findagrave.com/memorial/44004279.

blessing of March 1845, patriarch John Smith told Henrietta that, "The Lord hath looked upon thine afflicted condition & his bounds of compassion have been moved to bless thee" and "the Lord will give you a companion who shall hold the keys of the Holy Priesthood, he shall be able to give thee an endowment in the house of the Lord."[83] Henrietta's second anointing with Alpheus obviously fulfilled the promise of this blessing, and it underscores the tremendously important religious motivation for this plural marriage.

There does not seem to be any record of how or when Henrietta, now one of Cutler's plural wives, and Philinda got to the Mormon encampments at the Missouri. Yet, it is entirely possible, even likely, that she crossed Iowa with Alpheus Cutler's company.[84] During the winter of 1846/47 Henrietta and two-year-old Philinda were a part of Ward 18 at Winter Quarters.[85] Pregnant, presumably by her plural husband, Henrietta died in childbirth around 1851, probably at the Kansas mission, and there is no record of a surviving baby.[86] Referring to these Latter-day Saint missionaries, one report confirms that, "Death claimed a number of them, among whom were Mrs. Franklin Pratt [Emily Cutler Kimball Pratt], Mrs. Calvin Fletcher [Clarissa Cutler Kimball Fletcher], Mrs. Henrietta Cutler; and several children."[87] Philinda, now orphaned at about seven years old, became a ward of John and Eliza Daley, and she continued west to Springville, Utah, with them in 1852.[88]

---

83. Patriarchal Blessing of Henrietta Cutler by John Smith.

84. Philinda Cutler is listed as a member of Ward 18 at Winter Quarters, along with Abigail Andrews (Cutler) and her daughter, Margaret, as well as a "Sister Cox" (very likely Sally Cox Hutchings Cutler), one of Alpheus's married daughters, Louisa Elizabeth Cutler Rappleye, and a Clarinda Henrietta Cutler. See Winter Quarters Wards Membership Lists 1846–1848, Historical Pioneer Research Group, Early Latter-day Saints, A Mormon Pioneer Database, http://www.earlylds.com/showsource.php?sourceID=S8&tree=WinterQuarters. There is a Clarinda Henrietta Cutler among the Mormons at this time, but Philinda's mother does not appear to be listed, and either she is not there, which seems unlikely, or Philinda's care had been turned over to someone else.

85. Winter Quarters Wards Membership Lists 1846–1848, Church History Library.

86. Jorgensen, "Building the Kingdom of God," 203–7; also see William G. Cutler, History of Kansas (Chicago: A. T. Andreas, 1883), 499–500; and Elmer L. Brown, "Early History of Thompsonville," unpublished manuscript, Perry, Kansas, 1966. It is possible that Henrietta and her infant, like Clarissa Cutler Kimball Fletcher, died of the local cholera epidemic of 1852.

87. Emma L. Anderson, "History of the Cutlerite Faction of Latter Day Saints," Journal of History 13 (October 1919): 454–57, quoted from 455. Abraham A. Kimball, Finding a Father (Salt Lake City: Juvenile Instructor Office, Gems for the Young Folks, 1881), 2, further confirms that: "…the grim monster, death, visited us and deprived me of my mother [Clarissa], and a few months later my aunt Emily died, also Henrietta Cutler (widow of Moses Cutler) who left a girl now named Phelinda Rawlence."

88. Allen, "Henrietta Clorinda Miller and Moses Cutler." Henrietta recorded being baptized and sealed to Moses Cutler on December 21, 1845, but this remains unverified by any other source. Also see Ward J. Roylance, "Henrietta recorded being baptized and sealed to Moses Cut 'Roylance Family of Western America,'" FamilySearch, https://familysearch.org/photos/artifacts/14833088; https://familysearch.org/photos/artifacts/ 4926976.

Analysis and Interpretation

Marriage specifies the rights and privileges of the partners to one another forming a social institution composing culturally defined social structures.[89] Social institutions like marriage direct and delimit the decision-making and actions of individuals.[90] Americans often find polygamy morally abhorrent, yet it is an exceedingly common and socially functional form of marriage historically and cross-culturally.[91] Plural marriage, perhaps obviously, also is different, even in early Mormonism, from monogamous marriage. It was not, in other words, the same as a man marrying one woman or a woman marrying a man just with other wives; although exactly what this meant to the partners and community still was being defined and routinized.[92] Even so, early Mormonism mostly grafted a polygynous branch onto the monogamous tree of Christian marriage.[93]

Kathryn Daynes observes that most polygamous marriages enacted before 1852 were characterized by not taking the husband's surname, lack of open cohabitation

---

89. Sociologically, "marriage" comprises a set of cultural expectations and norms specifying the rights, obligations, and conduct of the parties to this relationship. See, for instance, Duran Bell, "Defining Marriage and Legitimacy," *Current Anthropology* 38, no. 2 (April 1997): 237–53.

90. This sociological perspective generally derives from Emile Durkheim, specifically as developed by Mary Douglas's *How Institutions Think* (Syracuse: Syracuse University Press, 1986). It asserts, contrary to American culture's pervasive emphasis on individual decision and choice, that individuals make choices within the parameters specified by the basic social institutions.

91. See George Peter Murdock, *Ethnographic Atlas: A Summary* (Pittsburgh: University of Pittsburgh Press, 1967); Irwin Altman and Joseph Giant, *Polygamous Families in Contemporary Society* (Cambridge: Cambridge University Press, 1996), 39–42; Embry, *Mormon Polygamous Families*, 3–16; Backman and Esplin, "Plural Marriage," 1091–95; and Peggy Fletcher Stack, "Globally, Polygamy Is Commonplace," *The Salt Lake Tribune*, September 20, 1998. In many of the societies permitting polygamy it is a minority practice and, under the conditions of modernity, it has become much less prevalent globally. The American preference for Protestant Christian imagines of marriage reflects a powerful ethnocentricism. While it is possible to evaluate the functionality of different forms of marriage, human studies grounded in the social sciences necessarily are agnostic about the ultimate morality of culturally defined and socially implemented institutions such as marriage, there being no independent epistemological basis for adjudicating such matters.

92. The "Revelation 12 July 1843" (section 132), normatively limits sexual relationship for both male and females exclusively to marriage, defining all other sexual relationships as adultery; and it requires the consent of the first wife for a husband to take additional wives, while otherwise leaving important features of these relationships almost entirely undefined.

93. Harline, *The Polygamous Wives Writing Club*, 22, appropriately concludes, for instance, that: "Most polygamous wives' personal writings provide evidence of the underlying tension between the expectations of monogamy and the practice of polygamy." Mormon polygamy did not redefine paternity, inheritance, economic obligations, dissolution (divorce), or any of the involved social roles (husband/father, wife/mother) among other possible normative features of marital and family relationships. Also see, Marie Cornwall, Camela Courtright, and Laga Van Beek, "How Common the Principle? Women as Plural Wives in 1860," *Dialogue: A Journal of Mormon Thought* 26, no. 2 (Summer 1993): 139–53. For an ethnographic sketch of Latter-day Saint marriage and family see Nels Anderson, "The Mormon Family," *American Sociological Review* 2, no. 5 (October 1937): 601–8. By way of comparison and contrast, Rachel Jones, "Polygyny in Islam," *Macalester Islam Journal* 1, no. 1 (Spring 2006): 61–79, observes that polygynous marriage in Islam is regulated by an elaborate set of values and norms.

or acknowledgement of the marriage except to a small intimate network of friends, and no public recognition of the marriage in the larger community. She further maintains, however, that husbands did endeavor to support these wives, most involved a marriage ceremony, and there were sexual relations in at least some cases.[94] The Cutler marriages conform to these general patterns and, in the absence of specific instructions, they indicate additional adaptations. These marriages seem to have operated as social investment accounts or as a form of cultural insurance. The accounts and roles of the wives beyond childbearing age (Margaret, Abigail, Sally, and probably Disey) necessarily were limited by their ages and biology, for example, while the accounts and roles of the two fecund wives (Luana and Henrietta) were more complex and costly. Once the Cutler marriages were formed, the partners were able to draw as needed, based on particular circumstances, on this investment in terms of a general cultural understanding of such monogamous institutions and Nauvoo Mormon theology. While this theology asserted the eternality of these relationships, it otherwise required adjustment based on earthly circumstances. The Cutler marriages consequently supply important new information about the enactment of Mormon plural marriage among the small, highly select, and thereby elite leadership circle around Joseph Smith at Nauvoo.

Marriage to Alpheus afforded Luana Hart Beebe, specifically, a means for crossing Iowa with her children and re-establishing a household, one slightly enlarged with the birth of a Cutler son, one whose paternity was disguised by a pseudonym. There is no indication that their 1849 separation was not amicable and mutually advantageous. This plural marriage would have been difficult to sustain in Iowa. Its dissolution enabled Luana to replace it with a conventional marriage, and it reduced Alpheus's marital obligations without diminishing their earthly or eternal status.

That Luana continued to reside among her ex-husband's family and schismatic followers for most of the rest of her life, even moving to Minnesota with them, strongly suggests that their divorce was not contentious or traumatic.

Margaret and Abigail Kerr as well as Disey McCall apparently did not require much, if any, assistance from their husband in crossing Iowa. Nevertheless, Margaret and Abigail lived out their lives adjacent to their husband, once again dispelling the idea that they were disowned and cast out. In spite of the lack of specific evidence, there is no sound reason to assume that they did not function as plural spouses in most all meaningful ways. Older people, contrary to popular youthful opinion, commonly appreciate emotional and physical relationships, including sexuality. Disey McCall's marriage to Alpheus, much like Luana's, probably ceased to be sufficiently rewarding to both of them here and now. The continued presence of Disey at Cutlerite Manti—more so than that of her mother and aunt—would have

94. Daynes, *More Wives Than One*, 31.

required a more elaborate rationalizing narrative; and, following the death of her sister Rachel's husband, these sisters found mutual support in forming a household lasting to the end of their lives in Utah with their surviving children and grandchildren.

Sally Cox drew little from her plural marriage investment, so far as is known, other than its promise of exaltation and eternal salvation. She continued west, perhaps not knowing that Alpheus would not, to reside among her adult children and their offspring. Henrietta Miller Cutler probably depended on Alpheus extensively for material support, although most all of the relevant facts of this situation remain unknown. Her youthful 1851–52 death in childbirth confirms her status as Alpheus's plural wife in the fullest sense.[95]

The actions of these plural marriage participants, notwithstanding the lack of supporting personal narratives, confirm the previous general finding that the Mormons were willing to deviate from monogamous American norms, sometimes reluctantly and under duress, for religious reasons—in order to achieve the promises of eternal marriage and family relationships as well as the glorious exaltation as kings and priests and queens and priestesses. These significant promises were no doubt especially appealing to those, like Mormons in general and specifically to these Cutler participants, lacking much social power or prestige in the larger society. Furthermore, this was a historical period in which high rates of mortality regularly deprived them of children, spouses, and many other loved ones. Their actions helped ensure the continuation of the radical theological innovations of Nauvoo Mormonism.

* * *

Alpheus Cutler's actions indicate that he, unlike about half of the anointed, did not enthusiastically embrace plural marriage, even though he and Lois were initiated very early into the novelty of eternal marriage and family relationships by Joseph Smith. Alpheus began marrying additional wives as a senior member of the anointed and fifty but only after the continuation of "Joseph's measures" became a critically important issue and a symbol of loyalty to this faction of Nauvoo Mormons. Marrying such a large number of women underscored and emphasized his commitment to this innovative theology while accruing considerable personal, social, and economic obligation to these wives. While all of these women were divorced or widowed, otherwise they were rather diverse with some older, younger, and about the same age as Alpheus. Multiple wives enhanced Cutler's religious prestige, and increased opportunities for all of the ordinary advantages of marital partnerships—affection, sexual relations, and contributions to gender-specific roles and labor. Numerous wives,

---

95. Knowing more about how Philinda Cutler came to be a ward of the Daley's would be a useful clue in ascertaining more about this situation. Did Alpheus help with this arrangement? Or, did the Daleys' assume responsibility for an abandoned orphan?

likewise, compounded and perhaps even amplified the ordinary disadvantages of marital contracts, as with additional demands on physical, emotional, and especially finite economic resources. Yet most importantly, taking plural wives would ensure to Cutler his promised eternal salvation and celestial glory. For the Cutler wives, a plural marriage to one of God's anointed offered an alluring and otherwise unavailable means to achieving eternal family relationships and salvation, especially including the utmost glory of reigning as priestesses and queens in the celestial world eternally. These findings are consistent with previous studies indicating that fulfilling the religious mandate to marry plurally was central to the participants' willingness to become involved in this Latter-day Saint practice.[96]

It is not surprising that Sally Cox Hutchings and Henrietta Miller Cutler may have been sealed to their deceased husbands in additional to their sealing and anointing to Alpheus—contrary to subsequent Mormon practices. Their former husbands had been dead for only about two years: Henrietta had been married a mere two years before the death of her husband Moses; and Sally had been married almost thirty years to Elias, a relationship consisting of almost unimaginable hardships and shared tragedies, especially the deaths of seven out of twelve children. If Sally and Henrietta were sealed to their deceased husbands, as temple records seem to indicate, then their celestial existence is polyandrous, since they also were sealed to Alpheus. This is a genuinely intriguing, if wholly unintended, consequence of Nauvoo Temple theology. Yet, it underscores the lack of routinization of the Mormon plural marriage institution during this period, a process that would continue without a suitable conclusion—or anything like full institutionalization—for the next fifty years. Even today, plural marriages in the United States lack the normative routinization and integration with the larger social structures characteristic of other forms of marriage and family as well as other patterns of societal institutions.

Lastly, it is important to note that the Cutlerites, with the formation of their 1853 schism, rejected the continuation of eternal and plural marriage, but not the other significant features of the Nauvoo Temple theology and the supporting rituals.[97] There is no indication that any of the founding members, other than Cutler and his wives, were actively involved in polygamous marriage. Nevertheless, it is likely that Margaret and Abigail resided at Cutlerite Manti if they were not deceased by 1853; and there is no indication that Alpheus or his wives rejected the eternal status of these marriages.

---

96. See, for example, Leonard J. Arrington and David Bitton, *The Mormon Experience: A History of the Latter-day Saints*, 2nd ed. (Urbana: University of Illinois Press, 1992), 199; and Embry, *Mormon Polygamous Families*, 41–32.

97. See Blythe, "Nearly All of the Factions," 168–201; and Blythe, "The Highest Class of Adulterers and Whoremongers," for important discussion of this matter.

DANNY L. JORGENSEN, PhD (sociology) is Professor of Religious Studies, University of South Florida, Tampa. He is a past president of the John Whitmer Historical Association and has published extensively on new religions in the United States, including the Latter Day Saints and especially the Cutlerites.

ANDREW LEARY, MS, is a longtime member of the John Whitmer Historical Association with an active interest in early Latter Day Saints, Cutlerite, and Reorganized Church of Jesus Christ of Latter Day Saints history. He is also an amateur genealogist whose family history is entwined with the early Latter Day Saints and Cutlerites.

Historical Empathy for Early Mormon Nauvoo, Illinois, 1839–1846

Richard P. Howard

A FRIEND ONCE ASKED ME, "Why do historians so often expose the mistakes of our predecessors and ignore their successes?" This question presupposes the use of history as *judgment.* I submit that the primary use of history is to deepen our understanding of persons and groups in their cultural contexts. *Understanding* opens the door to **empathy** for actors in the human drama, in **their** context, raising and exploring questions: who, what, when, where, and how. This process opens the most complex and elusive question of all—Why?—the question of motives. By the time historians build durable hypotheses approximating truth, the empathic goal is in sight: to enter into the actions and feelings of figures of the past.

Elisabeth Lazarakou's perceptive study[1] defines historical empathy as:

> ...the person's ability to comprehend the other's position, even though he does not have the direct experience to do so. In other words, empathy is one's ability to put oneself in another person's place even if the other is a stranger to him or even if he thinks differently [from] his own self.... empathy... is the ability of an individual to participate in the psychic experiences of another person as if he were reliving them himself.

Applying empathy to early Nauvoo history requires, for Community of Christ, discarding long-held, negative judgments based on ignorance and polemic agenda. The underlying premise for several RLDS generations was that things had gone dreadfully wrong in Nauvoo, and that church leader Joseph Smith was a fallen prophet. His assassination signaled divine intervention. Rejecting that stance requires sustained inquiry for new evidences and for finding viable ways to interpret sources, both old and new. Robert B. Flanders's 1965 analysis, *Nauvoo: Kingdom on*

---

1. Elisabeth D. Lazarakou, "Empathy as a Tool for Historical Understanding: an Evaluative Approach of the Ancient Greek Primary History Curriculum," *International Journal of Social Education* 23, no. 1 (Spring–Summer, 2008): 27–50.

the Mississippi, empathically contextualized Nauvoo's leaders, events, the military, the press, the temple, and the doctrinal, administrative, political and theological developments of the city. Flanders' treatment of Nauvoo is still in print, fifty-two years later!

For LDS Mormons the task is a bit different. The LDS church viewed early Nauvoo as the theological capstone of all that Mormonism was and could have become. The "New Mormon History," in my view, has done well to question that position, and then to frame inquiries into more accurate narratives. The late and beloved T. Edgar Lyon was an erudite LDS Mormon historian who helped recreate the *real* Nauvoo for skeptics, faithful believers, and curious onlookers. Lyon's meticulous scholarship nurtured empathic identification with early Nauvoo.

Empathy for figures of the past calls us to squelch presentism so we can enter their landscape. On arrival, we listen, look, and lean in so as to imagine and understand their troubles, stories, values, and feelings. We learn to weep, laugh, and sense their anxieties. We do not easily reach empathic levels of identity, but we strive to honor the discipline involved. This reflective paper attempts to look with empathy at three early Nauvoo contexts: Baptism for the dead, militarism, and plural marriage.

1. Baptism for the Dead (BD)

Joseph Smith Jr., in mid-September 1840 at Nauvoo, Illinois, launched the practice of baptism for the dead (BD). The context began in 1823 in Manchester County, New York. On November 24 Alvin Smith, firstborn of Joseph Smith Sr. and Lucy Mack Smith, died suddenly without Christian covenant. In preaching Alvin's funeral sermon, Reverend Stockton consigned him to hell, deepening the Smith family's grief and anxieties. Nine years later Joseph Smith Jr. and his confidant, Sidney Rigdon, wrote records of several visions or revelations (DC, sect. 76). Section 76:5–6 defined three heavenly glories, in descending order of eminence: Celestial, Terrestrial, and Telestial. By the terms of section 76, Alvin could rise only to terrestrial glory but would avoid the terrors of hell—also graphically portrayed in section 76:31–4. In August 1835 the church canonized section 76, along with more than a hundred other documents.

The Smith family's fears for Alvin's salvation endured, though eased somewhat by Joseph's record of another heavenly vision in 1836 in the Kirtland Temple. There he reported having seen Alvin in celestial glory. But even that vivid experience did not fully assuage the family's anxiety over Alvin's plight.

Final solace came as Joseph Sr. lay on his deathbed with family gathered round. Joseph Jr. entered and announced: "Father, you will be greatly pleased to know that the church can now practice baptism for the dead." (BD) The dying patriarch's wife, Lucy Mack Smith, later recalled this and also that her husband had asked their son

Joseph to be baptized immediately for Alvin. The family rejoiced that Alvin's presence in Celestial Glory was finally guaranteed.

The church responded eagerly to the good news. Soon scores of persons were being baptized in the Mississippi River and in the Chagrin River near Kirtland, Ohio, as proxies for their deceased spouses, relatives, and ancestors. At the October 1840 church conference, Joseph called his people to build a sacred temple to house BD. Hundreds of workers tithed their time weekly to construct the massive edifice. Its basement featured a majestic baptismal font on the backs of twelve oxen carved in stone—symbolizing the twelve tribes of Israel.

To comprehend the eager embrace of BD by the church at Nauvoo requires understanding the power of exclusive authoritarianism so central to the early Mormons' self-image. They walked together along the illuminated track of singular religious authority. Darkness and apostasy reigned outside their track. God had chosen them to build up the city of God, to which Christ would soon come to begin his millennial reign. At their helm was the Second Moses—Joseph Smith Jr.—to guide all their labors.

Also central to the BD context was the plague of persecution. The Mormons saw extremist religious zealots besieging them repeatedly since 1830. They were a beleaguered band, anxious for the survival of their blessed community. They widened their assurance of salvation to the celestial realm to include their deceased relatives and ancestors in Nauvoo Temple's waters of baptism. My empathic thesis today is this: Given the elements of the context, Joseph Smith acted understandably from premises of fear and anxiety to create a ritual designed to assure celestial salvation for Alvin Smith. By extension, that same assurance was also given on behalf of the beloved deceased relatives of every worthy church member at Nauvoo.

Early RLDS leaders believed in BD but never fully established it despite its apparent approval in early council minutes. They remained largely silent about it except to hold that the church must await a direct command of God to resume that Nauvoo ritual. This was due mostly to the RLDS church's financial inability even to consider building a temple.

The RLDS church's 1968 World Conference asked the First Presidency for a new format for the Doctrine and Covenants (DC). The First presidency responded in 1970 by proposing that the three documents in the DC (sections 107, 109, 110) authorizing BD be removed from the canon to an historical appendix. The 1970 World Conference almost unanimously approved. Why and what did that action mean?

In their proposal the First Presidency described BD as "not essential to salvation." The Presidency did not call BD a *mistake*. They knew the basic contours of the intricate context. Their course was gracefully to nudge the church in a different direction—one in which most of the members wanted to go anyhow.

To empathize with the context of the origin of BD is to avoid either the pain or the pleasure of accusing Joseph Smith Jr. of error in this regard. *Empathy* with those living in that context also dispels either embarrassment or regret over BD for the Community of Christ today; nor does empathy demand forgiveness, which would rest on a judgment of Nauvoo's BD as a major mistake. Community of Christ is thus freed to explore the hypothesis that BD presaged the temple's larger system of anointings, sealings, eternal marriage covenants, and plural marriage. The Nauvoo Mormons felt assured that no matter how violent future persecutions might become, their "Kingdom on the Mississippi" would forever endure.

2. The Church Militant: The Nauvoo Legion

Prior to Nauvoo, Joseph Smith and other church leaders had used military strategy to guard against religionists determined to destroy their church. The Ohio-based Zion's Camp expedition of 1834 represented a zealous move by church leaders to form a quasi-military force. Their aim: Redeem Zion—re-plant the Mormons on their lands—thus nullifying the church's violent expulsion from Jackson County, Missouri. Their motives were wrapped in (1) the garment of mercy for their exile; (2) their deep anguish at the loss of lands and opportunities to build Zion in Missouri; and (3) revenge for the relentless wave of economic and social injustices the church had endured. Their dream of Zion had been deferred but not crushed.

From 1835 to 1839 the Missouri Mormons suffered persecution and military actions launched against their communities in and near Far West, Missouri. They reacted during the summer of 1838 by forming their own military units. Sidney Rigdon's fiery Independence Day (July 4) sermon ignited flames of violence from the already angry populace. His rhetoric challenged the church's enemies to a "War of extermination." Finally, in October 1838 the Missouri governor, Lilburn Boggs, signed his heinous "Extermination Order," commanding the State Militia to drive five thousand Mormons from Missouri altogether. Their flight into Illinois during the severe winter of 1838–39, marked by unimaginable suffering of women and children, formed church leaders' resolve to take measures to put down any external threat to the safety and order of the exiled church.

Remembering relentless attacks against them in New York, Ohio, and Missouri, Mormon leaders framed a remarkably expansive charter for Nauvoo. The charter created instruments aimed at protecting their new city from peril. Executive, judicial, and legislative structures highly protective of the church's interests helped frame their *Kingdom on the Mississippi*. The Charter authorized the Nauvoo Legion—an independent militia of armed, uniformed troops composed of all of Nauvoo's healthy male citizens, ages eighteen to forty-five. An increasingly paranoid leadership team was sending strong messages to any external force intent on injuring the city: Attack us and you'll pay dearly! Viewing Nauvoo's militancy through empathic eyes, I imagine that had I lived there then and been called to serve in the legion, I would have rejoiced! I'd have been honored to bang the drums as we marched in review before Lt. General Joseph Smith and his brightly uniformed core of commanders. My broken heart would have mourned the 1845 revocation of the City Charter by the state legislature. The legion's proud and brief life ended unceremoniously. What next? What sorrowful fate might descend upon Nauvoo's anxious forebodings?

3. Plural Marriage Covenants

A notable cultural reality shaped the context of early Mormonism's essence as a religious movement. An entrenched patriarchy, transported across the pond from Great Britain, formed the nation and each of its sovereign states. Patriarchal control of Native Americans, negro slaves, and the rules of Christian marriage was a prominent feature of American culture from early colonial times. European and early American radical Christian groups led by charismatic, patriarchal men, framed polygamous marriage systems. Mormon patriarchy became clearly manifest via secret Nauvoo polygamy—the ultimate strategy for male dominance of women.

Permeating the early Mormon subculture was the conviction—deeper than bones in Joseph Smith and his followers—that their emerging movement embodied absolute, exclusive authority to represent God. In my view this doctrine, while not unique to Joseph Smith and his followers, shaped many of their encounters, both internally and with the outside world. Their "One and Only True Church" stance is also a vital element for understanding the ground of plural marriage's rise among Mormon leaders and elders at Nauvoo.

Credible evidence demonstrates that even earlier than Nauvoo, Joseph Smith participated in several extra-marital liaisons. Prominent among these was his affair with Fanny Alger, nineteen-year-old household servant to the Smith family in Kirtland. Later LDS Mormon apologists described this as the inception of polygamy, the "Divine Principle," among the Latter Day Saints. Other compelling evidences, however, indicate that the Fanny Alger affair was rather the most notable of several of Joseph's extramarital relationships, 1831–35.

Other church leaders—Oliver Cowdery and W. W. Phelps—knowing of the Smith/Alger connection, were determined to protect the church from more persecutions. In August 1835 while Joseph Smith was in Michigan, the church's general assembly at Kirtland, Ohio, ratified an article on marriage, written by Cowdery and Phelps. Their article (1) affirmed the church's embrace of monogamy, and (2) condemned fornication and polygamy of which the church (i.e., Joseph Smith) was then being accused.

An especially virile element of the early Mormon **patriarchal** subculture was Joseph Smith's luminous charismatic power. From 1829 until his death in June 1844 an enormously needy Joseph Smith emanated colossal personal magnetism that evoked adoring loyalties, both male and female. This cultic phenomenon had circular properties: the more compelling Joseph's charismatic impact, the more desperately he needed upward spirals of affirmation, wonder, fealty, and obedience from his devotees. With few notable exceptions, his followers gladly acquiesced, in the process sculpting an increasingly rigid, patriarchal, cultic system.

By mid-1843, this cyclic charisma/response pattern compelled Joseph to issue new revelations and celestial laws, eliciting ever-deeper loyalties and, understandably, alienations. His secret plural marriage commandment violated the Illinois anti-bigamy statute. Both Joseph Smith and other church leaders and elders, however, proudly proclaimed that the laws of God must often supersede mere laws of man. As George D. Smith ably documented in his 2008 tome, *Nauvoo Polygamy*, 186 Nauvoo elders entered into plural marriage covenants at Nauvoo with 793 women. Joseph Smith led the way, taking 38 plural wives. His first wife, Emma Hale Smith, endured unimaginable humiliation and angrily reacted—realities empathically described in Linda Newell's and Val Avery's landmark biography of Emma, first published in 1984, still in print.

Proxy baptisms at Nauvoo were mystically delivering hundreds of deceased ancestors and relatives into the celestial realm. Secret plural marriage, it was hoped, would broaden—also mystically—the scope and range of marital and family bonds, both in this life and especially in celestial realms beyond. Eventually, from these plural marriage covenants, countless eternal family units would surely emerge. They would nourish myriad patriarchal Mormon Kingdoms where the hatreds and violence of earthly persecution could never plague them again.

Community of Christ leaders have only lately begun to grasp Joseph Smith's central role in the advent of Nauvoo polygamy. They finally have been compelled by the weight of evidence to embark from the protective shell of 150 years of denial, across stormy waters toward the shores of acceptance of the truth on this and other matters. They seem, however, unable to embrace historical empathy as a possible response. Instead they have chosen 1) to sever Community of Christ's ties to the founding generation's paradoxes and 2) to extricate the church altogether from the burden (but sadly, the power) of its authentic history. For me, as historian emeritus, this new reality tortures me with a grief too deep to bear with equanimity. But bear it I will, and if possible, with empathy for leaders who have suffered agony over what for them must have been historiographical crises and traumas impossible to reconcile.

Conclusion

Doctrines evolve in time from human efforts to discern authentic models of community life. At their best, historians will do far more than chronicle social change. They will enter humbly, imaginatively, courageously, into the context of each notable shift. They may shed a few tears, and laugh aloud as they empathize with those who lived through turbulent seas of transformation.

Remember that lofty quote from the Gospel of John 8:32? "You shall know the truth, and the truth will make you flinch, before setting you free." Historical truth, via *empathic frameworks*, frees us to fashion equitable *progress* while also liberating us from stifling burdens of judgment. Finally, empathically derived historical truth garnered by historians of future generations will help people understand that what we do today will likely have been nearly the best we could have done.

The vocal artist, Laurie Anderson, wrote and performed the song, "The Dream Before," released on her *Strange Angels* record. She says succinctly what I've been trying to say today. Here are her lyrics:

> "She said, What is history?
> And he said, History is an angel
> Being blown Backwards Into the future
> He said: History is a pile of debris
> And the angel wants to go back and fix things
> To repair the things that have been broken
> But there is a storm blowing from Paradise
> And the storm keeps blowing the angel
> Backwards Into the future
> And this storm, this storm
> is called progress"

Charles Kettering, American inventor and holder of 186 patents, once said, "The price of progress is trouble." I submit that if every historian were to go to the trouble of doing empathic history, civilizations would live in a far-less troubled world. Maybe.

RICHARD P. HOWARD served as church historian of Community of Christ from 1966 to 1994. He is a founding member and past president of the John Whitmer Historical Association and past president of the Mormon History Association. He has published extensively in restoration history. The endowed lectureship of JWHA was recently renamed in his honor.

I Know What You Said Last Time: Reflections and Cogitations by a 46-year JWHA Charter Member

Paul M. Edwards

"The most effective way to destroy a people is to deny and obliterate their understanding of their own history."

—George Orwell

I CONSIDER IT one of the highlights of my life to have been inside the RLDS Auditorium during a citizens' march and boycott protesting William D. Russell, that "Communist" and advocate for integrated housing. Led by a used-car salesman of the same name, the crowd protested Russell's outspoken liberal attitudes and identified a serious clash within the church. It is the first time I remember the church being actively involved in a significant community outreach. Yet in looking over several decades of the association's programming, I have been concerned by how few such historical events are considered among the topics presented.[1]

Thus my thesis: *We have by reason of longevity and respectability established our identity as a professional association, and it is now time to stop dissecting our foundations and open up to the rest of the story.*

The John Whitmer Historical Association, deliberately named after a reactionary church historian, sponsored its first annual conference in Nauvoo. The initial program consisted of the film *Nauvoo: A Perception of the Past* by Alma Blair, a classic introduction to the "Prophet Puzzle" by Jan Shipps, and Robert B. Flanders's presidential address. Designed for members of the then-RLDS church, the doors were immediately opened to all interested.[2]

---

1. Acknowledgement must be made to Dr. Thomas Peterman, a cautious scholar who has examined my complete review of past annual JWHA meeting programs to verify the statistical points made here; an excellent worker and friend.

2. The purity and exactness of some accumulation figures are in jeopardy for despite an association-wide search for copies, there are some years for which no program could be located. The high percentage of programs avail-

* * *

The association's programs are the harvest of the circumstances of its birth in 1971.[3] The selection of the friends and colleagues who gathered at the Howard home was incidental but not arbitrary. Most were of a like mind, though not of a single mind. Most had grown up in a period of historical inquiry unfortunately known as the New Left. In their formal education most had moved beyond consensus history and had adopted a more conflicted view of the discipline: A view that identified the impact of dissent on social history and the expanding role of class, race and gender. Many would not be uncomfortable with identification as an 'outsider' in history and would share the suspicion that their community was a class struggle of religious priorities. Most of them had separated themselves from the methodological diseases of the social sciences, a view in which all aspects of human involvement, from theology to telemarketing, are rolled into a single science designed to replace the undependable art of the historian.

All were professionals and many had advanced degrees. They were all Community of Christ members, and all the men held the priesthood. The majority were or had been teachers. They were white, middle class, intelligent, and somewhat left of the average member. They shared a common heritage of history masquerading as theology and had reached some agreement on the balance of faith and reason. Most agreed with the premise of "historian as detective.'"

Some individuals reflected well-defined positions that continue to be evident in today's programs. Shades of legalism, progressivism, reductionism, and even historiography hovered about the presentations. All of those involved were on the move but miraculously non-competitive.

In the act of creation the group accomplished the first phase of their historical consciousness. They separated the church from its history. By common understanding, the church was no longer to be its history, but rather the history was set aside to be studied. For this purpose the association excluded the church name and avoided affiliation with other groups endorsed by the establishment.

* * *

A careful review of all available past JWHA meeting programs provided some interesting information. While most committees failed to identify themselves, there was no evidence of particular or collective agendas being pushed. Selection of pro-

---

able and the consistency of trends uncovered suggest, however, that my conclusions are primarily valid. When and if these additional programs can be located, the study should be updated.

3. The founding members include Robert Flanders, Alma Blair, Paul M. Edwards, Barbara Higdon, Barbara Howard, Bill Higdon, Richard Howard, Larry Hunt, Warren Jennings, Gerald Kruse, Mark McKiernan, Grant McMurray, William D. Russell, Geoff Spencer, and Pat Spellman. All but two, Hunt and Kruse, were active in the early years and delivered from three to sixteen papers in the following years.

gram committees seemed limited in the face of such a large membership. Each program had a theme but little continuity. The printed programs represented no agreement on little things—information on presenters, institutional and association identification, or mention of academic rank—with the exception of the inclusion of church rank. Some of the printed programs were elaborate and others downright skimpy.[4] There appeared to be a policy about location but it was poorly followed; localized and combined meetings appeared to provide a larger attendance, and yet the selection of chosen topics narrowed.

Without judgment I noted an increasing secularization. We have been less about religious history and more about the history of a religion. It was also noted that the closing worship service was included less often.

The membership has changed radically from the early days. That appears good. Many men and women have awakened to their heritage and have become involved. More universities are represented. I also have noted a strong LDS influence which, with its reputation for seriousness and high scholarship, has been a positive influence on the tone of meetings. I note as well the formalization of the procedures that may or may not be what we wish to continue.

There has been a serious gap in the involvement of some individuals. I refer to those who have delivered a variety of papers over a short period of time and then allowed a period of several years to pass before offering again. Some do not reappear. The list of such persons is surprisingly long. Some effort to keep them involved might be in order.

Meetings have become longer—not only more days and more papers, but longer sessions. At the first conference in 1973 there were five papers with no responses and also a worship service. During the last five years, the average has been fifty papers and fewer worship services. The number of responders has decreased while a contiguous second paper, often unrelated, has been added instead. The identification of visiting scholars has reflected wide tastes and careful selection, but their presentations, while enlightening, have not always been contingent to Mormonism.

* * *

The quantity of production has been incredible, with more than 865 presentations delivered by 411 individuals; an average of 2.08 per presenter. The top sixty-nine presentations were delivered by five persons with an average of 13.8 each. About 40 percent of all papers were delivered by persons making only a single presentation. .

The largest number of presentations was eighteen made by the esteemed William Shepard. Close runners-up included William Russell, Newell Bringhurst, Danny Jorgensen, Jessie Embry, and Jean Addams.

---

4. Reflecting the financial position, most likely, even though programs with handouts including more information and details appeared to correspond with programs that are more varied.

When responses were scheduled, William D. Russell led with twenty-four, followed by Ronald Romig, Alma Blair, Mark Scherer, Richard Howard, and Pat Spillman. Ninety-four persons delivered only one response.

When counting chair assignments, fifty-three members chaired more than one session and thirty-nine chaired fifty percent of the rest. William D. Russell leads the pack with thirty-six chair assignments. William Shepard, Barbara Walden, Newell Bringhurst, Mark Scherer, and Barbara Bernhauer follow closely behind.

* * *

The programs indicate a somewhat liberal bias, held in check by a lack of radicalism, a dependence on reductionist history, and a disturbing tendency to quote each other. The topics have naturally tended to focus on foundational evaluations and biography even though time has greatly widened the definition of Restoration. Indifference rather than interference best describes the relationship to the mother church. By virtue of some unspoken agreement, topics of personal relationships and dirty tricks that would have made great papers have been avoided.

Programs have reflected whatever was on the front page—murders, fake documents, new presidents—but they were short-lived. The majority of other topics fit rather easily into a dozen identified categories that represent 385 presentations, or 46 percent of the total. They have been somewhat predictable.

Including Canada and Mexico as foreign missions, the largest number of presentations reflected nondomestic efforts, usually portraying individual locations or missions. The second largest dealt with biographical studies that considered seventeen different persons. Of these, more than 50 percent related to the Smith family and reflected 8.5 percent of all programs. This list also included several papers that questioned the family's psychological health.

Thirty-two papers dealt with divergence movements. The Strangites did well, and the Cutlerites chalked up a statistically unexplainable twelve papers, half of them delivered by Danny Jorgenson or Biloine Young. Plenty of interest was evident in historic locations with more than three percent dealing with historic centers like Nauvoo; Kirtland was the most popular place.

Polygamy is still popular and was the focus of twenty-six discussions. Almost every conference had at least one such paper. Following polygamy in popularity were twenty-four papers identified as theological, assuming, it seems, if "Sacred Fudge" is really theology.[5]

Papers dealing with women's history have been sporadic and fewer than desired. The ordination of women did not produce the mass of papers that might have been assumed. The temples at Kirtland and Nauvoo continue to draw a lot of interest.

5. Over the years I have sensed a subtle reluctance to accept theological presentations as a significant part of the conference, and this feeling appears to be supported by the small number of theological presentations.

The most astonishing thing is the fact little or nothing has been provided on the temple in Independence.

Contrary to expectations, sessions dealing directly with the Book of Mormon numbered only twelve, fewer than 2 percent. The other basic scriptures—the Book of Abraham, the Doctrine and Covenants, and the Inspired Version—did even more poorly.

At the bottom of the list of popularity one finds some interesting avoidance. For example, only nine papers dealt with the history of worship or hymnody. For an institution proclaiming peace as a prerogative, only six such presentations were given, all hovering around 2006–2007. "Zion the beautiful" was considered in three papers, one of which was a panel discussing community. The Doctrine and Covenants held the penultimate post as the least considered subject with two papers. And number one in the neglected topic category was the Inspired Version of the Bible.

Adopting the theory expounded in *The Hound of the Baskervilles*, there may be more to be learned by the absence of something than by its presence.[6] If the association's goal is to explore church history, then there have been some obvious gaps that need to be addressed.

The mother church appears to undergo a significant reorganization about every seven years, and a good many of these changes and procedures reflect directly on theology. The recent roles of consensus and discernment bring into question the prime epistemological formation of the movement. Whatever happened to revelation?

There has been very little intellectual history considered even though a vast quantity of our belief structure has been borrowed. Note the underlying assumption of this year's "All Roads Lead from Nauvoo" theme: That the concepts forming our beliefs were born in the Nineteenth Century. Phil Marlow once addressed the influence of alchemy on the movement, but the history of formative thought has generally been ignored.

For a hundred years the Community of Christ has deliberately avoided its social programs while preaching community outreach. What happened to the Social Service Center, the Restoration adoption agency and orphanage,[7] the Credit Union, the Real Estate Division, Mound Grove, the Academy, Harvest Hills, the Sanatorium, the swimming pool, the White Masque players, the Boys' Choir, Herald House, the Book Store, Graceland's Rare Books Room,[8] assisted living, reading for the blind, the Messiah Choir, Rest Haven, and the current downgrading of the library, museum,

---

6. It was the belief in the limited nature of subjects under consideration that first led to this paper; I have begun to feel that I had heard it all several times before, and that so many topics have gone unaddressed. The hope is that the association can expand its offerings.

7. My sister, Ruth Fairbanks, was adopted in 1930 via the early church adoption agency.

8. This longtime collection of rare books and church archives was recently disemboweled to make room for another project.

and archives? One paper, on Rest Haven, was included in more than thirty years of study. What about chronicling the rest?

Biographies are wonderful historical tools, but surely we have heard enough about the founding mothers and fathers. What more can possibly be said about Joseph Smith to make him more or less a scoundrel? We must broaden the field even to include some pre-mortem subjects.[9]

Histories are made up of heroes and heroines, but also of villains and scoundrels. What does the church do when it is cheated, robbed, misinformed, betrayed, or sold out by persons with good expectations but criminal genes. Is it kindly good faith that allows the shady events to have remained in the shade? But like washing your feet with your socks on, this attitude betrays the intent of the association. What do we know about the scandal of the Marble Mine in Maine, or the source of the instruction to travel two by two, or who paid for the peyote used for early "higher powers" experiments, or who burned down Columbia school, or what were the cause and impact of today's financial speculation and the inappropriate investments?

And while we are at it, how about those clandestine movements that often shadowed and sometimes altered the church? Have we forgotten the church's struggle with the KKK, the John Birch Society, the America First, the American Nazi Party, McCarthyites, the Black Hand, the Order of Enoch, the Missouri Danites, and the Army of God (Joplin Branch), just to name a few.[10]

Beating my favorite dead horse, let me note that in our 185 years of history, the nation has been at war more than 71 percent of the time. Each conflict has affected our membership and our beliefs. How do we justify Fred M.'s commission as a colonel in the Missouri Militia, or the care and support of military chaplains, the joint council split over conscientious objectors, Joseph Smith's conscription policy, the 1940s War Bond Drives on campus, or selling Victory Stamps in Sunday school classes?

It is time for us to direct our creative minds to understand how we have responded to the great social issues. Few have taken a serious look at the significant impact of cultural and social alterations happening all around us. The influence of the Civil War, the impact of the trans-Pacific railway, the early impact of slaveholding on members, the depression, blacks and then women in the priesthood, name changes and new bonding, gender identification, and the intake of intoxicating drinks, just to name a few.

---

9. Such men as G. Leslie DeLapp, who not only kept the church from bankruptcy, but led the committee that build the Jackson Country Sports Complex (Chiefs, Royals), or perhaps Ruth Cobb or the highly significant Wayne Ham.

10. The protest march against William D. Russell at the auditorium is worth a paper in its own right, but more important, the role of the church in the integration of housing in Independence, Missouri, is a remarkable, if not pretty, story.

I believe the meetings and the topics have been too narrow. Since the association sponsors an international conference, it needs to move beyond the history of "the little mission at Chug-water, Wyoming." Every evidence suggests that we have revisited popular topics at the expense of breadth and variety. How many more versions of 'Emma stands by her man' do we need?

* * *

A good number of our members today come out of a post-restoration period. That is, they came to their interest in history after the emergence of what is generally known as "The New Mormon History." This post-awakening period is not the same history that formed the roots and assumptions of an earlier generation. The ancient models of which I speak began their quest from books written in the 1950s and 1960s that were still dealing with the stories of Inez Smith Davis and relying on documents held in secret or just "not available."

It was not an enlightened period—not really a better one—simply a different one. It is essential, however, that this new generation move ahead by employing the tools as well as the attitudes that have been given them, remembering that they stand on the shoulders, if not of giants, then certainly of creative dwarfs, that allows them to start where others have left off. It is time to move on, to grow, to emerge beyond the foundational questions that so traditionally have filled our programs.[11]

It would be beneficial to occasionally discuss the history of the scholarship involved: to consider how the views of a particular topic are altered not only by more information, but by the creation of the perfect storm: the evidence, the times and the inquirer coming together. Robert Flanders' book on Nauvoo, despite its significance, did not arise out of a vacuum; both the author and the artifacts seemed destined for that moment when they met in this investigation. We need reminding that the historian as well as the times intervenes in the investigation.[12]

The new playing field reflected in the publication of *Kingdom on the Mississippi* was not just a history of our founders struggling to create a kingdom of God; it is also the current story of the rising of a new generation of historians, matching their skills to their faith. It seems to me that the association is under some responsibility to teach as well as to profess; to keep our participants as up to date as possible about the historical profession. The association has some responsibility to teach its members skills as well as subjects.

In the process, perhaps we can illustrate some opposition to the slippery slope of the social sciences: that is, to put it in the simplest of terms, *to discount the idea*

---

11. A change in direction could be initiated by inviting half-a-dozen persons to make presentations on new and less generalized topics. Perhaps the association might consider the yearly assignment of a specific topic from which the group could learn.

12. Both science and philosophy has long held the idea that an object is altered when observed.

that the sum is the total of the parts, and to realize in the glaze of contingency, that history is primarily <u>more</u> than the sum of the parts. History is an art that has to be crafted, whereas social science is a science and needs only to be counted.

And last, I acknowledge the awful loss of most material: the Pilgrim's Progress that lies in some unacknowledged files. Some expanded effort needs to be made to distribute, if not to preserve, these presentations for future use.[13] The result of all this research is being lost. The association needs to make a greater effort to archive its own performance; perhaps to make an effort to locate and rescue significant presentations of the past.[14]

* * *

It is in its historical and literary consciousness that an entity preserves the attributes of a civilized memory. In our case literature is scarce and only minimally leads to performance. Few in the Community of Christ tradition compose novels, or short stories, or poetry, or music. So it has been left to the historian, whose job now is not only to investigate the institution's past and to make sense of its contribution, but to provide the stream of awareness upon which to float the remnants of our memories.

PAUL M. EDWARDS, a past president of the JWHA and the MHA, is currently senior fellow at the Center for the Study of the Korean War in Independence, Missouri.

---

13. Fewer than 4 percent of the articles presented are saved by publication in the association's journals.

14. The author would recommend the appointment of someone to serve as a liaison with the larger literary community.

The Relationship of Oliver Cowdery with Joseph Smith

William Shepard and H. Michael Marquardt

Introduction

IN THE FIRST NUMBER of the *Latter Day Saints' Messenger and Advocate*, Oliver Cowdery printed a September 7, 1834, letter he had written to his friend William W. Phelps. This became an anthem about the spirit of brotherhood that existed between Cowdery and Joseph Smith when the church was new:

> Near the time of the sitting of the Sun, Sabbath evening, April 5th 1829, my natural eyes, for the first time beheld this brother. He then resided in Harmony, Susquehanna county Penn. On Monday the 6th, I assisted him in arranging some business of a temporal nature, and on Tuesday the 7th, commenced to write the book of Mormon. These were days never to be forgotten—to sit under the sound of a voice dictated by the *inspiration* of heaven, awakened the utmost gratitude of his bosom! Day after day I continued, uninterrupted, to write from his mouth as he translated, with the *Urim and Thummim*, or, as the Nephites would have said, "Interpreters," the history or record, called "The book of Mormon."[1]

At the first church conference on June 9, 1830, Joseph Smith was designated an apostle and first elder and Cowdery as apostle and second elder.[2] With the joint bestowal of the keys of the kingdom they were unequaled in the church.[3] This article will focus on Oliver Cowdery's interaction with Joseph Smith and explore his struggle to retain the spirituality the above quote suggests.

1. "Dear Brother," *Latter Day Saints' Messenger and Advocate* 1, no. 1 (October 1834): 14, emphasis retained. Cowdery published Phelps's October 20 response in the November 1834 *Messenger and Advocate*. This general procedure would be followed in the exchanges of letters between Cowdery and Phelps in the *Messenger and Advocate* through November 1835.

2. Doctrine and Covenants (2013 LDS edition, hereafter LDS D&C) 20:2; Doctrine and Covenants (1990 RLDS edition, hereafter RLDS D&C) 17:1b–c.

3. LDS D&C 27:12–13; RLDS D&C 26:3a–b; text based upon the 1835 edition of the Doctrine and Covenants 50:3. Oliver Cowdery and David Whitmer were told by revelation in June 1829 they were not only apostles, their calling was comparable to the apostle Paul. They were commanded to "search out the Twelve." See LDS D&C 18:9, 37; RLDS D&C 16:3a–b, 6a.

While Cowdery is thought to be second only to Smith, we examine the level of responsibility Oliver possessed in church government and the emerging role of Sidney Rigdon. The dissension that occurred in Kirtland, Ohio is also examined as differences between Smith and Cowdery accumulated to the point that their relationship was threatened. They became enemies shortly thereafter at Far West, Missouri.

* * *

The first known example of Oliver Cowdery being conflicted with Joseph Smith came in the summer of 1830. While living with the Whitmer family at Fayette, New York, Cowdery discovered what he believed was an error in the manuscript of the articles and covenants of the church. He wrote Joseph Smith at Harmony, Pennsylvania, and demanded the offending portion be removed so there would be "no priestcraft" among them. As members of the Whitmer family supported Cowdery's criticisms, Smith wrote a response and afterward made a special visit and with considerable effort was able to convince them the writing was appropriate.[4]

Within a few weeks, Oliver Cowdery again took sides against the first elder when he joined members of the Whitmer family in defending messages received by Hiram Page about the upbuilding of Zion through the use of a seer stone.[5] The resulting revelation, proclaimed at the second conference of the church at Fayette, New York, specified Joseph Smith alone held the "keys of mysteries and revelations," and, thereby, he alone could receive "commandments and revelations" for the church. The message stipulated that Cowdery was subordinate to Smith—as Aaron was to Moses—and warned him to be obedient. Cowdery could testify to the truth of the revelations received by Smith and speak as led by "the Comforter" but could "not write by way of commandment." Cowdery was called to "go unto the Lamanites and preach my gospel unto them."[6]

Soon thereafter Peter Whitmer Jr., Parley P. Pratt, and Ziba Peterson were designated by revelations to join Cowdery on this mission.[7] They left Manchester, New York in mid-October 1830 and arrived in the greater Kirtland, Ohio, area two weeks later. The missionaries remarkably baptized some 130 persons during three weeks

---

4. Manuscript History, Book A-1:50–51, Church History Library, The Church of Jesus Christ of Latter-day Saints, Salt Lake City; B. H. Roberts, ed., *History of the Church of Jesus Christ of Latter-day Saints*, 2nd ed. rev., 7 vols. (Salt Lake City: Deseret News, 1932–51), 1:104–5. Both letters are not extant.

5. *History of the Church* 1:109–10 and 115. See Ezra Booth's description of the stone and its properties in Ronald E. Romig, *Eighth Witness: The Biography of John Whitmer* (Independence, MO: John Whitmer Books, 2014), 79. On Booth's letters see H. Michael Marquardt, "Ezra Booth on Early Mormonism: A Look at His 1831 Letters," *John Whitmer Historical Association Journal* 28 (2008): 65–87.

6. LDS D&C 28; RLDS D&C 27.

7. LDS D&C 30:5 and 32:1–3; RLDS D&C 29:2a and 31:1a–1c.

of preaching,[8] but Cowdery again lost his bearings and proposed marriage to an un-identified woman in the township of Mayfield in Cuyahoga County.[9]

The missionaries, with the addition of Frederick G. Williams, left the Kirtland area for Missouri near the end of November while Sidney Rigdon and Edward Partridge arrived at Fayette to meet Joseph Smith early in December. The fact that Rigdon was mature, knowledgeable, and had served a dozen years as a respected minister did not bode well for Cowdery.

After arriving on the borders of the United States in Missouri by January 1831, the missionaries were prevented by Indian Agents from preaching among the Native Americans. A few converts were made among the settlers, but the Mormons were greeted with suspicion. Oliver Cowdery wrote on May 7, 1831, from Kaw Township, that the "Universalists[,] Atheists, Deists, Presbyterians, Methodists, Baptists, and other professed Christians, priests and people: with all the devils from the infernal pit are united, and foaming out their own shame" in opposing them.[10]

Ezra Booth, who left in June with a group including Joseph Smith, traveled from Ohio to Jackson County, Missouri. Booth shortly afterward became disaffected, and wrote:

> If a pure and pleasant fountain can send forth corrupt and bitter streams, then may the heart of that man [Cowdery] be pure, who enters into a matrimonial contract with a young lady, and obtains the consent of her parents; but as soon as his back is turned upon her, he violates his engagements, and prostitutes his honor by becoming the gallant of another, and resolves in his heart, and expresses resolutions to marry her.[11]

Oliver would witness the arrival of missionaries, family groups, and the beginnings of settlements. The arrival of Joseph Smith, Sidney Rigdon, William W. Phelps, Edward Partridge, Ezra Booth and others in mid-July 1831 was shortly followed by the Colesville members. Cowdery doubtlessly joined in construction projects and witnessed the dedication of the temple site and the consecration of the land of Zion. When W. W. Phelps was directed by revelation to remain in Missouri and

---

8. See Richard Lloyd Anderson, "The Impact of the First Preaching in Ohio," in *Oliver Cowdery: Scribe, Elder, Witness*, eds., John W. Welch and Larry E. Morris (Provo, UT: Neal A. Maxwell Institute for Religious Scholarship, 2006), 195–220 and Milton V. Backman Jr., "The Quest for a Restoration: The Birth of Mormonism in Ohio," *BYU Studies* 12, no. 4 (Summer 1972): 346–64.

9. Cowdery's "transgression" was investigated by six High Priests at Independence, Missouri in May 1832. After he "frankly confessed" and assured his inquisitors he had "made his confession to the individuals injured & received their forgiveness" the previous year. Conference Minutes, and Record Book, of Christ's Church of Latter Day Saints, 27, Church History Library; see Donald Q. Cannon and Lyndon W. Cook, eds., *Far West Record: Minutes of the Church of Jesus Christ of Latter-day Saints, 1830–1844* (Salt Lake City: Deseret Book, 1983), 48–49, May 26, 1832.

10. *History of the Church*, 1:182.

11. Ezra Booth to "Rev. & Dear Sir" [Ira Eddy], December 6, 1831, *Ohio Star* 2 (December 8, 1831): 1, Ravenna, Ohio.

be "printer unto the church," Cowdery was assigned to be his assistant."[12] He was one of ten elders who accompanied Joseph Smith on his August 9–27 return trip to Kirtland. The day after his arrival he was ordained by Sidney Rigdon to be a high priest.[13]

While staying at the John Johnson Sr. home at Hiram, Ohio, Oliver was caught up in the flurry of activities relative to the arrangement and correction of the revelations for the printing of the Book of Commandments at Independence. Joseph Smith, Martin Harris, Oliver Cowdery, John Whitmer, Sidney Rigdon, and W. W. Phelps were told by revelation in November to be "stewards over the revelations and commandments" that had been and would be received.[14] This was the beginning of the Literary Firm whose members would be concerned with publication of church literature including Joseph Smith's revelations. A second November revelation assigned Oliver and John Whitmer to take the "commandments and the moneys … unto the land of Zion."[15]

Oliver and John left for Missouri on November 20 and arrived at Independence on January 5, 1832. As preparation for printing was a priority, a brick building was built soon after their arrival. They anxiously awaited the arrival of printing supplies.

As Oliver was laboring in obscurity in Missouri, it became apparent that Sidney Rigdon had replaced him as Joseph Smith's second in command. Rigdon had worked harmoniously with Smith as a scribe and advisor in the Bible translation and was dependable and loyal. David Whitmer retrospectively explained that Rigdon "had more influence over him [Smith] than any other man living" and became "brother Joseph's private counselor, and his most intimate friend and brother for some time after they met." He acknowledged "all the brethren … thought at the time just as Brother Joseph did about it."[16]

It was Sidney Rigdon who shared with Joseph Smith the reception of the great vision about "the three glories" on February 16, 1832.[17] Rigdon also took the lead in defending Smith against serious allegations made by Ezra Booth, who had withdrawn from the church after his return from Missouri. Publication of nine of Booth's anti-Mormon letters that had appeared in the *Ohio Star* of Ravenna, Ohio, from October

---

12. LDS D&C 57:11–13; RLDS D&C 57:5a–b.

13. Welch and Morris, "Chronology," *Oliver Cowdery: Scribe, Elder, Witness,* xi.

14. LDS D&C 70:1–4; RLDS 70:1a–c.

15. LDS D&C 69:1–2; RLDS D&C 69:1a. See accounts of pertinent conferences at Hiram, Ohio on November 8, 9, and 11, 1831 in Cannon and Cook, *Far West Record,* 28–32.

16. David Whitmer, *An Address to All Believers in Christ* (Richmond, MO: privately printed, 1887), 35. Cited in Romig, *Eighth Witness,* 120–21.

17. LDS and RLDS D&C 76.

13 to December 1831 influenced the withdrawal from the church of a significant number of Kirtland area members.[18]

Joseph Smith proclaimed a revelation in November 1831 that specified "that one be appointed of the high Priesthood to preside over the Priesthood."[19] Smith, therefore, became the Presiding High Priest over the church as he had been Presiding Elder over the church. The ordination occurred on January 25, 1832, at a conference at Amhurst, Ohio, when he was "acknowledged President of the High Priesthood" and was ordained to that office by Sidney Rigdon.[20]

On March 8 Joseph Smith selected Jesse Gause, a forty-seven-year-old recent convert, who had been a Shaker and also a Quaker, and thirty-nine-year-old Sidney Rigdon to be his counselors in the church presidency.[21] Historian Michael Quinn explained, "Smith ordained Gause a high priest, selected him and Sidney Rigdon as counselors instead of 'second elder' Cowdery, and placed Gause ahead of Rigdon."[22] Cowdery was in Missouri at the time.

While staying at the John Johnson Sr. farm at Hiram, Ohio, Joseph Smith and Sidney Rigdon were beaten, tarred, and feathered by a mob on the night of March 24.[23] Rigdon's injuries resulted in his temporally losing control of his mental faculties. Smith was influenced by unrest among the local population to leave for Missouri on April 1 with Bishop Newel K. Whitney, Peter Whitmer, and Jesse Gause. Rigdon joined them at nearby Warren. They purchased paper for the Missouri press at Wheeling, Virginia, and arrived at Independence on April 24.

Two days later Joseph Smith was "acknowledged by the High Priests in the land of Zion to be President of the High Priesthood, according to commandment and ordination in Ohio." Areas of conflict between Smith, Rigdon and Bishop Edward

---

18. Richard S. Van Wagoner, *Sidney Rigdon: A Portrait of Religious Success* (Salt Lake City: Signature Books, 1994), 109–11.

19. See Gregory A. Prince, *Power from On High: The Development of Mormon Priesthood* (Salt Lake City: Signature Books, 1995), 22. Prince explained, "This revelation, although received in November 1831 (see "Kirtland Revelation Book," 84–86), was not published until 1835, when it was included in an expanded revelation dated 28 Mar. 1835 (DC, 1835, III)."

20. D. Michael Quinn, *The Mormon Hierarchy: Origins of Power* (Salt Lake City: Signature Books, 1994), 40.

21. For biographical information on Jesse Gause see: Robert W. Woodford, "Jesse Gause, Councilor of the Prophet," *BYU Studies* 15, no. 3 (Spring 1975): 362–64; D. Michael Quinn, "Jesse Gause, Joseph Smith's Little-Known Counselor," *BYU Studies* 23, no. 4 (Fall 1983): 487–93; and Erin Jennings, "The Consequential Counselor: Restoring the Roots of Jesse Gause," *Journal of Mormon History* 34, no. 2 (Spring 2008): 182–227.

22. Quinn, *Origins of Power*, 41–42. Joseph Smith pronounced a revelation for Jesse Gause on March 15, 1832, which announced he was called to be a high priest, a counselor to Smith in the Presidency, and equally held the keys of the kingdom with the prophet. After Gause's apostasy, Frederick G. Williams was called to be his replacement. The text omitted Gause's name and added the name of Frederick G. Williams.

23. Van Wagoner, in *Sidney Rigdon*, 115, said the mob was composed of "infuriated Campbellites" possibly fortified by a "keg of whisky." Reasons for the assault are discussed in William Shepard and H. Michael Marquardt in *Lost Apostles: Forgotten Members of Mormonism's Original Quorum of Twelve* (Salt Lake City: Signature Books, 2014), 20–22.

Partridge were resolved and Partridge "extended the right of fellowship to Smith." Rigdon also "amicably settled" personal difficulties with the bishop.[24]

Oliver Cowdery, W. W. Phelps, and John Whitmer met with their brethren, Joseph Smith, Sidney Rigdon, and Jesse Gause on April 30 and agreed to print three thousand copies of the Book of Commandments. Significantly, Cowdery, Phelps, and Whitmer were not only authorized "to review" the Book of Commandments; they could also select which revelations should be printed and make grammatical corrections.[25] The print shop was consecrated in late May, and the first issue of *The Evening and the Morning Star* was printed in June.[26]

Historian Ron Romig explained that a previously known charge against Cowdery was now addressed, "Cowdery was brought before a church court in Independence, for either a sexual transgression or at least an impropriety with a young woman, which apparently occurred in the fall of 1830 at Mayfield, Ohio."[27] Smith and Rigdon had presumably left for Kirtland before a trial or hearing was conducted by Bishop Edward Partridge, Jesse Gause, and four other high priests on May 26. The account was apparently summarized from another source and later copied into the Far West Record. It stated that Cowdery had confessed his transgression to those present at the conference. It was recorded, "The reason why the above case was not taken into consideration by proper authority in the Church previous [to] this day, is that some of the Elders supposed that the affair had been adjusted last year when brother Oliver made his confession to the individuals injured & received their forgiveness."[28]

Oliver Cowdery married seventeen-year-old Elizabeth Ann Whitmer on December 18, 1832, at Independence.[29] He was shortly afterward passed over to be included in the church presidency. Joseph Smith received a revelation on March 8, 1833, indicating that Sidney Rigdon and Frederick Williams were equal with him "in holding the keys of this last kingdom."[30] These two brethren were ordained on March 18 and were counselors to Joseph.[31]

---

24. Cannon and Cook, *Far West Record*, 43–45, April 26, 1832.

25. Ibid., 46, April 30, 1832.

26. Ibid., 49, May 29, 1832.

27. Romig, *Eighth Witness*, 163.

28. Cannon and Cook, *Far West Record*, 48–49, May 26, 1832. After his return to Ohio Gause left Kirtland with Zebedee Coltrin on June 1 on a mission to the Quakers. He withdrew from Mormonism about August 19 and was excommunicated on December 3, 1832. See Dean C. Jessee, Mark Ashurst-McGee, and Richard L. Jensen, eds., *Journals, Volume 1: 1832–1839* (Salt Lake City: Church Historians Press, 2008), 10, cited hereafter as Jessee, *Journals, Volume 1*.

29. Romig, *Eighth Witness*, 191.

30. LDS D&C 90:6; RLDS D&C 87:3a.

31. Kirtland Council Minute Book, 16–17, Church History Library; Fred C. Collier and William S. Harwell, eds., *Kirtland Council Minute Book* (Salt Lake City: Collier's Publishing, 1996), 10–11, March 18, 1833. These minutes, also known as Minute Book 1, are available under Administrative Records on the Joseph Smith Papers web site

Cowdery saw the rise of anti-Mormon discontent, which exploded into mob violence during the summer of 1833. He was witness to the destruction of the printing establishment, the tarring and feathering of Edward Partridge and Charles Allen, the destruction of personal property, and how unmitigated violence affected the community.[32] Ron Romig said that with the destruction of the printing press, "three laborers lost their jobs and 'three families including Oliver and Elizabeth [were] left destitute of the means of subsistence.'"[33] Cowdery was sent to church headquarters in Kirtland, arriving on August 9 to explain the devastation and to seek advice. Elizabeth remained with family members in Missouri.

The destruction of the press in Missouri was a catastrophic loss for the Mormons. On September 11, when Oliver Cowdery met with Joseph Smith, Sidney Rigdon, and Newel K. Whitney, members of the Kirtland United Firm, it was determined that Cowdery would edit the *Latter Day Saints' Messenger and Advocate*, which would be published by the firm of F. G. Williams and Company.[34] Following his October trip to New York to purchase the press, Cowdery informed Ambrose Palmer of New Portage, Ohio, on October 30, that he would consecrate his time to the publication of the paper and hoped to make enough to obtain "the common comforts of life."[35] He also wrote his older brother Warren at Freedom, New York, on December 2 that his "every moment" was devoted to preparing for the resumption of printing.[36]

Cowdery met with members of the United Firm in the Kirtland printing office on December 18 for the dedication of the press. He received a blessing from Joseph Smith that included, "blessed of the Lord is bro Oliver nevertheless there are two evils in him that he must needs forsake or he cannot altogeth[er] escape the buffetings of the advers[ar]y if he shall forsak[e] these evils he shall be forgiven and shall be made like unto the bow which the Lord hath set in the heavens he shall be a sign and an ensign unto the nations."[37] There is no explanation what the "two evils" were.

---

at http://josephsmithpapers.org/the-papers. On October 12, 1833, at Perrysburg, New York, Smith told Rigdon that he had been appointed by revelation as "a spokesman unto this people," and in this capacity, would "know the certainty of all things pertaining to the things of my kingdom on the earth." LDS D&C 100:9–11; RLDS D&C 97:3a–b.

32. Ron Romig's account of violence against the Mormons, in *Eighth Witness*, 206–22, is compelling.

33. Ronald E. Romig, "Elizabeth Ann Whitmer Cowdery: A Historical Reflection of Her Life," in Alexander L. Baugh, ed., *Days Never to be Forgotten* (Salt Lake City: Deseret Book, 2009), 330.

34. Authorization for the renewal of printing is outlined in Collier and Harwell, *Kirtland Council Minute Book*, 18–19, September 11, 1833.

35. Oliver Cowdery to Ambrose Palmer, October 30, 1833, Oliver Cowdery Letterbook, 4, Henry E. Huntington Library and Art Gallery, San Marino, California.

36. Oliver Cowdery to Warren A. Cowdery, December 2, 1833, Oliver Cowdery Letterbook, 11, Huntington Library.

37. Jessee, *Journals, Volume* 1:21, 23. Cowdery would edit monthly issues of *The Evening and the Morning Star* from December 1833 through September 1834 and of the *Messenger and Advocate* from October 1834 to May 1835 and

The high council was formed by revelation on February 17, 1834, to settle cases "which could not be settled by the church or the Bishop's council to the satisfaction of the parties." The church president could singularly preside over the council or he could preside with his counselors who would also be referred to as presidents. Only Joseph Smith had the right to "inquire and obtain the mind of the Lord," but presidents Rigdon and Williams could preside over trials not meeting this criteria in his absence. Oliver Cowdery and eleven other high priests were chosen to be high councilors.[38]

Shortly after the organization of the high council, Joseph Smith left on a trip from February 26 to March 28, 1834, with Parley P. Pratt to raise money and manpower for what would be known as the Camp of Israel or Zion's Camp.[39] On March 9–11 they held several meetings at Freedom, Cattaraugus County, New York, and in the process spent time with Warren A. Cowdery, Oliver's older brother. Warren was not unknown as Oliver had printed several of his letters in *The Evening and the Morning Star* and had been attempting to convert him.[40]

On March 11 Heman Hyde was baptized, thus providing the groundwork for making Freedom a fertile area for spreading the gospel message.[41] Heman's son William, who was fifteen years old at the time, said his father in the early 1830s "began to hear something concerning the Book of Mormon." This information came "through Warren A. Cowdery, whose farm joined with ours, Warren A. obtained from his brother Oliver. at an early date, some of the proof sheets to the book of Mormon some of which we had the privilege of perusing."[42] Warren was baptized by the fall of 1834 after Smith and Pratt's March visit. In November he was selected to "be appointed and ordained a presiding high priest over my church, in the land of Freedom and the region round about."[43]

On April 19 Oliver was blessed "to assist brother Sidney in arranging the church covenants which are to be soon published."[44] Then on September 24 at a high council

---

from April 1836 to January 1837.

38. LDS D&C 102; RLDS D&C 99; Collier and Harwell, *Kirtland Council Minute Book*, 26–29, February 17, 1834.

39. LDS D&C 103; RLDS D&C 100.

40. Warren A. Cowdery was born in Poultney, Vermont in 1788. He and his wife Rebecca would have eleven children. He was a physician, pharmacist, postmaster, and farmer.

41. Jessee, *Journals, Volume* 1:32, 34; see also Scott Facer Proctor and Maurine Jensen Proctor, eds., *Autobiography of Parley P. Pratt* (Salt Lake City: Deseret Book, 2000), 133.

42. William Hyde Journal, 46, circa 1868–1873, MS 1549, Church History Library.

43. LDS D&C 106:1; RLDS D&C 103:1a. A critical study on Warren is lacking. See Lisa Olsen Tate, "Warren Cowdery D&C 106," *Revelations in Context: The Stories Behind the Sections of the Doctrine and Covenants*, ed. Matthew McBride and James Goldberg (Salt Lake City: The Church of Jesus Christ of Latter-day Saints, 2016), 219–23.

44. Jessee, *Journals, Volume* 1:41.

meeting presided over by Joseph Smith, the appointment was extended to Joseph Smith and Frederick Williams "to arrange the items of the doctrine of Jesus Christ for the government of the church of Latter-Day Saints."[45]

Oliver Cowdery "was ordained an assistant President of the High and Holy Priesthood" on December 5, 1834. Oliver recorded the wording of the ordination prayer of Joseph Smith, "My brother, in the name of Jesus Christ who ~~died~~ was crucified for the sins of the world, I lay my hands upon thee, and ordain thee an assistant President of the high and holy p[r]iesthood in the church of the Latter Day Saints."[46] Soon after the meeting Oliver made a record of it in a large book and titled it "Chapter 1." Oliver wrote about the December 5 meeting:

> Friday Evening, December 5, 1834. According to the direction of the Holy Spirit, Pr[e]sident Smith, assistant Presidents, Rigdon and Williams, assembled for the purpose of ordaining <first> High Counsellor Cowdery to the office of assistant President of the High and Holy Priesthood in the Church of the Latter-Day Saints.
>
> It is necessary, for the special benefit of the reader, that he be instructed <into, or> concerning the power and authority of the above named Priesthood.
>
> First. The office of the President is to preside over the whole Chu[r]ch; to be considered as the head; to receive revelations for the Church; to be a Seer, ~~and~~ Revelator <and Prophet—> having all the gifts of God:— ~~having~~ taking <Moses> for an ensample. Which is
>
> ~~Second~~ the office and station of the above President Smith, according to the calling of God, and the ordination which he has received.
>
> Second. The office of Assistant President is to assist in presiding over the whole chu[r]ch, and to officiate in the abscence of the President, according to ~~their~~ <his> rank and appointment, viz: President Cowdery, first; President Rigdon Second, and President Williams Third, as they <were> ~~are~~ severally called. The office of this Priesthood is also to act as Spokesman—taking Aaron for an ensample.
>
> The virtue of ~~this~~ the <above> Priesthood is to hold the keys of the kingdom of heaven, or the Church militant.
>
> The reader may further understand, that ~~Presidents~~ <the> reason why ~~President~~ <High Counsellor> Cowdery was not previously ordained <to the Presidency,> was, in consequence of his necessary attendance in Zion, to assist Wm W. Phelps in conducting the printing business; but that this promise was made by the angel while in company with President Smith, at the time they receivd the office of the lesser priesthood. And

---

45. Collier and Harwell, *Kirtland Council Minute Book*, 61–63, September 24, 1834.

46. Jessee, *Journals, Volume* 1:47–48.

further: The circumstances and situation of the Church requiring, Presidents Rigdon and Williams were presently ordained, to assist ~~the~~ President Smith.[47]

Historian Richard Bushman explained that Oliver Cowdery "took pains" to prove "his rightful place was at Joseph's side. Then he listed himself as the first assistant president ahead of Sidney Rigdon. The account of this reinstallation would be more persuasive if someone besides Oliver himself had written it. He was the one to underscore his own importance in the Church hierarchy."[48]

Cowdery's claim that he could not be ordained because he was "in Zion" assisting Phelps with the printing, is not convincing. He could have been ordained by Smith to be his "Assistant President" while he and Smith were together in Missouri in 1832, or while they served together at Kirtland anytime after August 9, 1833. The following day, December 6, Cowdery documented the ordinations of Hyrum Smith and Joseph Smith Sr. to the church presidency.

Although three new assistants had been added to the Presidency of the High Priesthood or church presidency, Sidney Rigdon continued as Joseph Smith's second-in-command. Just three weeks later on December 28, Rigdon was president of the high council in a matter of limited importance and Cowdery was a member of the council and served as clerk.[49] A high council meeting of January 18, 1835, reflected the revised composition with six presidents over the high priesthood. Presidents Joseph Smith Jr., Sidney Rigdon, and Frederick G. Williams presided over the high council. Presidents Oliver Cowdery, Hyrum Smith, and Joseph Smith Sr. served on the high council.[50]

Less than a month later, with the addition of Martin Harris, the command to Oliver Cowdery and David Whitmer to select the Twelve Apostles had been fulfilled as they had completed their selection from men who had participated in or supported Zion's Camp. On February 14, nine of the twelve candidates were ordained by the three witnesses. Cowdery told the men, "You have been ordained to the Holy Priesthood. You have received it from those who had their power and authority from an angel."[51]

---

47. Manuscript History, Book A-1:17 [separate section], CR 100 102, Church History Library, words written above the line are indicated by angled brackets <>. Also called History, 1834–1836; as cited in Matthew C. Godfrey, Brenden W. Rensink, Alex D. Smith, Max H Parkin and Alexander L. Baugh, eds., *Documents Volume 4: April 1834–September 1835* (Salt Lake City: Church Historian's Press, 2016), 194, 196. The manuscript volume was also used to copy Cowdery's letters to W. W. Phelps and third person entries from Smith's 1835–36 journal. In 1839 the volume was turned over to become the front cover for the manuscript history labeled A 1.

48. Richard L. Bushman, "Oliver's Joseph," Baugh, *Days Never to be Forgotten*, 4.

49. Collier and Harwell, *Kirtland Council Minute Books*, 67–68, December 28, 1834.

50. Ibid., 68–70, January 18, 1835.

51. Ibid., 70–84, February 14, 1835. See Shepard and Marquardt, *Lost Apostles*, 79–87, for the importance of the ordinations, the order in which the apostles were ordained, and the delayed blessings of Parley P. Pratt on February 21, while Thomas B. Marsh and Orson Pratt were ordained on April 26.

In a follow-up meeting with the nine newly ordained apostles on February 27, Oliver had reverted to his position as clerk and deferred to Joseph Smith, Sidney Rigdon, and Frederick Williams as the church presidency.[52] Rigdon gave "ordination blessings" to men called to be seventies on February 28 and March 1,[53] and on March 7, he was nominated to "officiate in laying on hands in the name of the Lord to bestow the blessings" on men who supported the building of the Kirtland Temple.[54] On March 16, Joseph Smith, Sidney Rigdon, and Frederick Williams presided over the high council and Joseph Smith Sr. and Oliver Cowdery served on the high council.[55]

Although Oliver Cowdery's desire to be Joseph Smith's primary assistant was not realized, there are no indications he was a malcontent. He appears to have been totally loyal at this time. Elizabeth had arrived at Kirtland from Missouri by October 1834.

The first apostolic mission began on May 4. Six pairs of apostles would take different routes for preaching, testifying, and holding conferences. They came together at Freedom, New York, for a conference from May 22–25 in the area Joseph Smith and Parley Pratt had successfully missionized the previous year.[56] Apostle William McLellin briefly noted in his journal, "Friday 22. We passed on to Elder [Warren] Cowdery's and there we met with our brethren the twelve and found them all well and proceeded to business and opened our Conference."[57] Records indicate that they established boundaries for the Freedom district, gave instructions on the Word of Wisdom, the gift of tongues, prophesying, and the redemption of Zion.[58]

As the first apostolic mission was taking place, Oliver Cowdery announced in the May 1835 *Messenger and Advocate*, "business and other duties" required him to give up the editorship in favor of John Whitmer "late of Missouri." He acknowledged the support he had received during his year and eight months of labor and referred to past and future events which had been and would be defined by Mormonism.[59] Ron Romig outlined Cowdery's changing duties:

52. Collier and Harwell, *Kirtland Council Minute Book*, 84–87, February 27, 1835.

53. Ibid., 87–104, February 28 and March 1, 1835.

54. Ibid., 104–7, March 7, 1835.

55. Ibid., 109–11, March 16, 1835.

56. In addition to the Smith-Pratt 1834 preaching at Freedom, Sidney Rigdon had recently presided over a large conference at Freedom. See "Freedom, April 3, 1835," *Messenger and Advocate* 1 no. 7 (April 1835): 101–2.

57. Jan Shipps and John W. Welch, eds., *The Journals of William E. McLellin, 1831–1836* (Provo, Utah: BYU Studies, Brigham Young University and Urbana and Chicago: University of Illinois Press, 1994), 178–79.

58. Ronald K. Esplin and Sharon E. Nielsen, "The Record of the Twelve, 1835: The Quorum of the Twelve Apostles' Call and 1835 Mission," *BYU Studies Quarterly* 51, no. 1 (2012): 33–34, minutes recorded in Patriarchal Blessing Book 2, Church History Library. See also "'The twelve' have been blest," *Messenger and Advocate* 1, no. 10 (July 1835): 153.

59. "To the Patrons of the Latter Day Saints' Messenger and Advocate," Ibid., 1, no. 8 (May 1835): 120–22.

John's assignment [to be editor of the *Messenger and Advocate*] freed Oliver Cowdery to once again function as Joseph's chief scribe and also concentrate on bringing out an updated edition of Joseph's revelations. This new work, to be called the Doctrine and Covenants, would combine the Lectures on Faith (the "doctrine"), delivered in Kirtland during December 1834, with Joseph's revelations (the "covenants"), many of which had formerly appeared in the interrupted Book of Commandments, but with the addition of fifty-seven new revelatory documents."[60]

The Kirtland and Missouri presidents, minus Frederick Williams, met on August 4 to consider a letter Warren Cowdery had written Oliver on July 29. Obviously shared by Oliver, the letter created a firestorm as it charged that the apostles did not solicit money for the Kirtland Temple during their recent visit at Freedom. Warren maintained that Jared Carter, a high priest and a member of the Kirtland high council, had arrived to collect money the apostles should have raised. According to Warren, Carter was so flustered when the money was unavailable that he could not preach effectively but added that he generously helped raise over $342. A letter from William McLellin to his wife added to the hierarchy's consternation as it maintained Orson Hyde had criticized Sidney Rigdon's school at Kirtland, and a Thomas Marsh letter came under fire for praising "the able" preaching of McLellin and Parley Pratt. The presidents, in a document composed by Oliver Cowdery, determined that the apostles had become "a kind of outlaws," acting independently of the Church Presidency. McLellin's and Hyde's priesthoods were silenced, and the remaining apostles were told to be humbler.[61]

During the course of the apostles' mission, and the absence of Joseph Smith and Frederick Williams on a mission in Michigan, a general assembly of the church was conducted on August 17, 1835, at Kirtland, at which Sidney Rigdon and Oliver Cowdery presented the 1835 Doctrine and Covenants for ratification by the church. After testimonies to the truth of the book by various quorum presidents and unanimous acceptance by the conference, W. W. Phelps read the "Article on Marriage." The article was evidently written by Oliver Cowdery, and after it was accepted unanimously, it was "ordered to be printed in said book." Cowdery then read the declaration, "Of Governments and Laws in General," which was also unanimously accepted.[62]

The intent of the Article on Marriage about rumors of "fornication and polygamy" continues to be debated. For example, Richard Bushman wrote, "No one in-

---

60. Romig, *Eighth Witness*, 256.

61. Warren Cowdery's letter to Oliver dated July 29 is quoted in *History of the Church* 2:239. The chastising response to the apostles is cited in Ibid., 2:239–41.

62. See Collier and Harwell, *Kirtland Council Minute Book*, 122–27, August 17, 1835 and LDS *History of the Church*, 2:243–50.

timated in 1835 that Joseph's actions caused the rumors."[63] Todd Compton believes the Article on Marriage was presented by Cowdery to counter the effects of Joseph Smith's polygamy and that "circumstantial evidence is strong that Cowdery's respect for Joseph diminished after that point."[64]

The "Council of the Presidency of the Church," which included the Kirtland and Far West Presidents, met with several of the Twelve Apostles on September 26 to investigate events which occurred on their inaugural mission. William McLellin and Orson Hyde "frankly confessed" and were forgiven for criticizing Sidney Rigdon's school. The governing body examined Warren Cowdery's accusation that the apostles did not solicit funds for the Kirtland Temple and ruled, "it was proved before the council that said complaints originated in the minds of persons whose minds were darkened in consequence of covetousness or some other cause other than the Spirit of truth."[65]

Oliver Cowdery was one of three presidents at a high council trial of William Smith on January 2, 1836. The presiding order was Frederick G. Williams, Oliver Cowdery, and David Whitmer.[66]

Oliver was not present at a dramatic meeting between the Church Presidency and the Twelve Apostles on January 16, 1836. The clerk, Warren Parrish, noted the apostles spoke "in a verry [sic] forcible, and explicit manner yet cool and deliberate." They complained about the disrespect they received on their recent mission. After Thomas B. Marsh, president of the apostles, "unbosom[ed] his feelings," the other eleven did the same. They remained furious about receiving during their mission a rebuking letter that suspended two of their number and "severely chastened" the remainder. The group of apostles continued to be angry because the Presidency rejected their counter-charges against Warren Cowdery and felt Oliver Cowdery had disrespected them "on a certain occasion, making use of language to one of the twelve that was unchristian." Joseph Smith said he and the Presidency had been disrespectful to the apostles but countered that the letter about Sidney Rigdon's school was also disrespectful. After apologies by the Presidency were accepted, a joyful covenant between the apostles and the Presidency was made to support each other.[67]

---

63. Richard Lyman Bushman, *Joseph Smith: Rough Stone Rolling* (New York: Alfred A. Knopf, 2005), 324.

64. Todd Compton, *In Sacred Loneliness: The Plural Wives of Joseph Smith* (Salt Lake City: Signature Books, 1997), 38.

65. Collier and Harwell, *Kirtland Council Minute Book*, 140, September, 26, 1835.

66. Ibid., 153–54, January 2, 1836. David Whitmer is referred to as a "Priesident" because he was a member of the Missouri Presidency.

67. Jessee, *Journals*, Volume 1:156–60.

As recorded in his Sketch Book on February 25, Oliver noted that his brother Warren and family "arrived this morning from Freedom, N. Y."[68] The next month Warren "confessed his mistake" about condemning the apostles in a meeting with Oliver, Sidney Rigdon, Joseph Smith, and "the Twelve" on March 5. It was explained by Oliver that the apostles had filed charges against Warren who, in turn, agreed to publish an apology.[69] The carefully worded apology, dated March 7, 1836, was published in the *Messenger and Advocate*:

> The undersigned although actuated by the purest motives at the time he wrote believing he had stated nothing but the truth, has since become satisfied from the best of evidence, that, that particular item in their instructions was not omitted as he had represented, he, therefore, most deeply regrets it, being sensible as he now is, that he was the cause (although innocent) of wounding the best of feelings, and depressing spirits buoyant with hope, while In the field of useful labor at a distance from home.[70]

Oliver Cowdery's Sketch Book, under date of March 19, indicates he and his brother Warren participated with Joseph Smith, Sidney Rigdon, and Warren Parrish "in writing a prayer for the dedication of the house [Temple]."[71]

At the Kirtland Temple dedication on March 27, Sidney Rigdon delivered the principal sermon and sat with Joseph and Hyrum Smith in the second pulpit at the west end of the Temple. It was Oliver Cowdery, however, who went with Joseph Smith "behind the veil" in the Temple on April 3, where they received a series of visions which were afterwards recorded by Warren Cowdery. The account told that the "eyes of their understandings were opened. They saw the Lord standing upon the breast work of the pulpit" and were told, "Behold your sins are forgiven you," and he accepted the dedicated building. The account also recorded that Moses, Elias and Elijah appeared and delivered keys or authority for the gathering of Israel, the gospel of Abraham, and "the keys of this dispensation."[72]

With the conclusion of the Pentecostal events, the hierarchy devoted themselves to facilitating renewed missionizing by the Twelve Apostles and Seventies and dealing with individual and church debt. The latter probably influenced a strange set of circumstances which led Joseph and Hyrum Smith, Sidney Rigdon, and Oliver Cowdery to leave Kirtland on July 25 for Salem, Massachusetts. J. Christopher Con-

---

68. Oliver Cowdery's Sketch Book, 17, February 25, 1836, MS 3429, Church History Library. Also in Leonard J. Arrington, "Oliver Cowdery's Kirtland, Ohio, 'Sketch Book,'" *BYU Studies* 12, no. 4 (1972): 425.

69. Ibid., 426, March 5, 1836.

70. "Notice," *Messenger and Advocate*, 2, no. 5 (February 1836): 263.

71. Arrington, "Oliver Cowdery's Kirtland, Ohio, 'Sketch Book,'" 426, March 19, 1836.

72. The third person account is in Jessee, *Journals, Volume* 1:219–22. First person account in *History of the Church* 2:435–36 and LDS D&C 110. Richard Bushman explained, "Joseph never mentioned the event in his other writings. There is no evidence he told the Kirtland Saints." Bushman, *Rough Stone Rolling*, 320.

kling, in his *Joseph Smith Chronology*, explained: "At this time the Church is in dire financial stress, the Kirtland Temple having cost between $40,000 and $60,000. A brother named Burgess comes to Joseph and says that he knows of a large amount of money hidden away in the cellar of a certain house in Salem, Mass., which had belonged to a widow. The woman had died, and he is the only person who knows of the whereabouts of the treasure." When the party arrived at Salem, Burgess "claims that the town has changed so much that he cannot find the house, and soon afterwards he leaves them there."[73]

Joseph Smith pronounced LDS D&C 111 at Salem on August 6, 1836 which reassured the party the trip was not made in vain and promised that "in due time" the "wealth pertaining to gold and silver shall be yours." The revelation also assured them the Lord would "give you power" to pay the church debts and "Concern not yourself about Zion" because the Lord would deal "mercifully with her."[74] They returned to Kirtland by September 13.

Historian Mark Staker explained that the revelation may have stimulated the men to consider "the idea of establishing a bank to raise money." A bank would foster "land development," which would enable the poor "to earn their way out of debt." As "gathering Saints" would be forced to purchase land from speculators at inflated prices, the Mormons reasoned it would be best if they controlled the process. He added, "The need to acquire land in Zion, which included Kirtland as its easternmost border, took precedence over paying for debts as leaders moved more actively into real estate investment."[75]

These financial realities were attested by Heber C. Kimball on his return to Kirtland after a mission in October 1836. He was "much grieved" by the "spirit of speculation" that was prevailing in the church as he found lots previously worth "about 150 dollars" were now "worth from 500 to 1000 dollars according to location." He also observed "some men who when I left could hardly get food to eat, I found on my return to be men of supposed great wealth." His observations included, "all seemed determined to become rich."[76]

Oliver Cowdery was one of the "committee of directors" of the Kirtland Safety Society and served in various capacities. On November 2, articles of the Society were drawn up, and the directors began to sell stock. Sidney Rigdon was designated president and Joseph Smith cashier. Cowdery was dispatched to New York to purchase plates for printing bank notes, and Orson Hyde was designated to go to Columbus

---

73. J. Christopher Conkling, *A Joseph Smith Chronology* (Salt Lake City: Deseret Book, 1979), 92.

74. LDS D&C 111:4–6.

75. Mark L. Staker, "Raising Money in Righteousness: Oliver Cowdery as Banker," in Baugh, *Days Never to be Forgotten*, 150.

76. "History of Heber Chase Kimball by His Own Dictation," 47–48, handwriting of Thomas Bullock, Heber C. Kimball Papers, MS 627, Church History Library, cited in Shepard and Marquardt *Lost Apostles*, 138.

to apply for a charter. Cowdery returned to Kirtland with the press and printed notes, but Hyde delayed his trip to Columbus until after the new year, thus missing the opportunity to ask potentially helpful Democratic representatives for help. Mark Staker explained, "Cowdery perhaps should have been selected to handle … getting a charter approved. He had been to the Democrats' Convention in Columbus and was a personal friend of influential party members. Instead, bank investors gave Orson Hyde that task."[77]

Assuming they would not receive a charter, the Kirtland Safety Society changed their strategy. Mark Staker explained that on January 2, 1837, they revised the "Articles of Agreement, transforming the society from a bank to a financial corporation." Presumably believing this would allow them to avoid the charter issue. They also "changed the name from the 'Kirtland Safety Society' to the 'Kirtland Safety Society Anti-Banking Company,' although it continued to be referred to in public discourse, private journals, letters, and historical memory as simply the Kirtland Safety Society."[78] The result was what Richard Bushman called a "partial land bank" whose notes, secured by land holding, "gave landowners liquidity to initiate commercial ventures when capital was lacking."[79]

On January 6 Wilford Woodruff visited the Kirtland Safety Society office and wrote in his journal:

> President Joseph Smith jr. declare in the presence of F Williams, D. Whitmer, S. Smith, W. Parrish, & others in the Deposit Office that he had receieved that morning the Word of the Lord upon the Subject of the Kirtland Safety Society. He was alone in a room by himself & he had not ownly the voice of the Spirit upon the Subject but even an audable voice. He did not tell us at that time what the LORD said upon the subject but remarked that if we would give heed to the Commandments the Lord had given this morning all would be well.[80]

Opening on January 9, the infusion of currency initially stimulated the Kirtland economy as public works, manufacturing, and a variety of businesses provided employment. It also allowed Joseph Smith, Sidney Rigdon, and others of the hierarchy to borrow money and buy area farms.[81]

The Kirtland Safety Society opened at a precarious time as out-of-control inflation, increasing debt, and growing dissension within the church began to threaten

---

77. Staker, "Oliver Cowdery as Banker," in Baugh, *Days Never to be Forgotten*, 156.

78. Mark Lyman Staker, *Hearken, O Ye People: The Historical Setting of Joseph Smith's Ohio Revelations* (Salt Lake City: Gregg Kofford Books, 2009), 477.

79. Bushman, *Rough Stone Rolling*, 330.

80. Scott G. Kenney, ed., *Wilford Woodruff's Journal*, 9 vols. (Midvale, UT: Signature Books, 1983–85), 1:120, January 6, 1837.

81. Staker, *Hearken, O Ye People*, 482–83.

Mormon stability. The greater threat, however, was the reaction by regional anti-Mormons. The Bank of Geauga in nearby Painesville, for example, refused to accept Mormon banknotes. Mark Staker explained:

> An 1834 law stated that unincorporated banks lending money could not collect their debts. Although this law was not widely known until the Kirtland Safety Society was in full operation and was apparently not enforced, any hint of impropriety made a financial institution less stable and easily destroyed through innuendo or blatant false accusations.[82]

Enemies would use this statute, banking without a charter, in law suits against them. Add to that, Grandison Newell, a Mormon hating industrialist from Painesville, led the attack by acquiring all the Mormon banknotes he could and then redeeming them for specie. This, of course, helped drain the Mormons' limited supply of specie. Richard Bushman acknowledged "the bank failed within a month."[83]

Wilford Woodruff attended a Seventies Quorum meeting on January 17 where president David Whitmer gave a dire prediction to the church:

> He warned us to humble ourselves before God lest his hand rest upon us in anger for our pride & many sins that we were runing into in our days of prosperity as the ancient Nephites did & it does now appear evident that a scourge awates this stake of Zion even Kirtland if their [there] is not great repentance immediately & almost every Countenance indicates the above expectation esspecially the heads of the Church.[84]

Woodruff mentioned that he heard "addresses from Presidents O Cowdery & J Smith Jr." on January 29. "JOSEPH blessed us in the name of the Lord & Said if we would be faithful we should rise above our [financial] imbarrements [sic] & be delivered from the hands of our enemies." Two days later he heard Joseph Smith and Sidney Rigdon speak "on the temporal business of the Church & Petitioned for a Charter to the Assembly of the State for the Kirtland Safety Society & the presidency of the Church bought the Monroe Charter."[85]

The *Messenger and Advocate* in an announcement, dated February 1, said "The late firm of O. Cowdery & Co. is this day dissolved by mutual consent. The entire establishment is now owned by Joseph Smith Jr. and Sidney Rigdon." It also mentioned "W. A. Cowdery takes the editorial chair."[86] This cleared the way for Oliver Cowdery to travel to Monroe, Michigan, and become affiliated with the Bank of Monroe.

---

82. Staker, "Oliver Cowdery as Banker," in Baugh, *Days Never to be Forgotten*, 165.

83. Bushman, *Rough Stone Rolling*, 330.

84. Kenney, *Wilford Woodruff's Journal* 1:122, January 17, 1837.

85. Ibid., 1:124, January 29 and 31, 1837, emphasis retained.

86. "Notice," *Messenger and Advocate* 3, no. 5 (February 1837): 458.

It was during Cowdery's brief stay at Monroe that he penned a final valedictory from Mormon newspapers which reaffirmed his belief in Mormonism:

> It is only requisite for me to add that the doctrines which I commenced to preach some seven years since are as firmly believed by me as ever; and though persecutions have attended, and the rage and malice of men been heaped upon me, I feel equally as firm in the great and glorious cause as when first I received my mission from the holy messenger.[87]

The Ohio Legislature rejected the Mormon application for a banking charter on February 10 while Joseph and Hyrum Smith, Sidney Rigdon, and Oliver Cowdery were in Monroe negotiating with Bank of Monroe officials. Cowdery was appointed "as a director and vice president to serve until the end of the business year in July." The following day financial adjustments were made between the organizations, and Cowdery remained in Monroe.[88] His stay would be short as he was back in Kirtland by March 6. Mark Staker felt the "departure was not voluntary," but also noted that the Free Banking Act on March 15 "made the Bank of Monroe's charter irreverent and required the bank officials to be legal residents of the state." He additionally noted, "it is not clear if Oliver retained his former position as bank director in Kirtland when he returned, but after coming back from Monroe he remained aloof from the institution."[89]

Cowdery arrived at Kirtland when the Kirtland Safety Society was drastically reducing the value of its bank notes, inflation was rampant, the church was floundering in debt, and important hierarchical members neared the end of their support for Joseph Smith. And a crisis was building in northern Missouri with the bishopric, high counselors, and apostles Thomas B. Marsh and David W. Patten forcing presidents William Phelps and John Whitmer to make concessions.[90]

Oliver Cowdery was elected Justice of the Peace in Kirtland on April 29, 1837, when dissent was becoming rebellion. He served from June 14 to September 15, 1837. Wilford Woodruff attended a meeting in the Temple on Sunday, May 28, and noted the "spirits of murmering, complaining, & of mutuny." It was "in the family Circle in the secret Chamber & in the streets untill many & some in high places had risen up against Joseph the servent whom God had raised up to lead Israel."[91]

The desperation gripping Kirtland was demonstrated the following day as president Sidney Rigdon attempted to conduct a trial for fellow counselor in the church presidency, Frederick G.Williams; president of the Missouri church David Whit-

---

87. "Valedictory," Ibid., 3, No. 11 (August 1837): 548, Monroe, Michigan, Feb. 1837.

88. Staker, *Hearken O Ye People*, 494.

89. Staker, "Raising Money in Righteousness," 186.

90. See Cannon and Cook, *Far West Record*, 107–9, April 3, 1837; 109–10, April 5, 1837; 110, April 7, 1837.

91. Kenney, *Wilford Woodruff's Journal* 1:147–48, May 28, 1837.

mer; apostles Lyman Johnson and Parley Pratt; and Warren Parrish, Joseph Smith's former trusted scribe and associate in the Kirtland Safety Society. They had been charged by loyalists Able Lamb, Nathan Haskins, Harlow Redfield, Artemas Miller, and Isaac Rogers, who said they had been "aggrieved" by the conduct of the accused "which for some time past had been injurious to the Church." They charged, "We therefore desire that the High Council should be assembled and we should have an investigation of their behavior." Rigdon faced a procedural nightmare as he had no answer for objections raised about legitimacy and jurisdiction. Added to that, four of the high counselors, to varying degrees, agreed with the accused and would withdraw or be removed from the church by 1838. After much discussion and confusion, Rigdon acknowledged that he had previously judged Parley Pratt and excused himself. Oliver Cowdery said he could not preside as he had previously "expressed his opinion" about some of the defendants. The meeting broke-up in confusion.[92]

On the same day, Lyman Johnson and Orson Pratt filed charges against Joseph Smith; Luke Johnson filed charges against Joseph Smith Sr.; and Warren Parrish filed charges against Sidney Rigdon. The charges were not acted upon by the high council.[93] Ron Romig indicated that David Whitmer left Kirtland for Missouri shortly after the trial. We can only speculate on Oliver Cowdery's reaction to the treatment his brother-in-law received.[94]

As Joseph Smith and his supporters struggled to keep the church from fragmenting, Warren Cowdery's editorials in the *Messenger and Advocate* appear to have been supportive of the dissenters. The editorial in the May 1837 issue frankly said that there were good and bad Mormons at Kirtland. He bluntly declared, "If you come here to see perfection in the church and all living like saints of God; you will be disappointed, sadly disappointed."[95]

Warren Cowdery's June editorial investigated the economic malaise that was gripping Kirtland. He contrasted the current economic status with that of the previous year. Calling the current period a "time of trial" because prices were nearly one hundred per cent higher than a year earlier and there was less employment. He ad-

---

92. Collier and Harwell, *Kirtland Council Minute Book*, 181–84, May 29, 1837. Wilford Woodruff noted the trial, "was considered not <law to> try <the president> before the high Council but before the Bishop. The Presidents withdrew. The council closed without transacting business." Kenney, *Wilford Woodruff Journal* 1:148, May 29, 1837.

93. Shepard and Marquardt, *Lost Apostles*, 141–43.

94. Romig, in *Eighth Witness*, 309–12, examined Lucy Smith's allegation that David Whitmer was one of several prominent Mormons who were deceived by a "young woman" at Kirtland who pretended to be able to see hidden things and to prophesy "by looking through a certain black stone." Romig sensitively outlined Whitmer's gradual slide out of Mormonism in "David Whitmer: Faithful Dissenter, Witness Apart." in *Differing Visions: Dissenters in Mormon History*, eds., Roger D. Launius and Linda Thatcher (Urbana: University of Illinois Press, 1994), 23–44.

95. "We, some few months since," *Messenger and Advocate* 3, no. 8 (May 1837): 507.

vised the readers to "indulge in no visionary schemes of worldly greatness," to support good leaders, and to "Remember that the great Creator never made an independent man, and with equal propriety we might add he never made an infallible one."[96]

Apostles Thomas Marsh and David Patten arrived at Kirtland in mid-July and, after dealing with their disappointment of not being able to participate in the English mission, Marsh helped convince Parley and Orson Pratt to make peace with Joseph Smith and resume their duties in the Quorum of Apostles. He probably influenced Luke and Lyman Johnson and John Boynton to briefly return to their Quorum.[97] For unknown reasons Patten, who was brother-in-law to Warren Parrish, took it upon himself to seek out Oliver Cowdery and question him about an alleged affair between Joseph Smith and a local girl. She is mentioned in a January 1838 letter as Fanny Alger.[98] Thomas Marsh later testified that Patten asked Oliver if Joseph Smith "had confessed to his wife that he was guilty of adultery with a certain girl, when Oliver Cowdery cocked up his eye very knowingly and hesitated to answer the question, saying he did not know as he was bound to answer the question yet conveying the idea that it was true."[99]

Richard Bushman wrote about this alleged affair between Smith and Alger explaining, "Alger was fourteen when her family joined the Church in Mayfield, near Kirtland, in 1830. In 1836, after a time as a serving girl in the Smith household, she left Kirtland and was soon married."[100] Leland H. Gentry and Todd Compton wrote that Cowdery may have started spreading the story in the summer of 1837 about the alleged adultery when he and Smith "were estranged over the bank failure."[101] Todd Compton credited the Smith-Cowdery estrangement of "Joseph's relationship with Fanny" as a marriage.[102]

Warren Cowdery's July editorial contained an extensive review of the Kirtland Safety Society and captured the feelings of many about Joseph Smith's financial

---

96. "A train of causes," Ibid., 3, no. 9 (June 1837): 522.

97. Shepard and Marquardt, *Lost Apostles*, 145.

98. Oliver Cowdery to Warren A. Cowdery, January 21, 1838, Oliver Cowdery Letterbook, 81, Huntington Library.

99. This visit of Patten with Cowdery is referred to at the church trial of Oliver Cowdery in Cannon and Cook, *Far West Record*, 167, April 12, 1838.

100. Bushman, *Rough Stone Rolling*, 323.

101. Leland H. Gentry and Todd M. Compton, *Fire and Sword: A History of the Latter-day Saints in Northern Missouri, 1836–39* (Salt Lake City: Greg Kofford Books, 2011), 79.

102. Todd Compton, "Fanny Alger Smith Custer: Mormonism's First Plural Wife," *Journal of Mormon History* 22, no. 1 (Spring 1996): 200; Compton, *In Sacred Loneliness*, 25–42. References to the Smith-Alger alleged affair are numerous. In part, see Brian C. Hales, "Fanny Alger and Joseph Smith's Pre-Nauvoo Reputation," *Journal of Mormon History* 35, no. 4 (Fall 2009): 112–90 and Don Bradley "Mormon Polygamy before Nauvoo?: The Relationship of Joseph Smith and Fanny Alger," in *The Persistence of Polygamy: Joseph Smith and the Origins of Mormon Polygamy*, eds., Newell G. Bringhurst and Craig L. Foster (Independence, MO: John Whitmer Books, 2010), 14–58. See also Brian C. Hales, "Guilty of Such Folly?" Accusations of Adultery or Polygamy Against Oliver Cowdery," in Baugh, *Days Never to be Forgotten*, 279–93.

abilities. He wrote, "If we give all our privileges to one man, we virtually give him our money and our liberties, and made him a monarch, absolute and despotic, and ourselves abject slaves or fawning sycophants." Warren said such a course would lead to "tyranny, and oppression" and the belief of infallibility. He reasoned:

> We are not bankers, bank stock holders, or financiers. We believe that banking or financiering [sic] is as much a regular science, trade or business, as those of law, physic or divinity, and that a man may be an eminent civilian, and know nothing of consequence of the principles of medicine. He may be a celebrated divine, and be no mechanic[,] no financier, and be as liable to fail in the management of a bank, as he would in constructing a balloon or the mechanism of a watch if he had never seen either.[103]

It was apparent when Warren Cowdery's penned his July editorial that Kirtland was becoming ungovernable. Mark Staker attributed this to the failure of the Kirtland Safety Society and noted, "At one end of the spectrum was an expanding group of members who rejected the First Presidency's leadership in economic affairs and viewed Joseph Smith as a fallen prophet even while accepting his earlier revelations." They went by the name "the Church of Christ." At "the other end of the spectrum" the loyalists were "known as lickskillets."[104]

It is not known if the July number of the *Messenger and Advocate* was published before Joseph Smith, Sidney Rigdon, and Thomas Marsh left Kirtland on July 27 to visit the Mormons in Canada. During their absence, a violent clash took place between the loyalists and dissidents in the Kirtland Temple on August 14. Lucy Smith recalled that Joseph Smith Sr.'s sermon on the bank affair incensed Warren Parrish who vigorously objected to the accusations. Joseph Sr. "appealed to Oliver Cowdery, who was justice of the peace," to control Parrish "but Oliver never moved from his seat." Apostle William Smith intervened and attempted to forcibly remove Parrish, but apostle John F. Boynton drew "a sword from his cane, presented it to William's breast," and threatened to run him through.[105]

John W. Welch explained that Parrish "preferred charges of riot, and the State of Ohio commenced a suit against nineteen defendants in Kirtland." The trial was on August 25–26 and "some seventy witnesses were called—twenty-two by the state, forty-eight by defense." Cowdery ruled "the charge against them [defense] was not sustained, and they were therefore discharged." Welch said Cowdery "simply let the two groups line up and shoot accusations at each other. And when the verbal assaults were over, he declared the Church-leader defendants the winners." He added, "only

---

103. "It is a well known and established fact," *Messenger and Advocate* 3, no. 10 (July 1837): 537–39.

104. Staker, *Hearken O Ye People*, 535.

105. Lavina Fielding Anderson, ed., *Lucy's Book: A Critical Edition of Lucy Mack Smith's Family Memoir* (Salt Lake City: Signature Books, 2001), 598.

two weeks later, on September 15, 1837, Oliver prematurely resigned as justice of the peace and left Kirtland for Missouri."[106]

After Joseph Smith returned to Kirtland in late August he warned the Mormons through the *Messenger and Advocate*:

> To the brethren and friends of the church of Latter Day Saints, I am disposed to say a word relative to the bills of the Kirtland Safety Society Bank. I hereby warn them to beware of speculators, renegadoes [renegades] and gamblers, who are duping the unsuspecting and the unwary, by palming upon them, those bills, which are of no worth, here. I discountenance and disapprove of any and all such practices. I know them to be detrimental to the best interests of society, as well as to the principles of religion.[107]

At a conference held in the Kirtland Temple on September 3 the Kirtland stake was reorganized. The first order of business was the sustaining of church officers. The gathering was predominately composed of loyalists recruited by Brigham Young.[108] The minutes stated that Sidney Rigdon "introduced Joseph Smith Jr to the congregation to know if he should still act as their Pres[ident]. as the presiding officer of the church." The vote was unanimous in his favor. Next Joseph Smith presented his two counselors Sidney Rigdon and Frederick G. Williams together with himself, "to constitute the three first presidents of the church." They were sustained. Then Oliver Cowdery, Joseph Smith Sr., Hyrum Smith and John Smith were introduced for assistant counselors and accepted by vote. Apostles John Boynton and Luke and Lyman Johnson were not sustained. Four High Counselors were removed from office: John Johnson Sr., Joseph Coe, Joseph Kingsbury and Martin Harris.[109]

The editors of the *Journals, Volume 1: 1832–1839* explained: "After December 1834, Cowdery ranked first among the assistants. Their separation here into counselors and assistant counselors with Cowdery among the latter clearly constituted a demotion for Cowdery, if not for Joseph Smith Sr. and Hyrum Smith, who were already ranked behind Rigdon and Williams."[110]

Joseph Smith wrote a letter on September 4 to be delivered by Thomas Marsh to John Corrill and the church in Missouri. It spoke of recent difficulties at Kirtland "which are now about being settled" and referred them to consult Marsh and Hyrum Smith "that you may know how to proceed to set in order & regulate the affairs of

---

106. John W. Welch, "Oliver Cowdery as Editor, Defender, and Justice of the Peace in Kirtland," in Baugh, *Days Never to be Forgotten*, 275.

107. "Caution," *Messenger and Advocate* 3, no. 11 (August 1837): 560.

108. See Shepard and Marquardt, *Lost Apostles*, 148.

109. Collier and Harwell, *Kirtland Council Minute Book*, 184–87, September 3, 1837. Not an exact presentation of the minutes is in Jessee, *Journals, Volume* 1:241–43.

110. Jessee, *Journals, Volume* 1:242, note 63.

the Church in zion whenever they become disorganized."[111] He enclosed the minutes from the previous day and added additional thoughts on Oliver Cowdery, David Whitmer, and others:

> Oliver Cowdery has been in transgression, but as he is now chosen as one of the Presidents or councilors I trust that he will yet humble himself & magnify his calling but if he should not, the church will soon be under the necessaty [necessity] of raising their hands against him Therefore pray for him, David Whitmer[,] Leonard Rich & others have been in transgression but we hope that they may be humble & ere long make satisfaction to the Church otherwise they cannot retain their standing. Therefore we say unto you beware of all disaffected Characters for they came not to build up but to destroy & scatter abroad

Joseph Smith then proclaimed a revelation which Thomas Marsh and others at Far West would interpret to mean they should punish John Whitmer and William Phelps:

> Revelation to Joseph Smith Jr Given in Kirtland Geauga Co[unty]. Ohio Sept 4th 1837 Making known the transgression of John Whitmer [and] W W. Phelps Verily thus saith the Lord unto you my Servent Joseph. My Servents John Whitmer & William W Phelps have done those things which are not pleasing in my sight. Therefore if they repent not they shall be removed out of their places Amen[112]

Luke and Lyman Johnson and John Boynton "made confession to the church" at Kirtland on September 10 and were restored to fellowship.[113] Lyman Johnson departed shortly afterwards for Far West with his family.[114] At a September 17 meeting of the Kirtland high council it was noted that "Pres. Rigdon then stated that it was necessary that the Church should have a general recorder & clerk, to fill the place of O. Cowdery who had lately removed to the West." It also noted, George W. Robinson, Rigdon's son-in-law, replaced Cowdery "as general clerk & recorder of the whole church."[115] Cowdery's resignation as justice of the peace and hasty departure from Kirtland gave rise to speculation he had no choice but to leave.[116]

In a conference of elders meeting in the Kirtland Temple on September 17, it was voted unanimously "that Presidents J Smith Jr & S. Rigdon be requested by this

---

111. Ibid., 241.

112. Ibid., 244–45.

113. Collier and Harwell, *Kirtland Council Minute Book*, 188–89, September 10, 1837.

114. Shepard and Marquardt, *Lost Apostles*, 152.

115. Collier and Harwell, *Kirtland Council Minute Book*, 189–90, September17, 1837.

116. Frederick G. Williams and Joseph Smith testified at Cowdery's trial at Far West that he was involved in counterfeiting and left Kirtland to avoid being prosecuted. See Cannon and Cook, *Far West Record*, 168–69, April 12, 1838.

conference to go & appoint other Stakes or places of gathering."[117] Smith and Rigdon, accompanied by Vinson Knight and William Smith, departed Kirtland for Far West on September 27.

The August and September numbers of the *Messenger and Advocate* included a "Prospectus For a new paper, to be published at Kirtland, Geauga co. Ohio, called the Elders' Journal of the Church of the Latter Day Saints." Signed by Sidney Rigdon, the Prospectus said it was to be edited by Joseph Smith.[118] Two issues of the journal were printed each in Kirtland (October and November 1837) and Far West (July and August 1838).

A General Assembly was held at Far West on November 6–7 that included the First Presidency; apostles Thomas Marsh, William McLellin, Lyman Johnson, and William Smith; the Far West high council and others. Oliver Cowdery was present, but his authority level, if any, was not mentioned, but he was clerk. This November 6 business included the decision that the greater Far West area had "sufficient room" for continued consolidation and that building a temple should be postponed. The minutes concluded with, "All difficulties were satisfactorily settled except a matter between J. Smith jr. Oliver Cowdery and T. B. Marsh which was referred to themselves with the agreement that their settlement of the affair should be sufficient for the Council."[119]

The second day of the assembly featured the unanimous sustaining of Joseph Smith as church president. Sidney Rigdon was sustained as one of the counselors, but Frederick G. Williams was objected by some of the brethren and was replaced by Hyrum Smith. David Whitmer, John Whitmer, and William Phelps were retained in the Far West Presidency after satisfying their critics.[120] Peace had been restored, but it would not last long.

Joseph Smith and Sidney Rigdon left Far West about November 10 and arrived at Kirtland a month later. During their trip, Oliver Cowdery was appointed standing

117. Collier and Harwell, *Kirtland Council Minute Book*, 190, September 17, 1837.

118. See "Prospectus," *Messenger and Advocate* 3, no. 11 (August 1837): 545, 547 and "Prospectus," Ibid., 3, no. 12 (September 1837): 571, 574. Historian Peter Crawley commented, "Implicit with this announcement is a dissatisfaction with Warren A. Cowdery, editor of the *Messenger and Advocate*, who had been publishing ponderous articles on ancient history and philosophy and in the July 1837 issue had criticized Joseph Smith and Sidney Rigdon for their roles in the Kirtland Bank fiasco." Peter Crawley, *A Descriptive Bibliography of the Mormon Church, Volume One 1830–1847* (Provo, UT: Religious Studies Center, Brigham Young University, 1997), 72. Phebe Woodruff wrote in her letter of March 1, 1838, "Doct[or] [Warren] Cowdery has withdrawn from the church." Phebe Woodruff to "Dear Wilford," March 1, 1838, Wilford Woodruff Collection, MS 19509, Folder 5, Church History Library. Phebe was summarizing a letter from Milton Holmes.

119. Cannon and Cook, *Far West Record*, 119–20, November 6, 1837. The unresolved issue concerned a meeting between Cowdery, Smith, and Marsh, evidently relating to a discussion about the girl Smith knew.

120. Ibid., 121–24, November 7, 1837.

clerk for the high council on December 6 at Far West, and the following day Oliver and David Patten made a report of their exploration of the "north country."[121]

During the journey of Joseph Smith, Sidney Rigdon and their party to Far West, Oliver Cowdery received information from his brother Warren at Kirtland informing him that Smith had broken his promise not to talk about the girl anymore. Oliver's January 21, 1838, response to Warren included a copy of a letter he had sent to Smith. The letter explained about his period of sickness and how he was finally able to keep his promise to explore the area north of Far West. It also said he had received "recent intelligence from Kirtland" which gave him "so much surprise." He continued, "I learn from Kirtland, by the last letters, that you have publickly [*sic*] said, that when you were here [Far West] I confessed to you that I had willfully lied about you—this compels me to ask you to correct that statement, and give me an explanation—until which you and myself are two." It is possible Cowdery's letter was not received by Smith.

Oliver's letter to Warren was to the point and in response to the information he received:

> You will see from the other page that your own and brother Lyman[']s requests concerning the Stated confession made to Mr. Smith, is, if I am to be credited, not so. From what he pretended to have made it, is to me unaccountable. I can assure you and bro. Lyman, that as God is to judge my soul at the last day, and as I hope for salvation in the world to come, I never confessed intimated <or admitted> that I ever willfully lied about him. When he was here we had some conversation in which in every instance, I did not fail to affirm that what I had said was strictly true. A dirty, nasty, filthy affair of his and Fanny Alger's was talked over in which I strictly declared that I had never deviated from the truth on the matters, and as I supposed was admitted by himself. At any rate, just before leaving, he wanted to drop every past thing, in which had been a difficulty or difference— he called witnesses to the fact, gave me his hand in their presence, and I might have supposed of an honest man, calculated to say nothing of former matters. Never believe that Oliver will disgrace the gray hairs of his father, or the high sense of honor in the bosom of his bothers, so much as to acknowledge to Joseph Smith Jr. that he has lied about him.

The letter continued with Oliver recalling his early financial assistance for the Smith family and the course he "pursued in defending him before all men with my ability and talent." Cowdery stated that when "Smith & Rigdon" arrived at Far West, "it will be my endeavor to seek a location for myself & friends some where else."[122]

---

121. Ibid., 127, December 6, 1837, and 132, December 7, 1837, respectively.

122. Oliver Cowdery to Warren A. Cowdery, January 21, 1838, emphasis retained; includes a copy of a letter of Oliver Cowdery to Joseph Smith Jr. also dated January 21, 1838. Oliver Cowdery Letterbook, 80–83, Huntington Library.

On January 26, Thomas Marsh, David Patten, and High Counselors received the report of the committee they had assigned to meet with Oliver Cowdery, John and David Whitmer, and William Phelps. The committee said the individuals under investigation collectively maintained that the word of wisdom was not a commandment, selling their land in Jackson County was not a revelatory violation, and that "they would not be controlled by an ecclesiastical power or revelation whatever in their temporal concerns." The council resolved to "no longer receive them as Presidents," and considered that "the case be laid before the Church at different meetings held for that purpose."[123]

Oliver Cowdery acknowledged to his brothers Warren and Lyman on February 4 that the "radical principles" of Joseph Smith and Sidney Rigdon have enabled the enthusiastic to "carry forward those damning doctrines to the subversion of the liberties of the whole church." Oliver said he, W. W. Phelps, and David and John Whitmer had been questioned by a committee of the high council about the word of wisdom, selling land in Jackson County, Missouri, and "in not teaching the church to fulfil the consecration law." He said if he had property and was sane, he "would not be dictated, influenced or controlled by any man or set of men by no tribunal of ecclesiastical pretences whatever. And when I or my family were sick or any other time, I would eat and drink what I thought would do me the most good: this was about the substance of what the others told them."[124]

From February 5–9, Thomas Marsh and David Patten chaired general assemblies at Far West and three satellite locations and overwhelmed the moderates with rhetoric based on Joseph Smith's directive and revelation of September 4, 1837. David and John Whitmer and William Phelps were almost unanimously rejected as presidents of the Far West stake. Only a few wanted to delay the sentencing until the arrival of Joseph Smith and Sidney Rigdon.[125]

At a meeting of the high council and the bishopric on February 10 it was determined that Oliver Cowdery, William Phelps, and John Whitmer "stand no longer as Chairman & Clerk, to sign and record licences [licenses]." Thomas Marsh and David Patten were also designated "Presidents, pro. tempor. of the Church of Latter Day Saints in Missouri" or until the arrival of Joseph Smith and Sidney Rigdon.[126]

---

123. Cannon and Cook, *Far West Record*, 135–36, January 26, 1838. The dissenters, Oliver Cowdery, Frederick G. Williams, David, John, and Jacob Whitmer, Lyman E. Johnson and W. W. Phelps, met on January 30, 1838 and determined to find a place "where they may live in peace." See enclosure dated January 30, 1838 in Oliver Cowdery to Warren A. and Lyman Cowdery, February 4, 1838, Oliver Cowdery Letterbook, 85, Huntington Library.

124. Oliver Cowdery to Warren A. and Lyman Cowdery, February 4, 1838, Oliver Cowdery Letterbook, 83–84, Huntington Library, emphasis retained.

125. Cannon and Cook, *Far West Record*, 137–40, February 5–9, 1838. The proceedings were printed in the *Elders' Journal* 1, no. 3 (July 1838): 44–45.

126. Cannon and Cook, *Far West Record*, 141, February 10, 1838.

Thomas Marsh wrote a letter to Joseph Smith on February 15, 1838, that informed the prophet things would be "a good degree straightened" by the time he arrived at Far West. They said the deposing of the Far West Presidency was accomplished to prevent "a rebellion" because the dissenters "undoubtedly" would have fractured the church. Responding to Smith's request, Marsh said that the previous November at Far West, he and George W. Harris had enclosed certified statements "relative to what Oliver Cowdery said about the girl"—Fanny Alger, mentioned in Oliver's January 21 letter to his brother Warren.

Thomas Marsh testified: "This may certify, that I heard O. Cowdery say to Joseph Smith Jr., while at George W. Harris' house, in Far West, that he (Joseph) never confessed to him, (Oliver) that he was guilty of the crime alledged [*sic*] to him. And O. Cowdery gave me to understand that Joseph Smith Jr. never acknowledged to him, that he ever confessed to any one, that he was guilty of the above crime." This was followed by George W. Harris's statement: "This may certify, that I heard Oliver Cowdery say, in my house, that Joseph Smith Jr. never confessed to him, that he was guilty of the crime alledged against him, and Joseph asked if he ever said to him (Oliver) that he confessed to any one that he, (Joseph) was guilty of the above crime, and Oliver, after some hesitation, answered no."

George M. Hinkle added his testimony that he sought out Oliver Cowdery the previous November to find out for himself if Joseph Smith admitted to him he was guilty of adultery:

> This may certify, that having heard the report about the crime referred to, I asked Oliver Cowdery, last fall, when Joseph Smith was in Far West, if the report was true, for said I, if it is, as he is to be presented before the church, I wish to know the truth of this matter before hand. And he gave me to understand, either in plain words or implications, that it was false. I bear this testimony for the good of the honest hearted in the east, and else where, and for the good of brother Joseph Smith Jr.[127]

Oliver Cowdery's February 24 letter to brothers Warren and Lyman said he continued to be "a victim to receive the displeasure of men who profess to hold the connecting link between earth and heaven!" He believed the dissenting actions he and his associates had taken "may be instrumental in preserving the church of Christ on earth."[128]

Joseph Smith's party was expected the first part of March, and the dissidents may have thought additional judgment would be put on hold until his arrival. They were mistaken, as four days before the Smith party reached Far West, John Whitmer

---

127. Thomas B. Marsh to "Beloved Brother Joseph," February 15, 1838, *Elder's Journal* 1, no. 3 (July 1838): 45.

128. Oliver Cowdery to Warren A. and Lyman Cowdery, February 25, 1838, Oliver Cowdery Letterbook, 89, Huntington Library.

and W. W. Phelps were charged with "persisting in unchristian-like conduct."[129] They, together with David Whitmer, sent a short letter dated March 10, 1838, to Thomas Marsh which said: "Sir: It is contrary to the principles of the revelations of Jesus Christ, and his gospel, and the laws of the land, to try a person for an offence, by an illegal tribunal, or by men prejudiced against him or by authority that has given an opinion, or decision before hand or in his absence."

The response was signed in a manner that was sure to infuriate, "Very Respectfully, we have the honor to be, David Whitmer, W. W. Phelps, John Whitmer: Presidents of the Church of Christ in Mo." The letter was attested by Oliver in the words "Clerk of the High Council of the Church of Christ in in [sic] Mo. I certify the foregoing to be a true copy from the original. Oliver Cowdery, Clerk of High Council."[130]

The charges against John Whitmer and William Phelps included misuse of $2,000 which had been subscribed "for the building a house to the Lord" in Far West. The verdict of the church trial was, "William W. Phelps and John Whitmer be no longer members of the church of Christ of Latter Day Saints, & be given over to the buffetings of Satan, until they learn to blaspheme no more against the authorities of God, nor fleece the flock of Christ."[131] Jurisdictional doubts about trying Lyman E. Johnson, Oliver Cowdery, and David Whitmer delayed their trials until after the arrival of Joseph Smith.

As the trials were being conducted, Oliver Cowdery wrote to brothers Warren and Lyman that a trial for two apostles presiding over the high council was their "new fangled council." He acknowledged, however, that the trial members, "will plead Smith's instructions and justify themselves in trying Presidents of the church before a rabble and call it legal!"[132]

Joseph Smith arrived at Far West on March 14 and shortly thereafter penned a statement for the church. It included, "But Wo to tyrants, Mobs, Aristocracy, Anarchy and Toryism: And all those who invent or seek out unrighteous and vexatious lawsuits under the pretext or color of law or office, either religious or political."[133] In a March 29 letter to the Presidency in Kirtland Smith acknowledged, "The difficulties of the Church had been a[d]justed before arrival here by a Judicious High Council With T[homas]. B. Marsh & D[avid] W. Patten who acted as Pres. Pro. Tem. of the Church of zion being appointed by the voice of the Council & Church." After stat-

---

129. See Cannon and Cook, *Far West Record*, 146, March 10, 1838.

130. Ibid., 146–47.

131. Ibid., 149.

132. Oliver Cowdery to Warren A. and Lyman Cowdery, apparently written March 10, 1838, Oliver Cowdery Letterbook, 91, Huntington Library, emphasis retained.

133. Jessee, *Journals*, Volume 1:238.

ing, "Wm W. Phelps & John Whitmer having been cut off from the Church," he said David Whitmer remains as yet.[134]

Historian Mark A. Scherer said that after Smith and Rigdon settled in Far West they "determined not to allow the internal dissent to emerge once again." He profoundly added, "Obedience became a test of fellowship."[135] Thomas Marsh became "President Pro tempore of the Church in Zion" at the April 6 Conference, and David Patten and Brigham Young became assistant presidents.[136]

The inevitable trial of Oliver Cowdery took place on April 12. Seymour Brunson filed nine charges against him and presumably Joseph Smith appointed Bishop Edward Partridge to preside over the high council. The charges were:

> 1st, For stirring up the enemy to persecute the brethren by urging on vexatious Lawsuits and thus distressing the innocent.

> 2nd, For seeking to destroying the character of President Joseph Smith jr by falsly [*sic*] insinuating that he was guilty of adultery &c.

> 3rd, For treating the Church with contempt by not attending meetings.

> 4th, For virtually denying the faith by declaring that he would not be governed by any ecclesiastical authority nor Revelation whatever in his temporal affairs

> 5th, For selling his lands in Jackson County contrary to the Revelations

> 6th, For writing and sending an insulting letter to President T. B. Marsh while on the High Council, attending to the duties of his office, as President of the Council and by insulting the whole Council with the contents of said letter

> 7th, For leaving the calling, in which God had appointed him, by Revelation, for the sake of filthy lucre, and turning to the practice of law.

> 8th, For disgracing the Church by ~~Lieing~~ being connected in the 'Bogus' business [counterfeiting] as common report says.

> 9th For dishonesty Retaining notes after they had been paid and finally for leaving or forsaking the cause of God, and betaking himself to the beggarly elements of the world and neglecting his high and Holy Calling contrary to his profession.[137]

The minutes said "It was not considered a difficult case" and only assigned one member of the high council to represent the plaintiff and one member for the de-

---

134. Ibid., 246.

135. Mark A. Scherer, *The Journey of a People: The Era of Restoration, 1820 to 1844* (Independence, MO: Community of Christ Seminary Press, 2013), 292.

136. Cannon and Cook, *Far West Record*, 158, April 6, 1838.

137. Ibid., 163, April 12, 1838.

fendant. Oliver Cowdery chose not to confront his accusers but instead sent a letter to Bishop Edward Partridge that said he wished "that those charges might have
been defer[r]ed untill after my interview with President Smith." Responding only to
charges number five, "Selling lands in Jackson County," and number four, "denying
the faith," Cowdery emphasized, "I will not be influenced, governed, or controlled, in
my temporal interests by any ecclesiastical authority or pretended revelation whatever, contrary to my own judgment." He added, he would not be controlled in his
"temporal interests" which would take away his "Constitutional privileges." He closed
with, "I do not charge you, or any other person who differs with me on those points,
of not being sincere; but such difference does exist, which I sincerely regret."[138]

The church court rejected the fourth and fifth charge with the sixth charge being withdrawn. The first charge, being guilty of using "vexatious Lawsuits" against
church members was sustained. The second charge of falsely insinuating that Joseph Smith "was guilty of adultery," brought forth sufficient testimony from George
Hinkle, George W. Harris, David W. Patten, Thomas B. Marsh and Joseph Smith
to have the charge sustained. The clerk, Ebenezer Robinson, for unknown reasons,
minimally recorded Smith's response to Oliver Cowdery's statements: "Joseph Smith
jr testifies that Oliver Cowdery had been his bosom friend, therefore he intrusted
him with many things. He then gave a history respecting the girl business."[139] Smith
also said Cowdery was dishonest in his business dealings. Since so little of Joseph
Smith's testimony about himself, Cowdery, and the girl is available, it is disappoint-
ing that there is no full record of what he said.

Frederick G. Williams, who was vacillating between factions, said Oliver
Cowdery admitted to him that "it was no harm to take that [bogus] money and pass
it." He added "it was reported Oliver was engaged in the Bogus money business."
Joseph Smith testified he was told by a non-Mormon at Kirtland that a warrant
would shortly be issued charging Oliver with "making a purchase of Bogus money &
dies to make the counterfeit money." Smith additionally testified he told Oliver "if he
was guilty he had better leave the country; but if he was innocent to stand a trial &
he should come out clear." He added, "but that night or the next he left the country."
Sidney Rigdon confirmed the allegations.

Bishop Partridge and his counselors decided, that the 1st, 2nd, 3rd, 7th and 9th
charges were sustained, while the 8th charge "was sustained satisfactoryly [sic] by
circumstantial evidence." Oliver "was, therefore, considered no longer a member of
the Church of Jesus Christ of Latter Day Saints." The high council sanctified the
decision.[140]

---

138. Ibid., 164–66.

139. Ibid., 168.

140. Trial minutes are in Ibid., 162–69, April 12, 1838.

Thomas Marsh, David Patten, and Brigham Young presided over the high council in the trials of Lyman Johnson and David Whitmer. In both cases charges were filed by Alanson Ripley, and both sent letters instead of attending. Johnson said he was withdrawing himself from the "society and fellowship" of the Mormons, and David Whitmer told the court, "I hereby withdraw from your fellowship and communion—choosing to seek a place among the meek and humble, where the revelations of Heaven will be observed and the rights of men regarded."[141] Both men were no longer considered church members.

The former Mormons did not move from Far West, and the passions which led to conflict continued to be exasperated. John Corrill wrote about the tense interaction:

> Notwithstanding the dissenters had left the church, yet the old strife kept up, and Smith and Rigdon, with others, complained much of the ill treatment which they had received from the dissenters and others, they said they had been persecuted from time to time with vexatious law suits; that mobs had arisen up against them, time after time; that they had been harassed to death, as it were, for seven or eight years, and they were determined to bear it no longer, for they had rather die than suffer such things[142]

Sidney Rigdon preached what was called the "salt sermon" on June 17. John Corrill wrote that President Rigdon "delivered from the pulpit what I call the salt sermon; 'If the salt have lost its savour, it is thenceforth good for nothing, but to be cast out and trodden under the feet of men,' was his text, and although he did not call names in his sermon, yet it was plainly understood that he meant the dissenters, or those who denied the faith, ought to be cast out, and literally trodden under foot. He, indirectly, accused some of them with crime."[143]

In the same month a strong letter was issued "To Oliver Cowdery, David Whitmer, John Whitmer, William W. Phelps and Lyman E. Johnson." Many of those who signed the warning were affiliated with an extra-legal group known as the Danites whose activities included cleansing the church. It was believed to have been written by Sidney Rigdon. It was a harsh assessment of their former friends:

> Out of the county you shall go, and no power shall save you. And you shall have three days after you receive this communication *to you,* including twenty-four hours in each day, for you to depart with your families peaceably; which you may do undisturbed by

---

141. Ibid., 173, 177, April 13, 1838.

142. John Corrill, *A Brief History of the Church of Christ of Latter Day Saints* (St. Louis: Printed for the Author, 1839), 29.

143. Ibid., 30. The text is similar to Matthew 5:13. See also LDS D&C 101:40; RLDS D&C 98:5; and LDS D&C 103:10; RLDS D&C 100:2.

any person; but in that time, if you do not depart, we will use the means in our power to cause you to depart; for go you shall.[144]

The document charged crimes to the dissenters. Oliver Cowdery was said to have been stealing, disturbing worshipers in the house of the Lord in Kirtland, taking away the rights of the members while justice of the peace, and "united with a gang of counterfeiters, thieves, liars and blacklegs." The warning ended with the words, "you have had the audacity to threaten us that, if we offered to disturb you, you would get up a mob from Clay and Ray counties. For the insult, if nothing else, and your threatening to shoot us if we offered to molest you, we will put you from the county of Caldwell so help us God."[145]

It was during this period that Sidney Rigdon is credited with writing a lengthy article in the August 1838 issue of the *Elders' Journal* that included public attacks on dissenters of the church. Historian Peter Crawley has written of those July and August issues of the church paper, "Rigdon undoubtedly did most of the editorial work on these two issues, and they reflect his militant stand against those who opposed the leaders of the Church."[146] The comments by Rigdon were of the lowest level against his former associates Warren Parrish, Leonard Rich, John F. Boynton, Luke Johnson, and Stephen Burnett. Warren Cowdery was considered worthy of notice. He was labeled a "pitiful beggar," incompetent and ignorant. On Warren the article said, "We have often heard it remarked by slave holders, that you should not make a negro equal with you, or he will try to walk over you. We have found the saying verified in this pious Doctor, for truly this niggardly spirit manifested itself in all its meanness; even in his writings, (and they were mean at best) … But such was the conduct of this master of meanness."[147]

In December Joseph Smith wrote a letter while in Liberty Jail, "To the Church of Latter day Saints in Caldwell County, and all the Saints who are scattered abroad." He said "Such characters as M'Lellin, John Whitmer, D, Whitmer, O, Cowdery, & Martin Harris who are too mean to mention and we had like to have forgotten." These individuals were to receive the final condemnation, "Therefore we say unto you, Dear Brethren in the name of the Lord Jesus Christ, we deliver these Char-

---

144. Testimony given in November 1838 before Justice Austin A. King and other documents relating to the Missouri-Mormon conflict were collected and published in 1841. Missouri General Assembly, *Document Containing the Correspondence, Orders, &c. in Relation to the Disturbances with the Mormons; and the Evidence Given before the Hon. Austin A. King, Judge of the Fifth Judicial Circuit of the State of Missouri, at the Court-House in Richmond, in a Criminal Court of Inquiry, begun November 12, 1838, on the trial of Joseph Smith, Jr., and others, for High Treason and Other Crimes Against the State* (Fayette, MO: Printed at the office of the Boon's Lick Democrat, 1841), 103, emphasis retained. See also Shepard and Marquardt, *Lost Apostles*, 178–80.

145. Ibid., 103–6.

146. Crawley, *A Descriptive Bibliography of the Mormon Church Volume One 1830–1847*, 74.

147. "Argument to argument where I find it, Ridicule to ridicule; and scorn to scorn," *Elders' Journal* 1, no. 4 (August 1838): 59.

acters unto the buffetings of Satan, untill the day of redemption, that they may be dealt with according to their works, and from henceforth their works shall be made manifest."[148]

Historian Jeffrey N. Walker traced Oliver Cowdery's early post-Mormon experiences and said by August 1838 he had determined to return to Kirtland and join his brother Lyman in practicing law. Walker indicated that Oliver was back in Kirtland "by late 1838." He studied law under Benjamin Bissell at Painesville who had "previously represented the Church's interests in various lawsuits," was admitted to the Ohio bar, and commenced practice with his brother Lyman as early as January 1840."[149] Oliver then moved from Kirtland to Tiffin, Ohio, in early 1842 where he continued practicing law, was active in Democratic Party functions, and at some point joined the Methodist Church.[150]

A revelation by Joseph Smith in January 1841, announced at Nauvoo, Illinois, was to transfer whatever blessings and priesthood that Oliver Cowdery once held to Smith's brother Hyrum who held the position of church patriarch. The document said that Hyrum may be a prophet, seer, and revelator to the church as well as Joseph, "that he may act in concert also, with my servant Joseph, and that he shall receive counsel from my servant Joseph, who shall shew unto him the keys, whereby he may ask and receive, and be crowned with the same blessings. I crown upon his head, the bishoprick, and blessing, and glory, and honor, and priesthood, and gifts of priesthood, that once were put upon him, that was my servant Oliver Cowdery."[151]

Phineas H. Young, who was married to Oliver's half-sister Lucy, had visited him three times that year and reported on December 14, 1842 to Willard Richards:

> Brother Oliver is well and doing well as far as this time is Concerned, and his heart is still with his old friends, and I believe he would be with them in person and that soon if Brother Joseph only knew the true state of affairs;- at the time brother Oliver was driven from far west, we are all aware of the fact that many were laying to break him down that they might rise there by; say George M. Hin[k]le George W. Robinson, Thomas Marsh and others who Brother Joseph thought to be his friends, and they told many things

148. Joseph Smith "To the Church of Latter day Saints," December 16, 1838, recorded in the Scriptory Book of Joseph Smith Jr., 107, Church History Library.

149. Jeffery N. Walker, "Oliver Cowdery's legal Practice in Tiffin, Ohio," in Baugh, *Days Never to be Forgotten,* 303–5. Stanley R. Gunn in *Oliver Cowdery Second Elder and Scribe* (Salt Lake City: Bookcraft, 1962) 169, quoted a newspaper clipping dated March 3, 1840 in the *Painesville Telegraph* 6, no.9 (March 3, 1840); which said: "L. & O. Cowdery, Attorneys and Counsellors at Law and Solicitors in Chancery, Kirtland, Geauga County, Ohio. Office a few rods South of the Stone Temple." Gunn indicates the ad was discontinued by September 17, 1840.

150. The issue of Oliver Cowdery joining the Methodist Church is discussed by Larry E. Morris, "'The Private Character of the Man Who Bore That Testimony': Oliver Cowdery and his Critics," *Oliver Cowdery: Scribe, Elder, Witness,* 282–88.

151. "Extracts," *Times and Seasons* 2, no. 15 (June 1, 1841): 428, same wording in Book of the Law of the Lord, 10–11, MS 22507, Church History Library. Compare wording with 1844 D&C 104:29; LDS D&C 124:95.

prejudicial to brother Oliver which he had no Chance whatever to Contradict, such for instance as that if he (Oliver) left the Church it would all go down, and all this sort of thing; which he never said, neither Came it into his heart[152]

Joseph Smith's last known mention of Oliver Cowdery occurred in an afternoon meeting on April 19, 1843, with Brigham Young and seven members of the Quorum of Apostles. The clerk of the meeting, Willard Richards, recorded the prophet giving dictation about the Nauvoo House, the Apostolic missions, and a statement about Oliver: "Write to Oliver Cowdery. & ask him if he has not eat[en] corn husks long enough: if he is not [illegible] ready to return & go up to Jerusalem, Orson Hyde hath need of him." Richards noted, "A letter was written & signed by the me[m]bers of the Quorum present."[153] Calling Cowdery "one of the witnesses to the Book of Mormon," "we reflect upon the time when we had met together, when we were brethren, when we were one, & took sweet counsel together." They asked him if he might abandon "his lonely solitary situation." After emphasizing they were brethren, not enemies, they told Oliver, "Your labor might be needed in Jerusalem, & you ought to be the servant of the living God."[154] For unknown reasons the letter was not mailed until December.

Oliver Cowdery's friendly Christmas day response was "strictly private— under no consideration is it to be exhibited to the public eye." He acknowledged he had been "a stranger in a strange land" but did not reply to the belated request to go to Jerusalem. He did refer to the time he left Far West and was concerned that his name be cleared and wrote:

There is another circumstance to which I must now adrest [address], in which you as members and principals in a great and increasing society, are interested: and in which also, whether in or out of that society, I feel, and must continue to feel sensibly and keenly. It is a certain publication, appended to which are many names who are, are were at the time, members of the Church of Latter Day Saints, charging myself with being connected with outlaws. I cannot speak definitely of this instrument, as I know nothing of it except what has been related by those who say they have seen it. Now, what I have to say concerning all the difficulty between myself and your Church, together with those charges last refer[r]ed to, is simply this: I believed at the time, and still believe, that ambitious and wicked men, envying the harmony existing between myself and the first elders of the Church, and hoping to get into some other men's birth right, by falsehoods the most foul and wicked, caused all this difficulty from beginning to

152. Phineas H. Young to "Dear Brethren's," December 14, 1842, Brigham Young office files, CR 1234 1, Box 44, Folder 5, Church History Library.

153. Andrew H. Hedges, Alex D. Smith and Richard Lloyd Anderson, eds., Journals Volume 2: December 1841–April 1843 (Salt Lake City: Church Historian's Press, 2011), 370.

154. Epistle of the Twelve to Oliver Cowdery, April 19, 1843, draft in Luna Y. Thatcher Collection, MS 6140, Reel 1, Folder 4, Church History Library.

<u>end</u>. They succeeded in getting myself out of the Church; but since they themselves have gone to perdition, ought not old friends— long tried in the furnase [furnace] of affliction, to be friends still, even laying out of view any and all religious consideration?[155]

Six months later Joseph and Hyrum Smith were murdered in Carthage, Illinois.

Summary

Oliver Cowdery's fall from grace apparently resulted from lack of control as opposed to malice. These lapses in concentration resulted in his not being retained as Second Elder and being placed in the undesirable position of attempting to reacquire past acceptability. His rehabilitation was hampered by Sidney Rigdon's reliability. To his credit, Cowdery made dramatic sacrifices to serve the church as scribe, newspaper editor, and High Counselor.

On December 5, 1834, Cowdery recorded minutes of a meeting in which he said he was ordained by Smith to be his "Assistant President." He said the ordination made him superior to Sidney Rigdon and Frederick G. Williams, authorizing him to preside over the church in Smith's absence, and be a spokesman for Smith like Aaron was to Moses. This subterfuge did not change his position in the hierarchy. Instead of becoming assistant president, he was a junior member of the Presidency. The following day Hyrum Smith and Joseph Smith Sr. were ordained to the Presidency and, like Cowdery, ranked below Rigdon and Williams. There was no real governing duties for these elders in actuality.

Although Oliver's passage through Mormonism is generally well documented, there are crucial gaps which have given rise to intense speculation. The authors could not determine when the relationship between Smith and Cowdery began to unravel but document why Smith decreed in November 1837 that Cowdery should be punished unless he repented. Oliver may have hoped he could reach an accommodation with Smith when he arrived at Far West. It is unknown why Smith did not meet with Oliver and seek reconciliation with his former associate.

Although there is evidence that Cowdery broke with Smith because of his alleged sexual relationship with Fanny Alger, the authors chose not to cite and interpret statements made about the subject many years later. Cowdery is often thought of as being weak because of his inconsistent journey through Mormonism. It is clear, however, that the Smith-Cowdery relationship degenerated to the point that each disrespected the other.

---

155. Oliver Cowdery to "Dear Brethren," December 25, 1843, Brigham Young Office Files, CR 1234 1, Box 39, Folder 11, Church History Library, emphasis retained.

WILLIAM SHEPARD is a longtime member of the John Whitmer Historical Association and is past president for 2008–2009. With H. Michael Marquardt, he has written *Lost Apostles: Forgotten Members of Mormonism's Original Quorum of Twelve*, which was published by Signature Books in 2014.

H. MICHAEL MARQUARDT (research@xmission.com) is an independent historian and research consultant. He is on the editorial board of the *John Whitmer Historical Association Journal*. He is the compiler of *Early Patriarchal Blessings of The Church of Jesus Christ of Latter-day Saints* (Smith Pettit Foundation, 2007); *Later Patriarchal Blessings of The Church of Jesus Christ of Latter-day Saints* (Smith Pettit Foundation, 2012); author of *Joseph Smith's 1828–1843 Revelations* (Xulon Press, 2013) and co-author with William Shepard of *Lost Apostles: Forgotten Members of Mormonism's Original Quorum of Twelve* (Signature Books, 2014).

———————— • ————————

The Appeal of Mormonism to Norwegian-American Immigrants: A Case Study

Thomas J. Morain

A LL FOUR OF my grandmother's grandparents migrated from Norway as children around 1840. The Danielsons and Thomasons came first in 1837. They headed directly to the Fox River settlement of Norwegians in north central Illinois. The Hayers and Elefsons followed in 1842. They went first to Wisconsin, but after a few hard years there, they too joined the Fox River settlement. Their travel arrangements were in keeping with the Norwegian pattern. (1) Norwegians were not loners or rugged individualists; they came in family groups. In all four cases, three generations of the family migrated together. (2) Beyond their own immediate family, they traveled and settled with neighbors from the same Norwegian district, often "those who had come out of the very valley…from which they themselves hailed in the old country."[1]

As the first wave of Norwegian-American immigrants, their travels and trials have been recorded extensively. Three of those families spawned extensive genealogies that continued well into the latter twentieth century.[2] Beyond the data on the

1. Theodore C. Blegen, *Norwegian Migration to America, 1825–1860* (Northfield, MN: Haskell House 1931), 75. See also Theodore C. Blegen, *Norwegian Migration to America: The Transition* (New York: Haskell House, 1969).

2. Following Norwegian genealogies is not for the faint of heart. Last names in Norway took the name of the farm on which the family was living and changed when the family moved. Fortunately, that practice stopped in America and last names became permanent (at least for men), usually taking what had been the middle name as someone's son or daughter. Early in an account of the Elefson family, the author provides this explanation of the interconnectedness of the immigrating families. The Jorisdals would become Elefsons. Three Elefson children would marry three Hayers to further complicate matters. "In 1839, several families named Luras emigrated to Wisconsin. Among them were several descendants of Halvor Eilefsen Jorisdal's (Halvor Elefson's) aunt, Ingeborg Oldsdatter Jorisdal. In 1841, Ole Kittilson Luras and wife, Anne Christiansdatter Hayer, with children immigrated. Ole was the first cousin to Halvor Eillefsen. Anne was a first cousin to Halvor's wife, Gro Oldsdatter Bakka. Anne was also a niece to Lars Hayer. Also in 1841, Oysteinson Sjotveit came to Wisconsin. He was a nephew to Lars Hayer's wife, Anne Oldsdatter Haugen. And in 1842, the rather large Elefson and Heyer families ['our' Hayers] came to the United States." Got that? Vern Elefson, *Everything You Ever (Never) Wanted to Know About the Elefson Family History* (Kearney, NE: Morris Publishing, 1998) 4–5.

family tree charts of who begat whom, however, we want to place these pioneers within a larger historical context to understand *why* they made some of their major decisions.

There are, of course, more questions one would like to ask of one's ancestors than can be explored in one paper. The question that most unites *JWHA Journal* readers is why all four of those family lines of Norwegian immigrants were attracted shortly after their arrival to the Mormonism of the 1840s, and beyond that, to the Reorganization or the westward migration with Brigham Young. To keep the project manageable, I will limit the scope to just one of the family lines—the Hayers. The family included Lars and Ann Hayer and their eight children ranging in age from 11 to 30. Their oldest daughter Caroline was accompanied by her husband and four small children. Lars and Ann, daughter Caroline and her six siblings and their spouses all converted to Mormonism. Only one son, Christian, left for Salt Lake City. What is their story?

In that absence of smoking-gun evidence that explains their mindset in detail, I am experimenting with an approach shamelessly adapted from John Wesley's formula for evaluating the merits of theological propositions. He urged his Methodist followers to approach an issue from four different angles: scripture, reason, tradition, and experience. Does it make sense from each perspective? In place of Wesley's four, however, I will substitute a historian's four. I will examine the data in terms of economics, theology, ethnicity, and family. What influence did each of these four factors play? How and how much might each factor have shaped the conversation around the Hayer family supper table?

The Norwegian Background

Like the three other families, the Hayers converted to Mormonism in the American Midwest—not in Norway—but I would argue that their Norwegian background made them receptive to this new religion. In the Norway of the first half of the nineteenth century, small farmers like the Hayers were struggling. Taxes were high. Norwegian laws on land inheritance were leading to the divisions and redivisions of family farms into ever smaller parcels. The number of farms grew from around 80,000 in 1802 to nearly 113,000 in 1845. While the oldest son inherited the farm's title, he was expected to buy out or otherwise provide for his siblings. Along with exorbitant interest rates and low farm prices, many farms struggled under unsustainable debts. Again, statistics tell the story. By the mid-1840s, two-thirds of Norwegian farms had mortgages. Facing bleak futures, farm owners accounted for the bulk of the immigrants as they were the ones who could raise the cost of the move via the sale of their lands.[3]

3. Blegen, *Migration*, 165–74.

In Telemark in south central Norway, the Hayers' home turf, farmers had the additional challenge of poor grain harvests from 1836–39, the years immediately preceding their migration to America.[4] There were even reports of famine in 1838. One account describes the region "as having utilized and exhausted all the resources that a primitive and tradition-bound agricultural system could muster." A rapidly growing population further exacerbated the problem. In the Tinn district in Telemark, the population increased 37 percent between 1801 and 1835, from eighteen hundred to twenty-five hundred.[5] The conservative government was aligned with the wealthy few and did little to alleviate the economic pinch on the poor.

However, liberal winds were stirring discontent. The roots of the movement were at first more religious than political or economic. In 1796, at the age of twenty-five, a young farmer by the name of Hans Hauge described a religious vision he experienced while he was "plowing a field and singing a hymn." Hauge told his own story this way:

> I stood transformed…my soul experienced something supernatural, divine, and blessed …a joy which no tongue can describe… No one can convince me otherwise; for I know the spiritual fruits of this experience, especially the deep burning love for God and my neighbor, that I experienced a change of mind, a sorrow for all since, a desire that all men should partake with me in the same grace; a keen desire to read the Word of God as contained in Holy Writ, especially the teachings of Jesus, coupled with an increased power to understand, and to direct all religious instruction toward the one basic truth, the Christ has come as our savior; that we can be born again through his Spirit. A voice echoed in my soul: Thou shall make known My Name for mankind, warn them to repent and seek me while I can be found…repent from darkness and enter into Light.[6]

The state religion in Norway was Lutheranism, with its emphasis at this time on correct beliefs. Although Norwegian law forbade any but ordained Lutheran clergy to preach, Hauge began a dynamic one-man revival traveling the length of Norway to spread a pietistic message—a personal relationship with God, awareness of sin, repentance, righteous living—that stood in stark contrast to the rationalist formulas of the state church. Hauge also promoted an economic as well as spiritual gospel encouraging the formation of co-op arrangements to help the poor.

The one-two punch of economic stress and religious awakening proved powerful to the rural poor like the Hayers who chafed under the economic policies of the conservative political and church elites. Historians argue over which factor—eco-

---

4. Blegen, *Migration*, 168.

5. Odd S. Lovoll, *The Promise of America: A History of the Norwegian-American People* (Minneapolis: University of Minnesota Press, 1984), 16. I acknowledge an unpublished paper on family history written by Dr. Kay Mussell as my introduction to this fact.

6. Gerald M. Haslam, *Clash of Cultures: The Norwegian Experience with Mormonism, 1842–1920*, American University Studies, series IX (History), vol. 7 (New York: Peter Lang, 1984), 1–2.

nomics or religion—supplied the prime motivation for immigration.[7] A more fruit-ful approach for our purposes might be to consider how the combination of the two factors severely weakened the attachment of struggling farmers to both church and government institutions, "a forceful emancipation of the common people…from the control and dominance of the elite…an important manifestation, and a reinforce-ment, of the…now reawakened quest for freedom and independence."[8] If they were typical of early Norwegian immigrants, Lars and Ann Hayer and their children hoped to leave behind the economic, spiritual, and political restrictions of Norway. If they were typical, their dreams were *not* to recreate in America conditions they had experienced at home. They were open to something new. Letters from fellow countrymen who had already made the voyage, passed from hand to hand, were pub-lished in newspapers, and discussed at length among families and neighbors.[9] Cheap lands, democracy, social equality, and low taxes looked good. So did the prospect of finding a more congenial spiritual home. L. DeAne Lagerquist summarizes the ethos succinctly:

> The common people were most receptive to the [Haugean] revival's pietistic impulse. Without attention to this movement, the religious character of the Norwegians who immigrated to the U.S. …and their descendants is incomprehensible."[10]

Upon arriving in America, the Hayers and others in their party sailed up the Hudson River to Albany, boarded Erie Canal boats to the Great Lakes, and arrived in September at the small town of Milwaukee, Wisconsin. From there they headed southwest to join a small Norwegian settlement near Muskego in Rock County that included both relatives and neighbors from Telemark.

The newcomers had little time to prepare for the winter, and their first couple years were brutal. The Muskego land was swampy, and the immigrants struggled. Lars's wife Ann Hayer died in 1843 and so did their oldest daughter's husband, leav-ing widowed Caroline with four young children. In that same year, Caroline also lost a baby boy, possibly in childbirth. The following year her three-year-old son died.

---

7. A good example of the two approaches are the in the writings of Rasmes B. Anderson and George T. Flom. Anderson gives primacy to religious considerations in *First Chapter of Norwegian Immigration, 1821–1840* while Flom challenges the theory in *A History of Norwegian Immigration to the Unites States* (Iowa City, IA: printed by the author, 1992), 66–67.

8. Peter A. Munch, "Social Class and *Acculturation*," in *The Strange American Way: Letters of Caja Munch from Wiota, Wisconsin, 1855–1859*, quoted in L. DeAne Lagerquist, *In America the Men Mil the Cows: Factors of Gender Ethnicity and Religion in the Americanization of Norwegian-American Women* (Brooklyn, NY: Carlson Publishing, Inc. 1991), 27.

9. Theodore Blegen, *Migration*, 175–76.

10. L. DeAne Lagerquist, In America the Men Milk Cows, 25. See also Theodore C. Blegen, "The Religious Im-pulse" in Norwegian Migration to America: The American Transition (Northfield, MN: Haskell House, 1940).

Their three-year-old had been baptized in Norway, but the younger one certainly had not. Did the death of an unbaptized infant weigh on their minds?

After two years and four deaths in Wisconsin, the Hayer family decided to relocate and start over in what they hoped would be a better location. Over the next three years, several Muskego families, Hayers among them, began migrating south to the Fox River settlement, the largest and most established Norwegian community in the country at that time. Wisconsin immigrants had kept in contact with their Illinois countrymen. Younger males sometimes went down to Illinois during the haying season. While they may have decided as a family to relocate, this time the Hayers did not travel as a group or all move at the same time. Over the course of the next few years, however, the entire Lars Hayer family in Muskego and some extended relatives relocated to La Salle County. Lars moved in 1845 with his youngest daughter Ann and lived with his son Hans until Lars's death in 1863. Caroline also moved with her four children, remarried in 1847 and bore four more children, three of whom survived to adulthood.[11]

Their decision to relocate involved economic, ethnic, and family factors. By 1843, Fox River had a population of six hundred, almost all Norwegian immigrants. Many Fox River families had passed the primitive pioneer stage, were living in good houses, and were raising crops and livestock. There were exciting new developments. The Illinois and Michigan Canal that connected Chicago with the Mississippi River was nearing completion and would soon provide cheap, easy access to Chicago markets. Its western terminus was Ottawa, the county seat of La Salle County, some ten miles from the heart of the Fox River settlement. There were also plans to add a railroad line along much the same route. Both the canal and the proposed railroad ran through or very close to Norwegian land holdings. Choice prairie lands were still available, and in view of the newly opened transportation options, their farms would soon become prime real estate.[12]

In addition to those considerations, there was now an important new factor in their decision. During their time in Wisconsin, most if not all of the family had converted to Mormonism, and Fox River had a thriving branch of the church. How that came to be takes us back again to Fox River.

La Salle County lies approximately 180 miles northeast of Nauvoo and 80 miles west of Chicago. In 1842, a Mormon elder from Nauvoo, George Dykes, made a missionary trip to Fox River and was directed to see one Goodman Hougus, perhaps a Baptist minister at the time, whom Dykes described as "a man of strong mind

---

11. Annie Hyer Kemp, *What We Know About the Hayer (Hyer) Family* (Logan, UT: printed by the author, 1954), 10.

12. Ikdal, 129. See also Vickie Cleverley Speek, "Forgotten Waterway: The Illinois and Michigan Canal and Its Connection to Early Mormon History," *John Whitmer Historical Association Journal* 31, no. 2 (Fall/Winter 2011): 103–16. The reference to prime real estate comes from Oliver Hayer, The Hayer Family (self-pub, 1922), 8.

and well skilled in scriptures."[13] He was known to have been strongly influenced by Hauge's call to lay preaching and personal examination. Hougas and his wife, along with several others, were converted, and the Mormon congregation met in their home for the next seven years. Hougas was more than just a religious leader. With no formal medical training, he became the frontier doctor for the community, dispensing medicines and prescribing cures. Another convert played a special role in this narrative. Dykes converted Ole Hayer, a nephew to the Lars Hayers. Like Hougas, Ole was known as a minister, a "pious Haugean preacher."[14]

Burning with converts' zeal, Goodman Hougas and Ole Hayer themselves set off the on a mission to share their new faith with their fellow countrymen in the small Norwegian enclave of Sugar Creek in Lee County, Iowa. According to family historian Vern Elefson, one son of Lars and Ann Hayer, also named Ole Hayer like his missionary cousin, was living there at the time of the Hougas/Hayer visit. Elefson writes that son Ole "moved to Sugar Creek shortly after arriving in America. He lived there for some ten years and several of his children were born there. But [he] eventually moved back to La Salle County, Illinois."[15] The missionary team achieved some limited success. Ole Hayer was probably converted on that Iowa mission as were members of the Eric Hogan family who would become related to the Lars Hayers by way of the plural marriage of two of their daughters to Ole's brother Christian.[16]

From Sugar Creek, the Mormon missionaries headed north to Muskego. According to the narrative as it was passed down through the family, Muskego residents had been warned not to talk to the Mormon missionaries. When Ann Hayer saw the two elders walking toward the house, the story goes, she fled up to the loft and listened through cracks in the floor boards. The account has it that when the conversation "seemed so reasonable," she declared to herself, "What a fool I am, I shall go down and visit them, too."[17] Lars and Ann's son Christian dates his baptism to June 23, 1843, probably the occasion of the Hougas/Ole Hayer visit. Data drawn from scattered sources strongly suggests that Lars, Ann and all their children eventually converted to the Mormon fold as did their spouses and several extended family members.[18]

---

13. Gerald M. Haslam, *Clash of Cultures*, 59.

14. Vern Elefson, *Family History, from Vern Elefson to his brothers and sisters* (unpublished paper, November 7, 1974), 16.

15. William Mulder, "Norwegian Forerunners Among the Early Mormons," http://newsarch.rootsweb.com/the/read/NORWAY/1999-10/0940528858

16. Vern Elefson, Family History, 17.

17. Annie Hyer Kemp, *What We Know about the Hayer (Hyer) Family*, 6.

18. Older daughter Caroline and the five older sons received Nauvoo Temple endowments in 1846. "Nauvoo Temple Endowment Name Index," https://user.xmission.com/~research/family/familyh.htm. Kemp's Hayer genealogy identifies youngest son Austin and youngest daughter as church members. Kemp, *What We Know*, 19–20.

Elefson provides additional support for the assertion that conversion was a family affair. He notes that while Ole Hayer was related to the Lars Hayers, Hougas was related to a Gitle Danielson also living in Muskego who also converted on that trip. He writes: "I am guessing that Goodman's success with Gitle, under the circumstancers, rested in part on the influence he would have as a close relative. And that would also explain why [Hougas] made the trip in the first place."[19]

When the Hayer family decided to leave Wisconsin, it is significant that they did not choose to relocate to Nauvoo. Nauvoo had the top Mormon church leaders, but the city was in turmoil following the death of Joseph Smith. Fox River had a thriving Mormon congregation and_Norwegians. George Dykes reported that the La Salle congregation numbered over a hundred members by 1844 and witnessed "prophecy, healing, speaking in tongues and the interpretation in remarkable degree."[20]

The Hayers took their religion seriously in Fox River. On February 6, 1846, Lars, daughter Caroline, and sons Andrew, Christian, Ole, Hans, Oliver and Oliver's wife Julia all traveled to Nauvoo where they received their endowment in the temple. Christian was ordained a Seventy.[21]

Among the factions that emerged following Joseph's assassination, the Fox River congregation became a hotbed of contention. In the fall of 1844, Mormon apostles Brigham Young, Heber C. Kimball, and Parley P. Pratt all visited the community. Young purchased a hundred acres of land from Goodman Hougas and his son-in-law Jacob Slogvik (Anderson) on which to build a temple for the gathering of Scandinavian Saints who, the residents were promised, would receive their endowments *in their own language.* The plan was to send Hougas to Norway as a missionary. They also proposed and laid out a plat for the city of Norway with the two main streets named Young and Hougas.

James J. Strang threw a wrench into Young's plans when he persuaded both Ole Hayer and Hougas of his own claim to church leadership. It appears that Strang was already intent on setting up an independent church structure. Strang was listed as "president" when he presided at a church conference in the newly-platted Norway on April 17–18, 1846. Goodman Hougas was ordained an apostle and Ole Hayer, an elder before the conference, was ordained and appointed High Priest over northeast-

19. Vern Elefson, *Family History*, 7. Elefson dates the trip to Muskego to 1844, but that is probably incorrect since it would have been a year after Ann Hayer's death in 1843 and son Christian Hayer's recall of his conversion. Elefson also claims that Lars and Ann's son Ole never converted to Mormonism. However, Nauvoo Temple records show Ole receiving a temple endowment along with his family in 1846.

20. Haslam, Clash of Cultures, 4–5. Haslam also cites another source that lists the membership at 150 in 1845.

21. "Nauvoo Temple Endowment Name Index."

ern Illinois. Christian, Austin, and Hans Hayer were all ordained elders during the two-day conference.[22]

Later in 1846, Strang issued a call for Mormons to relocate to his home in Voree, Wisconsin, but neither Hougas nor Ole Hayer took him up. Hougas announced his decision to join the Utah migration but died on July 28, 1849, one of the first victims of the cholera epidemic. None of the Hayers took up Strang's offer to resettle on Beaver Island. Ole Hayer, Hougas' missionary partner, abandoned both the Mormons and Fox River and joined the Baptists. Eventually, perhaps because of Strang's embrace of polygamy, Strang lost his support in Fox River. The opening of the I & M canal in 1848 through La Salle County and the plans for a railroad connect to Chicago were economic considerations also weighing against a relocation to distant and unknown Utah.[23]

Brigham Young renewed his appeal in 1848 by sending George B. Bratton with instructions to organize a company to head west. A party of twenty-two did leave from Fox River for Utah that year, including one—but only one—son of the Lars Hayer family. It was the Norwegian tradition that young men did not marry until they owned or had access to a farm on which they could support a family. Christian was thirty years old, single, and owned no farm land. He had traveled considerably since his arrival in America, to Wisconsin, to visit a brother in Iowa, and to Nauvoo to receive his endowment and priesthood ordination. All his brothers, older and younger, were either married or engaged as was his older sister Caroline. Was Christian's decision based on theology or, with fewer attachments than his siblings, the opportunity to try something new?

Christian joined a company of seven wagons headed by Ezra Taft Benson departing from Sugar Creek in the spring of 1849. He spent little time upon his arrival in Utah in finding a wife. He arrived on October 25 and on November 23 married Caroline Hogan from the Norwegian settlement in Iowa across the Mississippi from Nauvoo. Shortly after that, he also married her sister Lovina. A few years later, he married a third time. Just for the record, the third wife was Rosina Shepherd, but since she was apparently not Norwegian, who cares?[24]

Back in Fox River, the Illinois Hayers would become a pillar of the early RLDS Mission congregation, named for Mission Township in which it was located. It became the second largest RLDS congregation in northern Illinois, second only to nearby Plano after Plano became church headquarters. The Hayers are cited as a significant influence in the life of the family of Bertha Madison, another daughter of Norwegian immigrants and the future wife of Joseph Smith III. Bertha's parents had

22. Data on the 1846 conference comes from a photocopy of a manuscript in the possession of Betty Johnson in Lamoni, Iowa, as of January 18, 2018.

23. See Speek, "Forgotten Waterway," 103–116.

24. Kemp, *What We Know About the Hayer (Hyer) Family*, 15–16.

moved frequently around the Midwest but finally relocated back in La Salle County by the early 1860s. In an account by Bertha's older sister Ann, their father

> got acquainted with the Hayers and other church people [sometimes called "Mormons"]. He became very intimate with them and began going to church with them.... Father was in with anyone ... that was a Latter Day Saint.... So when he heard from the Hayers about the Reorganization, he was baptized in 1864.[25]

When Joseph III needed a housekeeper to care for his ailing wife and young children, it was not unusual that he sought an immigrant girl who knew the household routines and didn't cost much, all the better if from an RLDS family near at hand to Plano. The Hayers continued to play an active role in congregational life and intermarried with other Norwegian families within the RLDS Church, forming an intricate network united by religion, ethnicity, and family.[26]

Long, long ago, at the beginning of this exploration, we raised the tough question: why? Why did the Lars Hayer family find the Mormonism of the 1840s appealing? Family ties were important. Their first encounter was with a trusted family member, nephew Ole Hayer. Once the conversions began, the entire family joined in, and except for Christian Hayer, the family was united in support of the Reorganization. Their Norwegian ethnicity played a role. Again, if they were typical, they were disaffected from the Lutheran Church and government before they arrived in America. They eagerly embraced American democracy in opposition to the restrictive policies they had left. They were promised a temple of their own where endowments would be given in Norwegian, a sure sign of God's favor. Their decision to relocate to the fertile Illinois prairies that would soon have canal and railroad access connecting the Great Lakes and the Gulf of Mexico made economic sense. (As a descendant, I wish they hadn't traded their Illinois farms now selling for $14,000 an acre for the hills of Decatur County, Iowa.) Hans Hauge had encouraged the poor to create economic organizations for their own advantage and spiritual communities of the like-minded. Mormons proclaimed the imminent coming of the City of Zion in these "the latter days."[27]

And yet beyond these visible shreds of evidence, how does the historian explain the internal religious experience? With a great deal of reticence and humility, we

---

25. J. Hart Rosdail, *The Ikdal Family History: The American Branches of the Ikdal Family with an Account of their Origins in Western Norway and Information Concerning Norwegian Relatives* (Chicago: printed by the author, 1947), 213. Bertha Madison herself would inherit Hayer in-laws when her cousin Bertha Danielson married Lorenzo Hayer, grandson of Lars and Ann.

26. See Charles A. Reedy, Church History of the Mission Branch (Illinois), 1861–1961). Reedy's record of baptisms and other events place Hayers firmly in active congregational roles.

27. For more information on the communitarian impulse among early Norwegian immigrants, see Mario S. De Pillis, "Cleng Peerson and the Communitarian Background of Norwegian Immigration," Norwegian-American Historical Association, online at https://www.naha.stolaf.edu/pubs/nas/volume21/vol21_5.html.

hope. We can document that several factors in their Norwegian past had Mormon parallels. Hans Hauge's vision was remarkably similar to Joseph's account in the grove. Both Hauge and Mormonism stressed an inner examination of one's faith and yearning for assurance for salvation. Death was a frequent guest on the frontier for old and young alike. The Lars Hayer family alone lost four members in just their first two years. Did Mormonism's offer of salvation through posthumous baptism for those who hadn't heard the Restoration message appeal to the Hayers? We know it did to Bertha Madison's Norwegian grandfather who was baptized by proxy for an infant grandson who died in childbirth.[28]

I offer another possibility for the appeal of Mormonism, sparked by an article by H. O. Mathieson entitled "Belonging in the Midwest: Norwegian-Americans and the Process of Attachment, 1830–60." Mathieson distinguishes between adjustment and belonging. Adjustment is what one does; belonging is how one internalizes, understands those actions. Mathieson describes how Norwegian-Americans could think of themselves as fully American without giving up their Norwegian heritage. He credits historian Jon Gjerde with the term "complementary identity," holding simultaneous allegiances to national and ethnic identities in a pluralistic society. In the grand American myth, immigrants from many lands come together united by their belief in democratic equality and liberty, two concepts Norwegian arrivals passionately embraced. Norwegians were eager to enter into the great American democratic experiment.[29]

In this context, Mormonism was one more ingredient of Gjerde's "complementary identity" mix: American, Norwegian, Mormon. What was new was the expansion beyond the secular, temporal world to the sacred, eternal. If there is merit in this perspective, Mormonism sanctified that emerging American identity for recently arrived Norwegians, clothing it with a spiritual dimension. In Mormon thought, America became a sacred landscape. Mormon America had its own scripture in the Book of Mormon. And most important, the Mormon elect had a front-row seat on the coming realization of Zion and the return of Christ. On one level, Norwegian-Americans were aware of the social inferiority ascribed to them by native-born Yankees. But in Midwestern Mormonism, the important distinction was not between Yankees and Norskies. The *big divide* became that between Saints and gentiles. The Hayers' embrace of the Restoration gave them a new identity among God's elite and a citizenship that enfolded their Norwegian heritage into an exuberant and hopeful American context.

---

28. J. Hart Rosdail, *The Ikdal Family History*, 211.

29. H. O. Mathieson, "Belonging in the Midwest: Norwegian-Americans and the Process of Attachment, 1830–1860," *American 19th Century History*, 15, no. 2 (2014): 119–46.

But do our speculations about the motivations and decisions of the Hayers have any relationship to the actual historical reality of the family? Ja, there's the rub. Vil vi noensinne vet? Will we ever know?

TOM MORAIN serves as Director of Government Relations at Graceland University where he has taught Iowa history, writing and critical thinking. He completed his doctorate in American Civilization from the University of Iowa and was director of history at Living History Farms in Des Moines for fourteen years. In 1995, he became head of the State Historical Society of Iowa until returning to Graceland in 2001. He has authored several books and numerous articles on Iowa and church history and served as JWHA President.

The Tragedy of William Hodges

William Shepard[1]

Introduction

I SUSPECT MOST HISTORIANS encounter a research subject who captivates them emotionally. I found myself in this situation when I extensively researched four brothers named Hodges who died violently in the greater Nauvoo area in the summer of 1845. I was drawn to William Hodges, a twenty-five-year-old developmentally disabled young man. His mother called him tender, he could not sign his name, and when observed with his twenty-two-year-old brother Stephen, people believed he was younger because he was smaller and subservient.[2] It was unfortunate Stephen was his main role model because of his violent temper and mental instability. To make matters worse, his older brothers, Amos and Ervine, were committed thieves and demonstrated limited reasoning ability. Although the brothers were baptized Mormons, allegiance to their religion's strict tenets had apparently been replaced by values dictated by a criminal society composed of both Mormons and non-Mormons.[3]

This article will outline events that culminated in the destruction of the Mormon portion of the criminal society in the summer of 1845 and the destruction of the non-Mormon portion later that year. It will include the murder of two Mennonite men in May, the murders of Ervine and Amos Hodges in June, and the murder of Col. George Davenport in July. Stephen and William Hodges were hanged in July, and Granville Young and Aaron and John Long followed them to the gallows in October.

---

1. The author wishes to thank H. Michael Marquardt for his help with this article.

2. I was a teacher of the developmentally disabled for twenty-nine years at a state residential care facility in Wisconsin. In the early years, I was responsible for a program in which "high functioning" individuals (those with an IQ just below eighty) learned work and social skills preparatory to community living. I gained and still retain a high degree of empathy for this population.

3. It is impossible to know the degree of faith the Hodges brothers retained in Mormonism during this period. Amos was the president of the Thirteenth Quorum of Seventy and William Hodges was a member of that quorum. See "70s Rec, Bk B Sel, 13 Qrm, 1844–45," Church History Library, The Church of Jesus Christ of Latter-day Saints, Salt Lake City, Utah.

The personal tragedy of William Hodges, however, is the centerpiece of this article. Living in a society without understanding, public empathy, or treatment facilities for the intellectually compromised, he was dependent upon the dictates of others.

In January 1845, William's parents, Curtis Sr. and Lucy Hodges, and other family members left Nauvoo for Pennsylvania to fellowship with Sidney Rigdon. Daughter Elisa Jane Hodges apparently lived with her widowed sister Emeline Campbell, and sons William and Stephen Hodges lived with their brother Amos and his wife Lydia in a poor area by the Mississippi River. Ervine Hodges and his wife Luzette lived at Mechanicsville some twenty miles inland from Nauvoo. Stephen, Amos and Ervine had been accused of stealing in Iowa, and all were members of a small criminal cabal of Mormon and non-Mormon thieves headquartered at Nauvoo.[4]

It was unremarkable that thieves would be drawn to Nauvoo because of its location on the Mississippi River and its population of some 10,000 persons. Philip D. Jordan, a professor of history from the University of Minnesota, wrote:

> During the 1840's, counterfeiters, horse thieves, stage robbers, and murderers plagued western Illinois and eastern Iowa. Singly and in well-organized bands, desperadoes disrupted the peace not only in the immediate vicinity of Nauvoo but also in the trans-Mississippi towns of Fort Madison, Montrose, Burlington, and Davenport in Iowa Territory.[5]

Mormon historian Truman G. Madsen added, "At this time [1844] Nauvoo was the largest city in Illinois; hence, counterfeiters, blacklegs, bootleggers, slave traders, gamblers and every other disreputable type of person found their way there trying to exploit the possibilities for dishonest profits, trying to gull recent and sometimes naïve converts who had come from far and near."[6]

Joseph and Hyrum Smith fiercely made war on thieves in Nauvoo and the countryside, removing those so identified from the church. They failed, however, to identify and expel this particular criminal society of Mormons and non-Mormons who carefully guarded their identities. Joseph read his proclamation dated March 25, 1843, at a special conference in Nauvoo twelve days later about "a band of desperadoes, bound by oaths of secrecy, under severe penalties in case any member of the combination divulges their plans of stealing…" He pledged protection to anyone

4. The inconsistent journey of the Curtis and Lucy Hodges family through Mormonism is outlined in Bill Shepard, "The Notorious Hodges Brother: Solving the Mystery of Their Destruction at Nauvoo," *John Whitmer Historical Association Journal* 26 (2006): 260–86.

5. "Introduction by Philip D. Jordan," in Edward Bonney, *The Banditti of the Prairies or, The Murderer's Doom!! A Tale of the Mississippi Valley* (Norman: University of Oklahoma Press, New Edition 1963), ix.

6. Truman G. Madsen, *Joseph Smith the Prophet* (Bookcraft: Salt Lake City, 1989), 112, cited in Kenneth W. Godfrey, "Crime and Punishment in Mormon Nauvoo, 1839–1846," *BYU Studies* 32 (1992): 196.

intimidated by the secret band and demanded he be supplied with information so he could eradicate them. He declared, *"Thieving must be stopped."*[7]

Joseph Smith's 1843 Journal, kept by Willard Richards, recorded Hyrum Smith adding to his brother's warning about this group of criminals, alleging that:

> a man who formerly belonged to the Church. Revealed to me there are a band of men & some strong in the faith of the Doctrine of Latter Day Saints. & some who do not belong to the chu[r]ch, <were bound to~by secret oaths &c> that it is right to steal from any one who does not belong to the church if they gave ¼ to the temple. If they did not remain steadfast — they ripped open their bowels & gave them to the cat fish. — and they are the very gadianton robbers of the last days.[8]

The identity of the thieves Hyrum Smith referred to as "Gadianton robbers"[9] was not divulged while he and his brother Joseph lived. However, in the aftermath of the May 10, 1845, murder of a Mennonite minister at West Point in Lee County, Iowa Territory, the identity of the "robbers" came into clearer focus. Mormons William and Stephen Hodges, Thomas Brown and Artemus Johnson were accused of murder, and Mormons Ervine and Amos Hodges, William [Bill] Hickman and Return Jackson Redden were identified as their criminal associates.

The murder of Col. George Davenport at Rock Island on July 4, 1845 by non-Mormon members of this group set in motion events that would reveal their identities as well. John and Aaron Long and Judge Fox had been members of the notorious William W. Brown criminal gang at Bellevue, Iowa. After Brown and gang members were killed in a gun battle with the sheriff and vigilantes in 1841, Fox and the Longs made their way to Nauvoo.[10] By 1845, Robert Birch, a former member of the Josh Driscoll criminal gang of Ogle County, Illinois, was using Nauvoo as a base of operations. He had also seen the wrath of vigilante justice.[11] There would have been other

---

7. "Special Conference," April 6, 1843, *Times and Seasons* 4 (May 1, 1843): 184. Emphasis retained.

8. Joseph Smith Journal kept by Willard Richards, April 6, 1843 in Andrew H. Hedges, Alex D. Smith and Richard Lloyd Anderson, eds., *Journals Volume 2: 1841–April 1843* (Salt Lake City: Church Historian's Press, 2011), 334–35. William Clayton recorded Hyrum Smith as saying: "… there was a gang of thieves down [by] the river are plundering on the credit … They are also making bogus money. They have some 3 or 4 amongst them who denied the faith, would talk, they ripped up their bowels & gave them to the Cat fish & that was their Oath. I wish to warn you all not to be duped by such men, for they are the Gadianters of the last days." Hyrum Smith, April 6, 1843, as reported by William Clayton in Church Historian's Office, General Church Minutes, CR 100 318.

9. The Gadianton Robbers are prominently referred to in the Book of Mormon as the incarnation of evil: secret societies featuring secret oaths, procedures and murder which made them enemies of godly society.

10. In 1841 at Bellevue, Iowa, arrogant law breaking and challenging civil authority led to Brown's death and the lashing and exile of Judge Fox, John and Aaron Long. See Susan K. Lucke, *The Bellevue War: Mandate of Justice or Murder by Mob?* (Ames, IA: McMillan Publishing, 2002) and James W. Ellis, *History of Jackson County, Iowa* (Chicago: S. J. Clark, 1909), 470–75.

11. After members of the Driscoll gang burned the new courthouse at Oregon in Ogle County, Illinois, and murdered a vigilante, Driscoll and a son were executed by a vigilante firing squad in 1841 and the gang was scattered. See Robert Huhn Jones, "Three Days of Violence: The Regulators of the Rock River Valley," *Journal of the Illinois*

transitory non-Mormon thieves involved. Mormons George Grant Redden and his son William, fringe criminal associates, provided their secluded home at Devil's Creek, across from Nauvoo in Iowa Territory, as a place for the thieves to secretly assemble.[12]

The Banditti of the Prairies

Edward Bonney, a former non-Mormon member of the Council of Fifty, author, successful bounty hunter, and eyewitness to many of the criminal activities of these thieves would refer to the group Hyrum Smith labeled the "Gadianton robbers" as the "Banditti of the Prairies."[13] This hybrid group agreed to do everything possible to obtain the release of any incarcerated member in exchange for group loyalty. They clustered on the western limits of Nauvoo and quietly fellowshipped with other undesirables. To be sure, Nauvoo citizens were uneasy with rumors of their activities, but the fact that they kept a low profile served them well. But each robbery they committed in Iowa and the Illinois countryside would cause the already suspicious non-Mormons to blame the Mormons.

Murder in Iowa

William and Stephen Hodges, Artemus Johnson, and Thomas Brown were drawn to the community of West Bend, in Lee County, Iowa, by rumors that a Mennonite minister named John Miller [Johannes Mueller] had $1,000 with which to buy land and build a church.[14] They located the newly constructed log home built by Miller's son-in-law Henry Leiza [Leize, Leisa or Leise] and brazenly asked the occupants if they could change a bank note for them. Neighbors of the Mennonites

State Historical Society 59 (1966): 131–42 and Rodney O. Davis, "Judge Ford and the Regulators, 1841–42," *Select Papers in Illinois History* 2 (1981): 25–36. It is possible the four exiles may have worked together as thieves in other locations prior to gathering at Nauvoo.

12. See Bonney, *Banditti of the Prairies*, 66.

13. Bonney, *Banditti of the Prairies*, Title and Introduction by Philip D. Jordan, vii–xxi. See Jordan's biographical essay about Bonney in *Banditti of the Prairies*, vii–xxi and Michael Quinn's comments about Bonney's connections with the Mormons in *The Mormon Hierarchy: Origins of Power* (Salt Lake City: Signature Books in association with Smith Research Associates, 1994), 127.

14. Judge Charles Mason, in an extensive account of his interaction with the brothers prior to their execution, maintained Stephen told him that "a man by the name of Jackson" was with the brothers in Iowa on the day of the murder. This could only refer to fellow Mormon gang member Return Jackson Redden. See "The Hodges," Burlington *Hawk-Eye* 7 (September 25, 1845): 2. The possibility of Redden's involvement is strengthened in a confidential letter of attorney Daniel F. Miller from Fort Madison, Iowa, to Judge Charles Mason. Miller, an associate of Jonathan C. Hall, the Hodges' lead lawyer, told Mason, "I might not be justifiable in my moral behavior [*sic*] to informant, to detail to you all the particulars of the murder, but I can briefly assure you that Wm. & Stephen Hodges were at Millers & Leisis [Leiza's] on the night of the murder. There were six [robbers] in all..." As Miller named only four participants, Redden presumably was one of the two unnamed thieves. See D.[aniel] F. Miller to Hon[.] Charles Mason, July 23, 1845, typescript, Iowa State Historical Society, Des Moines, Iowa.

remembered being approached by the would-be thieves, being asked if they had seen their "lost ox," and raising questions about the Mennonites. The thieves thus determined that the stories about Miller's $1,000 were true and reasoned that they could enter the house at night to silently relieve him of his money. They apparently hadn't considered that the peace-affirming Mennonites would resist.

They blackened their faces and made their move about midnight on May 10 and with a "dark lantern" entered their intended victims' home. They encountered the stoutly built Miller, born about 1787 in Bavaria, and his wife Mary Anna, their daughter Elizabeth and husband Henry Leiza, and a second daughter Amelia and her husband Jacob Risser sleeping on the floor. Mary Anna heard the door unlatch and screamed a warning. A desperate fight ensued. Leiza overpowered one invader and was beating him while Miller flailed at the others with an uncharged rifle. According to Apostle John Taylor, Miller "struck one of the villains over the head [with the rifle] and felled him."[15] As the fight spilled out of the house, the thieves desperately fired pistols and stabbed with their Bowie knives — Miller died after being shot and stabbed in the heart. Leiza, also shot and stabbed, died three weeks later.[16] Miller's other son-in-law Jacob Risser was despised by the Iowans as they believed he had chosen not to engage the invaders.[17]

Methodist Reverend Elnatan Corrington Gavitt, indicted in a retrospective anti-Mormon account, related that "the screams and shrieks of the terrified women" caused the murderers to flee "without accomplishing more than the death of their victims."[18]

Aftermath

Iowans quickly coalesced under the leadership of Sheriff James Estes of Lee County, Iowa, and found "a cloth hat … trimmed with fur and without a front piece"

---

15. "The John Taylor Nauvoo Journal — January 1845 – September 1845," *BYU Studies* 23 (Summer 1983): 48. Dr. Holmes, who arrived at Miller's at day light on May 11, testified, "I observed the gun, it was shattered and the stock held on by a wire." "Trial for Murder, *Burlington Hawk-Eye* 7 (June 26, 1845): 2.

16. News of the murder of Miller and the mortal wounding of Leiza was being communicated by individuals on commercial and private boats plying the Mississippi River within hours. It spread like wildfire inland in Illinois and Iowa and then became national news as accounts in area newspapers were circulated.

17. Colonel J. M. Reid, in *Sketches and Anecdotes of the Old Settlers and New Comers, the Mormon Bandits and Danite Band* (Keokuk, IA: R. B. Ogden, Publisher, 1877), 40, sarcastically said if Jacob Risser, "the other cowardly son-in-law," would have joined the fight, the thieves "would have been defeated and repulsed." Instead, according to Reid, "he covered up his head while the fight went on as he laid still on one corner of the cabin and trembling with fright let his father-in-law and brother-in-law be murdered." Jacob Risser testified at the trial of Stephen and William, "My wife was awake when I awoke; she tried to pull me back and prevent my getting out of bed. She said: 'there are murders — we will all be murdered.'" Jacob added when he got up a shot passed through his shirt sleeve as the robbers retreated from the house. *Burlington Hawk-Eye*, "Trial for Murder."

18. Rev. Elnathan Corrington Gavitt, *Crumbs from My Saddle Bags or, Reminiscences of Pioneer Life and Biographical Sketches* (Toledo, OH: Blade Printers and Paper Co., 1884), 220.

in Leiza's yard. When fresh tracks were followed to an area on the Mississippi River opposite Nauvoo, the searchers predictably concluded that the murderers were Mormons.[19]

Artemus Johnson and Thomas Brown wisely went into hiding, but the brothers returned to Nauvoo the next morning to ask Brigham Young for protection. When Young told them instead to turn themselves into the law, they foolishly threatened to kill him.[20] Mormon apostle William Smith, who had known the family since 1832,[21] advised them to leave the area, but they instead went to the secluded home of their brother Amos and his wife Lydia.

William and Stephen Hodges quickly emerged as prime suspects because they were in the neighborhood the day before the murder and had been inquiring about Miller. Added to that, the brothers had worked on the courthouse at West Point during its construction, may have briefly lived in the area, and were generally well known. Some of the Iowans were also certain that the cap left by one of the assailants belonged to William.[22]

Iowans familiar with the brothers infiltrated Nauvoo on May 12 and learned that William had been seen without his cap and that Stephen had been observed with blood on his shirt.[23] Stephen Markham, the police watch commander, was notified of the circumstances by the Iowans, and the search was on for the brothers. Hosea Stout, captain of the Nauvoo Police, recorded that he was with Brigham Young at his home at the time he was notified that "some men by the name of Hodges who were suspected of being guilty of murdering a man in the Iowa" were hiding in Nauvoo. Doubtless with Young's blessing, Stout, the Iowans and Nauvoo police cooperatively searched Nauvoo. Stephen and William were located at their brother Amos's house and were observed to be heavily armed. They "refused to be taken until day light," so Stout and company "guarded the house" until morning when the three brothers surrendered and were "conducted away by Col[.] Markham."[24]

19. Bonney, *Banditti of the Prairies*, 31–32.

20. Jessee, *John Taylor Nauvoo Journal*, 48.

21. See Kyle R. Walker, *William B. Smith: In the Shadow of a Prophet* (Salt Lake City: Greg Kofford Book, 2015), 91.

22. Bonney, in *Banditti of the Prairies*, 32–33, credits himself with these conclusions but they were the result of consensus agreement.

23. *The Iowa Territorial Gazette and Advertiser* [of Burlington, IA] 8 (May 17, 1845): 2, under the heading, "Murder and Attempted Robbery," said, "The cap left at the theatre of bloodshed has been recognized as belonging to one of them, and the hair (red) which adhered to the gun used upon one of them by Miller, corresponds precisely with that of one of the persons arrested.… It is also said that there is testimony to prove that the red haired Hodges was seen to enter Nauvoo about day light bare headed, the morning after the Murder."

24. Juanita Brooks, ed., *On the Mormon Frontier: The Diary of Hosea Stout —Volume One 1844–1848* (Salt Lake City: University of Utah Press, 1961), 1:38–39.

As Nauvoo did not have a jail, the brothers were held under guard in the Mansion House.[25] Shortly thereafter William Smith unsuccessfully attempted to get members of the Nauvoo police to release William and Stephen from custody.[26] On the morning of May 15, a showdown of sorts took place at Nauvoo with a trial before justices of the peace Aaron Johnson and Isaac Higbee.[27] The brothers were represented by well-known Mormon attorney Almon Babbitt who would have been hired by Erwin Hodges and other gang members to keep Stephen and William from being released to the Iowans. At some point in the trial, Amos Hodges was released from custody. Regardless, a large contingent of Iowans led by Sheriff Estes arrived with a bill of indictment from the grand jury of Lee County, Iowa, specifying that William and Stephen be released to Sheriff Estes's custody. Hosea Stout recorded the tense encounter:

> There was great excitement about this murder in Iowa and our enemies taking the advantage of us endeavoured [sic] to lay this thing to the Mormons and when they found that those men were in Nauvoo, raise a hue & cry that we were harboring the murderers and that it was no use to come after them, this was when there was an opportunity [to] raise evil reports against us, hence the people of Iowa was jealous and expected we would let them go, but when the Court decided against them and they [William and Stephen Hodges] were being conveyed by the police to [Fort] Madison [Iowa] the same evening, they saw we were willing to do justice by all and they all as with one accord, declared that we were abused and misrepresented[.] so the matter turned in our favor and they instead of being our enemies as the mob intended became our friends.[28]

A letter from one of the Iowans who witnessed the release of the brothers, said they were offered the choice, "either to go to Carthage jail and wait a requisition, or proceed immediately to Fort Madison. They preferred the latter and are now safely lodged in strong quarters."[29]

The May 21 *Nauvoo Neighbor* printed an article from the *Lee County Democrat* of Fort Madison, Iowa under the heading, "The Iowa Murder," which read in part:

---

25. In "Trial for Murder," *Burlington Hawk-Eye* 7 (June 26, 1845): 2, Mormon D. M. Repsher, who was testifying against the brothers and referred to himself as a "Nauvoo town constable," said after the brother's surrendered he "took them to the Mansion House."

26. John Taylor recorded a meeting between William Smith and Brigham Young, other apostles and members of the Nauvoo police at the Masonic Hall on June 25, 1845, to settle a variety of difficulties related to William's disruptive activities. Young's comments about Smith included, "William Smith had no right to counsel those men to let the Hodges go, they were men acting under the town police, fulfilling the law, harboring men in their custody, who I believe to be murderers, and who had threatened my life. They came to me asking what they should do. I told them to fulfil the law." See Jessee, *John Taylor Nauvoo Journal*, 62.

27. See Bonney, *Banditti of the Prairies*, 38.

28. Brooks, *Diary of Hosea Stout*, 1:44.

29. "Late Murder in Lee County," *Warsaw Signal* 2 (May 21, 1845): 2.

After a hearing before Esquires Johnson and Higbee, they were surrendered to the Sheriff, who brought them to this town last evening and secured them in the penitentiary. Their name is Hodges they are brothers. Two other persons named Tom Brown and A. Johnson, are suspected as indicated and the most strenuous endeavors are being made for their arrest. It is due to the Mormon authorities, to state that they made every exertion to further the ends of justice, and cooperated most cordially with the Sheriff to that effect.

The *Neighbor* editorialized, "We [Nauvoo authorities] always have and always will help men execute the laws and bring the offenders to justice." It incorrectly added, "Let it be known throughout the land, that *these two young Hodges are not Mormons, nor were: neither are Johnson or Brown.*"[30]

Interlude in the Fort Madison, Iowa Prison

After being initially held in the Fort Madison prison, the brothers were taken by Sheriff Estes and Hawkins Taylor, former sheriff of Lee County,[31] on a heavily guarded trip to West Point where the members of John Miller's family were asked to identify Stephen and William from a six-person lineup. The dying Henry Leiza identified Stephen Hodges as the one who had clubbed him and said that William had shot John Miller. Widow Anna Miller came to a different conclusion. She "sank down" when she saw "the smaller Hodge" [William], and, speaking through an interpreter, cried out, "My God that man killed my good husband."[32] Hawkins Taylor also spent three days in Nauvoo taking "testimony to be used in court" with William and Stephen Hodges' initial lawyer Lyman E. Johnson of Keokuk, Iowa, a former member of the first Quorum of Twelve Apostles.[33] Unsurprisingly, Artemas Johnson's wife Almira, sisters Emeline Campbell and Eliza Jane Hodges, and assorted friends swore William and Stephen Hodges were in Nauvoo on the night Miller was murdered. John and Aaron Long and Judge Fox, non-Mormon criminal associates of the Hodges brothers, boldly attempted to provide the brothers with an alibi as well.

---

30. "The Iowa Murder," *Nauvoo Neighbor* 3 (May 21, 1845): 2, emphasis retained. The *Iowa Territorial Gazette* also praised the Mormons, "The two Hodges suspected in the murder of Miller in Lee County were delivered up by the authorities of Nauvoo, it is said, acting well in the matter—refusing to wait until a formal requisition was made on them by our Governor for the delivery of the prisoners." "Arrest of the Murderers," *Iowa Territorial Gazette* 3 (May 24, 1845): 2.

31. See John E. Hallwas and Roger D. Launius, eds., *Cultures in Conflict: A Documentary History of the Mormon War in Illinois* (Logan: Utah State University Press, 1995), 51–55, for information on Hawkins Taylor.

32. *Autobiography of Hawkins Taylor*, 1876, Archives and Special Collections, typescript, Western Illinois University, Macomb, Illinois, 55–56.

33. See William Shepard and H. Michael Marquardt, *Lost Apostles: Forgotten Members of Mormonism's Original Quorum of Twelve* (Salt Lake City: Signature Books, 2014), 251 and William Shepard and H. Michael Marquardt, "Lyman E. Johnson: Forgotten Apostle," *Journal of Mormon History* 36 (Winter 2002): 128.

Taylor later related, "There probably never was a worse lot of thieves in any one court then in during this time."[34]

In a change of venue, Stephen and William Hodges were taken in chains on June 11 from Fort Madison to Burlington, Iowa, by the steamer *New Purchase* where they were greeted by "a vast crowd" who had gathered to see the murderers. They were released to Sheriff John H. McKinney of Des Moines County, Iowa, and taken to the jail on North Hill Public Square.[35]

Trial at Burlington, Iowa

On June 17, Lyman Johnson and Hawkins Taylor witnessed a legal document stating that five Mormons and one non-Mormon had transferred property valued at $1,000 to Frederick D. Mills and Jonathan C. Hall of Burlington, Iowa, to defend the brothers. Those participating were Mormons Ervine and Amos Hodges, Return Jackson Redden, William (Bill) Hickman, W. Jenkins Salisbury and non-Mormon Robert Birch. Except for Salisbury, the individuals were members of the criminal gang.[36] According to Hawkins Taylor, Lyman Johnson made it clear from the start, "that nothing could save them [William and Stephen Hodges] but the testimony establishing an alibi, given by the high officials of the church."[37] William and Stephen's crude threats to Brigham Young had eliminated that possibility.

Jurors were empaneled on Thursday, June 19, and the brothers' trial began the following day at the Old Zion Methodist Church in Burlington, Iowa, with Judge Charles Mason presiding.[38]

Information about the trial is incomplete since the minutes have apparently been stolen from the Des Moines County Court House in Burlington.[39] It is therefore necessary to rely upon accounts in two Burlington newspapers.

---

34. *Autobiography of Hawkins Taylor*, 56.

35. "Great Crowd—Arrival of the Prisoners," *Burlington Hawk-Eye* 7 (June 12, 1845): 2.

36. Bonds and Mortgage document, Bonds & Mortgages, Vol. 2, 1844–1848, pp. 66–67. Original in Hancock County Court House, Carthage, Illinois. Microfilm no. 954,776, Family History Library, Salt Lake City, Utah.

37. *Autobiography of Hawkins Taylor*, 56.

38. Judge Charles Mason, October 24, 1804 – February 25, 1882, was chief justice of Iowa Territory when he presided over the trial of William and Stephen Hodges. He graduated from West Point in 1829 with a higher rating than his classmate Robert E. Lee. In addition to being chief justice of Iowa, Mason taught engineering, was a patent attorney, president of a railroad, and a noted Copperhead or Peace Democrat. He unsuccessfully ran for governor of Iowa in 1867. In part, see *Life and Letters of Charles Mason: Chief Justice of Iowa, 1804–1882*, ed., Charles Mason Remey (Washington, DC: Charles Mason Remey, 1939); *The History of Des Moines County, Iow...* (Chicago: Western Historical Co., 1879); and Emlin M'Clain, "Charles Mason," Iowa's First Jurist," *Annals of Iowa* 4 (1901): 595–609.

39. Philip D. Jordan, in his introduction of Edward Bonney's *Banditti of the Prairies*, xv, wrote, "Thirty-four years ago, I compared Bonney's narrative [about the apprehension, trial, and execution of the Hodges brothers] in the Des Moines County Courthouse [at Burlington, Iowa] and found no significant contradictions. Moreover, accounts in two local journals, the *Burlington Gazette* and the *Burlington Hawk-Eye* agreed essentially with Bon-

The brothers' lawyers emphasized that because the house was dark and the encounter took only minutes, making a positive identification would have been difficult. Stephen and William would have been encouraged when Judge Mason would not permit the dying declaration of Leiza "that the prisoners were the Killers" to be admitted as evidence.[40] In retrospect, however, they had no chance of being acquitted. The testimony of Amelia and Jacob Risser, Elizabeth Leiza, and Mary Anna Miller was sufficient to win over the jury. Accounts of Miller's neighbors placing the brothers in the area the day of the murders and the belief that the distinctive cap left at the murder scene belonged to William Hodges reinforced the belief that they were guilty. Further, the fact the brothers were Mormons appears to have strengthened the desire to convict.

The *Burlington Hawk-Eye's* coverage of the brothers' trial included two items of testimony William Hodges made about himself which was incriminating. John Court said that William had told him that he "would rob, steal and murder before he would work on a steam boat." John Walker testified that William attempted to get him to join his "company" because, "there was a better way to make money than by work, that they could make a living and meant to have it, without work." William purportedly explained to Walker, "when one [of the company] got into a scrape they would help one another out: if they could not one way, they would another." Walker was also told, "if any of the company ever told anything [secrets], that he or the balance would kill him: if ever I told any of the conversation they would kill me." When William asked him to "join the company," Walker courageously refused but was terrified. After John Miller was murdered, it was rumored that Walker was withholding information and only told of his interaction with William after "citizens" threatened to "raise a mob" and make him talk.[41]

Amos Hodges did not attend the trial of his brothers because he had been indicted for a previous robbery in Iowa.[42] His brother Ervine was at Burlington but there is no record he attended the trial.

Witnesses for the defense were not taken seriously. Sisters Emeline Campbell and Eliza Jane Hodges and a variety of neighbors repeated their pre-trial testimony and swore the brothers were in Nauvoo on the night of the murders. Unfortunately, they gave different accounts of the brother's locations and activities, and the type

---

ney's version …" During a thorough search of documents in the Des Moines Courthouse I only located two documents of minor importance about the Hodges brothers. After asking for assistance, a curator told me the records of the trial had been stolen.

40. Barbara Howard and Junia Braby, "The Hodges Hanging," *The Palimpsest* 60 (March–April, 1979): 53.

41. "Trial for Murder," *Burlington Hawk-Eye* 7 (June 26, 1845): 2.

42. Remey, *Charles Mason*, 91–93.

of hat William wore.[43] Horace Braffett said he saw William wearing a straw hat at Nauvoo on May 10, while Amelia Johnson said he always wore a "wide rimmed hat." Emeline Campbell said she had burned William's cap "in February 2 miles this side of Nauvoo," and Peter Munjar testified William told him during his incarceration at Nauvoo that "he burned his cap" and replaced it with a new one."[44]

Judge Mason said Amos Hodges's wife Lydia told Jonathan Hall, the brother's lead lawyer, by confidential letter not to call her to provide an alibi for Stephen and William on the night of Miller's murder. She said the brothers were gone all night and when they returned, "said they had been unsuccessful and perhaps got themselves in trouble." Lydia also confirmed the cap left at the Millers' belonged to William.[45]

On Saturday morning, June 21, the lawyers for the defense began their extensive summary to the jury, followed by the prosecution's three-hour rebuttal. Judge Mason delivered his charge to the jury at nine o'clock that evening, and after a short consultation the jury agreed to give their verdict the next morning. The courtroom was full early Sunday morning when Mason asked the jury to pronounce their verdict. Editor James G. Edwards of the *Burlington Hawk-Eye* said, "breathless silence prevailed in the audience." The verdict was, "*We, the Jury, find William Hodges and Stephen Hodges GUILTY of Murder.*" Edwards said, "The feeling of the large crowd so long kept in painful suspense, and their anxiety kept at such a fearful stretch, could not now be restrained and many of them joined in clapping and other signs of approbation."[46] The other Burlington newspaper, the *Gazette and Advertiser*, said, "It is conceded on all hands that the proof against the prisoners was such as to justify the verdict. If not positive it was as nearly so as can well be imagined. Not a doubt is entertained by any of the justness of the verdict, or the guilt of the wretched men now under sentence of death."[47]

Prior to the sentencing that afternoon, Judge Mason asked William Hodges if he would like to address the court. The *Hawk-Eye* quoted him as saying, "I have nothing more to say except that I am innocent of the charge; I have had the benefit of a fair trial by a Jury of my country—I have been found guilty and I am prepared to submit myself to my fate." Stephen also asserted "their entire innocence of the charge." Mason's sentence stipulated:

---

43. Reid, in *Sketches and Anecdotes,* 41, said "the prisoners were prosecuted "with great vigor and on the cross examination of the witnesses to prove an alibi for the defense completely entrapped them, as no two witnesses could agree to the particular place the prisoners were at Nauvoo on the night of the murder."

44. "Trial for Murder," *Burlington Hawk-Eye.*

45. Remey, *Charles Mason,* 91–93, 94.

46. "Trial for Murder," *Burlington, Hawk-Eye.*

47. "Trial, Conviction and Sentence of the Hodges, *Iowa Territorial Gazette and Advertiser* 8 (June 28, 1845): 2.

I direct that you William Hodges and Stephen Hodges, be taken from this place to the Jail of the County of Des Moines, there to remain until Tuesday, the 15th day of July next, that on that day you be taken by the proper officer of this County to some convenient place within the same, and there, between the hours of 10 o'clock A. M. and 4 o'clock P. M. that you be hung by the neck until you are dead; and may God have mercy upon you.[48]

The account in *The Iowa Territorial Gazette and Advertiser* was not as extensive as the *Burlington Hawk-Eye* but it captured the demeanor of the brothers during their trial:

The deportment of the Hodges throughout the trial, was marked by a singular manifestation of apparent indifference as to the result. A stranger, unacquainted with the circumstances, never would have dreamt, judging from their looks and conduct, that they were on their trial for life and death. Indeed, when the verdict of "guilty" was rendered by the jury, they received it without the slightest perceptible change of countenance and as though they would have been disappointed by any other result. And while listening to the touching and melting sentence of the judge, dooming them to the felon's death, they manifested but little sensibility. Both avowed their innocence, and expressed a readiness to meet their fate. The younger brother, Stephen, it is apparent, however, is the master spirit in daring and crime, and the foregoing remarks relative to the hearing of both throughout the trial will apply with more force to him than to William.[49]

At an unknown time after the sentencing of the brothers, Jonathan C. Hall told Judge Mason that "he had no idea of asking for a new trial" as the brothers were guilty.[50]

Deaths of Ervine and Amos Hodges

Edward Bonney said Ervine Hodges was seen at Burlington after the trial making "strong efforts" to "rouse the Mormons" to rescue his brothers. According to Bonney, Ervine made it known he would "confess all he knew" about Mormons stealing from the Gentiles if the Mormons did not obtain the release of his brothers.[51] His reasoning was bizarre, as he was threatening to inform on the criminal gang to which he and his brothers belonged to embarrass the Mormons. It is inconceivable that he

---

48. "Trial for Murder," *Burlington Hawk-Eye*, emphasis retained.

49. "Trial, Conviction and Sentence of the Hodges," *Iowa Territorial Gazette*.

50. Remey, *Life and Letters of Charles Mason*, 91–94.

51. Bonney, *Banditti of the Prairies*, 50. John D. Lee substantiated this account by saying, "This answer recalled to my mind the threat [to take Young's life] that Erwin [*sic*] made during the day, at the trial of his brothers, who were sentenced and hung at Burlington, Iowa." See John D. Lee, *Mormonism Unveiled: or The Life and Confessions of the Late Mormon Bishop, John D. Lee* (St. Louis: Bryan, Brand & Co.—New York: H. Stellie & Co, 1877), 158.

did not realize the Mormons wanted nothing to do with him or his brothers. After all, William and Stephen had threatened to kill Brigham Young, were arrested by Mormon police, and were released by Mormons to Iowa officials. It is also inconceivable that he did not realize his fellow gang members would kill him if he told about their criminal activities.

On Monday morning, June 23, Ervine was recognized on the ferryboat to Nauvoo. An employee of the *Burlington Hawk-Eye* later noted, "We were on the same boat and little did we think that before another sun would rise that tall and athletic frame, full of strength and animation would be cold in death."[52] He made his way to Brigham Young's home and, in a state of rage and devoid of reasoning, demanded Young obtain the release of his brothers from the Burlington jail. When Young refused, Ervine threatened to take his life. Zina Diantha Huntington Jacobs, a plural wife of Young noted, "The said Hodge was direct from Burlington. He has a Brother there, sentenced [*sic*] to be hung on the [blank] of Sept next for Murder, said ~~Hodge has threatened Brigham Youngs life which~~ He was a man of unbounded temper."[53] After Ervine's violent encounter with Brigham Young, he conferred with William Smith, who presumably urged him to keep his mouth shut and leave Nauvoo.[54]

According to John Taylor, about 10:00 pm that night Ervine was cutting through a cornfield near Young's home when Nauvoo policemen Allen Stout and John Scott, who were guarding Young's home, heard screeching and distinct blows being struck. Ervine managed to stagger from the field and make it into Young's yard where he collapsed. He had been beaten with a club and savagely cut with a bowie knife.[55] Hosea Stout said, "he had been knocked down & then stab[b]ed 4 times in his left Side with his own knife."[56] John Taylor said John Scott asked Ervine who stabbed him and the response was "they were men whom he took to be friends, from the river." Taylor additionally recorded that a non-Mormon named Clapp asked Ervine "if he knew the perpetrators." After Ervine acknowledged he did, "the only answer he [Clapp] received was; he could not tell." Taylor added that Ervine had told Young "if his brothers were hung," he "would die next."[57]

The Nauvoo Sexton, William Huntington, said that on the day after the murder Ervine had been murdered "by some ruffians – as Hodge was supposed to be of the

52. "Irvine Hodges — Tragical," *Burlington Hawk-Eye* 7 (July 3, 1845): 2.

53. Maureen Ursenbach Beecher, ed., "All Things Move in Order in the City": The Nauvoo Diary of Zina Diantha Huntington Jacobs," *Brigham Young University* Studies 19 (Spring 1979): 314. The editor did not include the crossed-out portion of Jacob's diary.

54. John Taylor recorded on June 24, William Smith was with Ervine "a short time before" his death and added William "soon arrived" after Ervine expired. See Jessee, *John Taylor Nauvoo Journal*, 58.

55. *Allen Stout Remembrances and Journal 1845–1889*, Church History Library, Salt Lake City, Utah.

56. Brooks, *Diary of Hosea Stout*, 1:49.

57. Jessee, *John Taylor Nauvoo Journal*, 58.

same gang."[58] Attorney Daniel F. Miller told Judge Mason a month later that Ervine "was killed unquestionably by one of the Band … He was murdered because he threatened exposure."[59] The identity of Ervine's murderer became common knowledge that Fall when Robert Birch, a non-Mormon criminal associate of the Hodges, turned state's evidence during his trial for the murder of Col. James Davenport of Rock Island, Illinois, and testified that gang member Return Jackson Redden had murdered Ervine Hodges.[60]

Amos Hodges also lost his life in this overlapping timeframe but, as his body was never located, details are unavailable. He disappeared after he had informed Brigham Young that two non-Mormon gang members, Robert Birch and Judge Fox, were planning to rob a Mormon merchant named Rufus Beach at Nauvoo. He apparently did so in order to influence Young to secure the release of William and Stephen from their Iowa imprisonment. The *Iowa Territorial Gazette*, mixing Amos with Ervine, confusingly said:

> Of the fact of the murder there seems to be no question, but the circumstances attending it are not so well understood. Conflicting reports are in circulation on this point. The story told is, that upon arriving at home Hodges was approached, by two or three persons and solicited to engage in the contemplated robbery of a store—that H. consented, or seemed to consent—that, in the meantime he advised the owner of the store of the mediated robbery, and a guard was placed in the house—that, upon ascertaining their intentions were discovered, the robbers as is supposed, sought vengeance of H. for their betrayal, and killed him.[61]

John Taylor recorded on June 21, "A man of the name of Amos Hodges was taken up on a charge of theft. I am afraid he is connected with a gang of villains that are lurking about, stealing on our credit." He added on June 23, Amos had been "since cut off [from the church]."[62] Amos was jailed at Carthage, Illinois, but his incarceration was brief, as William Clayton recorded on June 24, "Wm. Smith has given

---

58. *William Huntington Autobiography*, typescript, Harold B. Lee Library, Brigham Young University, Provo, Utah.

59. Daniel Miller to Charles Mason, July 23, 1845, typescript, Iowa State Historical Society, Des Moines, Iowa.

60. For example, see, untitled, *Sangamo Journal* [of Springfield, Illinois] 15 (November 6, 1845): 2, "There is another of the Reddings concerned in this [Davenport's] robbery—a son—he is still at large—and is said to be the one who murdered Irvine Hodge in Nauvoo, to prevent a revelation of the crime of the gang to which he belonged." *Quincy Whig*." See also, *Shepard* and Marquardt, *Lost Apostles*, 252–54 and Shepard, "The Notorious Hodges Brothers," 268–69.

61. "A Brother of the Murderers Murdered," *Iowa Territorial Gazette*. The *Gazette* concluded this was not a "probable tale," and said it was more likely Ervine was murdered "by a gang of scoundrels to which he and his brothers are supposed to have belonged to prevent disclosures which it was feared the execution of Stephen and William might provoke."

62. Jessee, *John Taylor Nauvoo Journal*, 53 and 59 respectively.

bail for another brother of the Hodges, who was in custody for robbing."[63] Reliable documentation of his presence ends at this point. The *Warsaw Signal* of July 23, 1845, inadvertently confirmed Amos's disappearance when it wrote, "it appears that Amos Hodges who was under arrest in Nauvoo was permit[t]ed to escape or [is] held as a hostage, for he has not been publicly heard of since the murder of his brothers."[64]

In July 1846, when William Smith was bitterly opposing Brigham Young, he charged in the *Sangamo Journal* that, "Amos Hodge was murdered, it is said, between Montrose and Nashway, in Iowa by Brigham Young's guard, who pretended at the time to escort him out of Nauvoo, for his safety, under cover of women's clothes, who then pretended that he had run away." Evidence strongly indicates that he was killed by Birch and Fox because he had informed Brigham Young that they were planning to rob Beach's store.[65]

Final Days of William and Stephen Hodges

The brothers remained in the Burlington Jail following their June 22 sentencing and were housed separately. The *Lee County Democrat* of June 28 reported, "One of the Hodges attempted to destroy himself on Tuesday last by strangulation."[66] This was surely William after he learned of Ervine's death.

Time would have moved rapidly for the imprisoned brothers in their final three weeks of life. Judge Charles Mason was likewise under pressure to prevent the hanging of William Hodges, as it was apparent to him that William became a criminal at the urging of his brothers. He realized that the only possibility of saving his life was to get him to provide information which would lead to the destruction of his criminal accomplices. Another person under pressure was Emeline Campbell, sister of William and Stephen. She was now alone at Nauvoo as her sister Eliza Jane Hodges had eloped with a married doctor, James H. Lyons, of Ft. Madison, Iowa.[67]

---

63. *An Intimate Chronicle: The Journals of William Clayton*, ed., George D. Smith (Salt Lake City: Signature Books in association with Smith Research Associates, 1995), 169.

64. "Irvine Hodges," *Warsaw Signal* 2 (July 23, 1845): 2.

65. Bonney, in *Banditti of the Prairies*, 215, quoted Robert Birch as confessing during his October 1845 trial for the murder of Col. George Davenport: "[Judge] Fox and myself attempted to rob Beach in Nauvoo, and would have succeeded, had not Brigham Young told Beach the plan. We came near being caught, but escaped, and crossed the river [Mississippi River] to Old [Grant] Redden's." He added in Banditti, 55–56, "Fox and Bleeker [alias for Robert Birch] accomplished in their hazardous profession, entered the house of Beach with so much silence and skill that, notwithstanding the careful look kept for them, they had nearly succeeded in escaping with a large leathern trunk, which they had taken from the top of a bureau, before they were discovered. The trunk contained between three and four thousand dollars. The guard fired several shots at them, but they escaped without injury, and with no other loss than one of Bleeker's shoes, which was afterwards found in a mud-puddle near the house."

66. Untitled, *Lee County Democrat* 4 (June 28, 1845): 2.

67. Remey, *Life and Letters of Charles Mason*, 91–94. Dr. James H. Lyons was mayor of San Antonio for several nonconcurrent terms; was a successful doctor and an officer in the Mexican War. For additional information on

Despite the stresses associated with dealing with their rapidly approaching deaths, the doomed brothers came to appreciate the kind treatment they were receiving from Sheriff McKenney and his staff.[68] They were also visited by different clergymen and developed a strong friendship with Reverend J. G. White of the Cumberland Presbyterian Church.

Members of the Burlington community held a meeting in early July to take measures "to protect themselves from the Mormons, on the occasion of the execution of the two Hodges, on the 15th inst." The *Bloomington Herald* said, "Sheriff McKenny passed up the river a few days since to procure a hundred stand of arms for the same purpose."[69] The *Burlington Hawk-Eye* of July 10 noted that "a vast concourse" was expected to descend on Burlington in five days that would be composed of "all characters." It wished "it would be" that "no intoxicating drinks would be allowed to be vended on that day."[70] The *Bloomington Herald* ran this ad on July 12:

> The two Hodges are to be executed in Burlington of Tuesday <u>next</u>, the 15th, inst. The Steamer *Mermaid*, Cap. Glein in order to accommodate such as wish to be present at the execution, will make a trip from this place to Burlington on that day, leaving Bloomington at 5 o'clock, A. M. *precisely* and returning at an early hour of the evening. Cap. Glein always gives his passengers plenty to eat and drink, and all who wish to go cannot find a better opportunity.[71]

After the brothers' deaths Judge Mason publicized his interactions with them in the final two days of their lives in the *Burlington Hawk-Eye*. He said he thought he had convinced William on July 13 to provide evidence about other gang members in exchange for a prison sentence. He explained:

> I spoke to him kindly for in his then awful situation, I could harbor no feeling towards him but that of pity. I told him I regarded crime as very frequently the offspring of misfortune, or the result of a train of circumstances often difficult to be withstood— not from his appearance I would not suppose him capable of engaging in a career of crime from a feeling of wanton wickedness—that he must have been urged on by his necessities, or by the persuasions of others, from one step to another, to the final commission of the act for which he was then doomed to suffer; and in all this I had reason to believe that he had rather been acting as the instrument of others, then the originator of any criminal purpose of his own.

Lyons see "Handbook of Texas On line," "Lyons, James H." http://tshaonline.org/handbook/online/articles/flyby.

68. Stephen Hodges said shortly before he died, "If he had been a boarder at Mr[.] Painter's the jailor, he could not have had better fare. He acknowledged that he had received the most tender treatment from Sheriff McKenney." "The Execution," *Burlington Hawk-Eye* 7 (July 17, 1845): 2.

69. Untitled, *Bloomington Herald* 1 (July 5, 1845): 2.

70. "The Execution," *Burlington Hawk-Eye.*

71. "The Two Hodges," *Bloomington Herald* 1 (July 12, 1845): 2, emphasis retained.

At this juncture, William "burst into tears" and told Mason he would comply with his request if "Amos Hodges' wife Lydia should be removed from Nauvoo as he said they [gang members] would kill her the moment that he had made a confession." Mason guaranteed he would have Lydia removed and placed in protective custody. William, however, refused to dictate the information until the next morning. Mason said he found William "in great agitation" and was informed "he would make no revelation as he had previously promised." He said informing on gang members would result in the "destruction" of "all his friends" and his parents in Pennsylvania. William also concluded that the penitentiary "could furnish no protection to himself."

Mason then attempted to talk with the brothers together, but William resumed his subordinate role to Stephen, and the brothers mutually denied "knowing anything of the murder—anything of the recent robberies in Lee county—anything of a gang or association for any criminal purpose." The judge was terribly perplexed when attempting to interact sensibly with Stephen. For example, "the day previous to his execution," Stephen told Reverend White that, "he had it in his power to save William, but that he would not do so." When Mason confronted Stephen about the remark, "he denied in the most positive manner that he had ever made any [such] statement."[72]

The Hanging of William and Stephen Hodges

The public hanging of William and Stephen Hodges was the most remembered event in frontier Burlington history. One account said: "No incident has been more talked and written about by the people of Des Moines County than the trial, sentence and execution of William and Stephen Hodges. Theirs was the first and only legal execution in the county and marked an epoch by which old settlers regulated their calendars, events in their lives happening either before or after the hanging of the Hodges."[73] The community of over two thousand persons was invaded by an estimated eight-to-ten thousand excited visitors focused on watching William and Stephen die. James G. Edwards, the editor of the *Burlington Hawk-Eye*, wrote an extensive account of the events of July 15 and proudly proclaimed that he had never seen "more decorum or behavior exhibited at a public execution."[74] The thousands of

72. "The Hodges," *Burlington Hawk-Eye* 7 (September 25, 1845): 1. A Unitarian Minister named J. A. Gurley attended a Territorial Convention of Universalists at Burlington and visited William and Stephen at the Jail. He mistakenly called William "the younger brother" and referred to his promising to reveal the names of members of the criminal association and then refusing to do so. Gurley said he saw William's sister at Burlington. Assuming this is true, Emeline visited with William and Stephen at least on Sunday and Monday, July 13–14, and attended the hanging the following day. See "Journey to Burlington, Iowa," *Star in the West* [Cincinnati] (July 26, 1845): 126.

73. Augustine M. Antrobas, *History of Des Moines County and Its People …* (Chicago: S. J. Clarke Publishing Co., 1916), 150.

74. "The Execution," *Burlington Hawk-Eye*.

attendees came overland and by steamers and other types of boats. The *Hawk-Eye* said:

> The Steamer Mermaid brought a large number from Bloomington—the Shockoquon, after bringing an immense load from the place whose name she bears, proceeded to Oquawka, from whence she landed at our wharf with a crowd from Illinois. In the meantime[,] one of the Steam ferry boats from Fort Madison—the Caroline—came loaded to the guards with passengers—the "New Purchase" with a large multitude from Nauvoo, and places adjacent, arrived too late for the passengers to witness the execution.[75]

The *Hawk-Eye's* long and important account of this seminal event said the gallows was on Mount Pleasant road immediately west of Burlington and was situated in an area that formed a natural amphitheater. This location was "in full view of and immediately contiguous to the thousands of spectators who covered the hills" and "nothing could be said that all could not see and hear."[76]

The brothers were removed from jail in their white death shrouds, white caps, and heavy shackles at noon. They were seated on their coffins in a wagon and quietly talked. Other than looking pale, they seemed unconcerned. The Burlington *Iowa Territorial Gazette and Advertiser* observed that their "dogged indifference" was astounding and concluded, "it may be doubted whether an instance ever occurred in which men similarly situated exhibited more nerve and resolution."[77]

The procession, escorted by militia, excited observers, and a band playing funeral music slowly made its way to the execution site. They were met by a multitude of men, women, and children crowded around the gallows on elevated areas and even in trees. Ministers of the Cumberland Presbyterian, Methodist, Catholic, and Congregational churches, the brothers' lawyers, the sheriff, and one deputy awaited them on the platform. After prayers, hymn singing, and the reciting of a psalm about guilt and forgiveness, the brothers addressed the multitude.

James G. Edwards of the *Hawk-Eye* said Stephen was "very much agitated," and his "address was so different from anything we [he] anticipated from a dying man." He was startled by Stephen's "bitterness and maliciousness" which became "so maniacal" that he dropped his pencil "in utter astonishment." Stephen proclaimed his innocence, said he had been unjustly convicted and that he and William were being hanged because they were Mormons. His rage grew as he condemned Judge Mason and the jury and became so angry "froth issued from his mouth." The reporter said

---

75. "The Execution," *Burlington Haw-Eye*. Reid, in *Sketches and Anecdotes*, 42, alternately said, "The 'New Purchase came in just before the execution, loaded down with passengers from Nauvoo, and its whistle was heard just before the execution, at the levee. The passengers had time to get to the execution before it took place."

76. "The Execution," *Burlington Hawk-Eye*.

77. "Execution," *Iowa Territorial Gazette and Advertiser* 9 (July 19, 1845): 2.

it appeared he might break the ropes binding his arms. Showing signs of "extreme madness and rage," Stephen turned on the crowd and "said the curses of God would rest upon them." Edwards attempted to explain his feelings about Stephen's histrionics:

> It was our intention—and we believe that thousands felt as we did,—to have left the ground or to have turned our back upon the dreadful tragedy as soon as the preliminary exercises were over; but the speech and conduct of Stephen dissipated those tender sympathies in their behalf which we had all along felt. This change was wrought in us by having been in possession of admissions made by both the prisoners to different individuals entirely opposite to the statements made on the gallows. These admissions clearly prove their guilt.[78]

The account in the *Iowa Territorial Gazette* said William spoke "in a subdued voice, and in a different spirit than Stephen."[79] The account in *the Burlington Hawk-Eye* was more explicit and said that he attempted to convince the audience he and Stephen were not guilty of murder by imitating the mannerisms and arguments his lawyers used during his trial. He even addressed the crowd as "Gentlemen of the Jury." This was followed by a short address in which he advised the audience "to repent of their sins." Edwards said his final words included, "I am prepared to go—and when I drop I expect to go right into Heaven. I bid you all farewell. I am going home to glory. I die in peace and hope to meet you all in that better world of glory." William then, "claimed the forgiveness of all and said he forgave all, and again bid the audience farewell."[80]

As the 3:00 pm time of execution had not been reached, hymns were sung and the ministers preached. For example, Bishop Loras of the Catholic Church, "read the story of the penitent thief, … admonishing all to serve and fear God and never sin against him and thus avoid the doom that awaited the young men so soon to be executed." Edwards said:

> Their chains were then knocked off, and the Sheriff conducted William to the drop and put the rope around his neck. While the rope was being put around the neck of Stephen we could see that William was apparently engaged in prayer. The caps were pulled over their faces, and in a few moments the Sheriff with one blow severed the cord, the drop

---

78. "The Execution," *Burlington Hawk-Eye*.

79. "Execution," *Iowa Territorial Gazette*.

80. "The Execution," *Burlington Hawk-Eye*. J. M. Reid, in *Sketches and Anecdotes*, 42, writing thirty-two years after the execution, said "Stephen was a tall finely formed, dark complexioned man with black hair, with a loud ringing voice, in which there was not the slightest tremor when he spoke." He said William "spoke well but was excited and trembled slightly, and his voice was not so loud or his manner so decided."

fell, and both were launched into eternity. Stephen's neck broke and he died without a struggle. William struggled nearly ten minutes before he was apparently dead.[81]

In 1914, a letter of an unidentified young lady who witnessed the hanging was discovered which said, "One of the brothers promised Mr. [Rev.] Coleman [of the Methodist Church] to confess if he could have a conversation with his brother. After that was allowed, he refused to say anything."[82] Eyewitness Henry Smith remembered William's death:

> He [William] stood near the north end of the trap and when the south end fell, it made an inclined plane down which his feet began to slide, until the tightening rope checked the motion the consequence was his neck was not broken, and he died of strangulation. He struggled in his agony, drawing up his limbs, relaxing them and again drawing them up, his muscles twitching and his limbs, relaxing them and again drawing them up, his muscles twining and his body in contortions.

Smith said it was a "sickening sight which the crowd gazed on the gruesome spectacle with horrified interest, varying of course with temperament and age." He added, "One woman fainted. It was said it was their sister."[83]

The editor of the *Hawk-Eye* attempted to express his tangled feelings about the way the brothers died. Commenting, "Thus ended the scene of their mortal existence," he expressed the hope "that the impression of it on the minds of all will be beneficial." After acknowledging, "public executions ordinarily in our opinion have a different tendency," he explained:

> Executions should be so conducted as to hold no inducements for the culprit to make a hero of himself. Are we uncharitable in thinking that the whole conduct of these young men at the gallows and on their way there, was to gain for themselves the title of heroes? Are we, after we knew that they had held out encouragement to one of their counsel and to others that they would confess, and that nothing probably but the presence of their sister prevented it?—When called upon to fulfil his special engagement to do this, William, who had seen and conversed with Stephen, declared that he could not do it— that if he revealed the secret the whole family would be murdered. At another time one

81. "The Execution," *Burlington Hawk-Eye* 7 (July 17, 1845): 2. Reid, in *Sketches and Anecdotes*, 42, said "wild crys [sic] of despair from their sisters [sic] rend[ed] the air as they fell, and a death like stillness outside of this reigned in the crowd of thousands …"

82. "Extract from a Letter Written Sixty-Nine Years Ago by a Young Woman Who Witnessed the Gruesome Spectacle. The Document was Found, Faded and Dim, in a Trunk in a Burlington House Recently," *Burlington Hawk-Eye* 201 (January 25, 1914): 1.

83. "Henry Smith's Story," *Burlington Hawk-Eye* 201 (January 25, 1914): 2. Smith added, "My sister, Mrs. Elsa Mast, who was present at the hangings, said, "I was only a little girl then but I remember many of the circumstances. Near everybody went, and I was foolish enough to go—to my regret afterwards for it was too or three weeks before I could banish the scene from my mind. It troubled me in my sleep. I never want to see another hanging."

of them said that they had taken an oath, and they might as well die with the secret as to break that oath. There must be some horrid secrets and oaths binding these secret societies at Nauvoo, which sets human life and common human allegiance at defiance. Nothing but the revelation of the righteous judgment of heaven can detect and bring to justice men thus bound together.[84]

Afterward

In what would have been a traumatic endeavor, Emeline Campbell returned the bodies of her brothers to Nauvoo on one of the steamers and had them buried in the Old Nauvoo City Cemetery.[85] Their presence was immediately objected to, and John Taylor said on July 20 during a public meeting that there was, "a great deal of dissatisfaction expressed to the people in general." William Smith objected and said, "We ought to show mercy to them after they were dead: from what he had heard of the evidence, it was not sufficient to hang them, and thought they might be innocent." Brigham Young ended the controversy by saying, "he knew them to be murderers and not innocent men; and he would not want them buried in his lot; he said he would sooner they buy a piece of ground remotely situated for the purchase." Taylor said he, "called a vote to know whether they should be moved or not," and then acknowledged "it was carried that they should be moved."[86]

Demise of the "Gadianton robbers"

The murder of John Miller set into motion a series of events in which William and Stephen Hodges were hanged, and Ervine and Amos Hodges were murdered. Thomas Brown remained in hiding and rejoined the Mormons in Iowa in 1847. Artemus Johnson quietly returned to Nauvoo and later accompanied the Mormons to Utah. Return Jackson Redden and Bill Hickman were compelled to remain within the Mormon society until they too joined in the move to Utah.

---

84. "The Execution," *Burlington Hawk-Eye* 7 (July 17, 1845): 2.

85. Emeline's nightmarish accomplishment is hard to quantify. It would have been compounded because of the physical changes William underwent as he slowly strangled. Dick Haws in, *Iowa and the Death Penalty: A Troubled Relationship 1834–1965* (Lexington, KY: Dick Haws, 2011), 8, explained, "when hanging goes wrong, the person dies a much more hideous death from strangulation, often with the eyes bulging, the face blue-grey, the tongue swollen and bitten in two."

86. Jessee, *John Taylor Nauvoo Journal*, 78, emphasis retained. Hosea Stout, in Brooks, *The Diary of Hosea Stout*, 1:53, said, "Elder Taylor Spake [sic] and mentioned about the dissatisfaction which was caused by the two Hodges who were hung at Burlington being buried here that he had been requested to mention it[.] there [sic] was remarks made for & against them remaining[.] the vote being put to the congregation it was almost unanimously decided that they should not remain in our burying ground." The *Nauvoo Neighbor* reported, "By a unanimous vote of the citizens of Nauvoo, the Hodges are to be removed from the graveyard of the saints, in a place to be specifically purchased for that purpose." See "Removal of the Hodges," *Nauvoo Neighbor* 3 (July 23, 1845): 2. It remains unclear if the bodies were removed.

Just as the murder of John Miller resulted in the shattering of the Mormon portion of the Banditti, the murder of Col. James Davenport led to hangings, imprisonment, and dissolution of the non-Mormon Banditti. The initial planning of the Davenport robbery took place at Nauvoo by the combined Banditti.[87] However, with their Mormon associates unable to participate due to the after-effects of the murders of Miller and Leiza, a group including Granville Young, John and Aaron Long, Judge Fox, Robert Birch and John Baxter carried out the robbery on July 4, 1845. Davenport was mortally wounded when a pistol accidentally discharged, and the gang widely scattered but were captured and returned to Illinois.[88] Granville Young and John and Aaron Long were hanged at Rock Island on October 29, 1845.[89] Judge Fox and Robert Birch either bribed their guards or broke jail, and John Baxter received a sentence of life in prison. William Redden was incarcerated for a year, but his father Grant escaped punishment when a juror refused to convict him. The demise of the non-Mormon part of the criminal association was guaranteed when Birch and Young freely disclosed gang secrets to impress the judiciary. The latter-day "Gadianton robbers" ceased to exist.

A few thoughts about some of the participants may be in order:

ARTEMUS JOHNSON—born on April 18, 1809 at Remsen, Oneida Co., New York, Johnson was ordained an elder at Commerce, Illinois, on October 5, 1839,[90] and married Almira Ayers the following month at Nauvoo.[91] Identified along with Thomas Brown's father Alanson as "notorious thieves," he defaulted on a $500 bond and fled Nauvoo.[92] Joseph Young indicated in a January 26, 1846, meeting with the Seventies, that Artemus Johnson was "cut off five years ago."[93] If that was the case, he may have been rebaptized, as Almira testified during the trial of Stephen and William Hodges that "he was a

---

87. Bonney, *Banditti of the Prairies*, 214.

88. The best source for the murder of Davenport, the capture of those accused, and their trials remains Bonney's *Banditti of the Prairies* and newspaper accounts. See for example, "Arrest and Trial of the Murderers of Col. Davenport," *The Davenport Gazette* 5 (October 16, 1845): 2.

89. The execution of Aaron Long did not go well. His rope broke and he was injured in the fall. Confusion reigned and a "shouting match" erupted as some in attendance loudly proclaimed being hanged once fulfilled the law. The majority, however, countered that a bad rope did not overturn a death sentence. Confusion reigned when the word spread that "a rescue had been attempted," and people "fled in all directions." The editor of the *Davenport Gazette* wrote, "evil teams dashed pell-mell through the crowd" but "not a person was hurt." Summarizing the chaotic event, the account said, "no accident occurred save the breaking in pieces of one wagon, Hats, shawls, chairs, and not a few shot guns belonging to the brave rifle company, who guarded the prisoner, were afterwards picked up on the field of bloodless confusion. The rope was quickly adjusted about the neck of Aaron Long, the plank upon which he stood knocked from under him and his cries were hushed in the spasmodic efforts of a dying man." "Trial and Execution of the Murderers," *The Davenport Gazette* 5 (October 30, 1845): 2.

90. "Proceedings of a General Conference ..." *Times and Seasons* 1 (December 1839): 30.

91. "Married," *Times and Seasons* 2 (February 1840): 64.

92. "Look out for Thieves," *Times and Seasons* 2 (December 15, 1840): 256.

93. "Jany. 26. 1845 Quorum of 70. In the 70 Hall 10 a.m.," typescript, Leonard J. Arrington Papers, series 9, box 12, folder 2, 3–4, in Special Collections, Merrill Library, Utah State University, Logan, Utah.

Mormon."[94] Since he was not identified with the murders as thoroughly as Thomas Brown and Stephen and William Hodges, he apparently quietly reintegrated into the Mormon community. He accompanied Brigham Young to Utah, and upon his return to Council Bluffs received a patriarchal blessing from Isaac Morley in December 1847. Historian Andrew Jenson said Johnson is thought to have died in Utah "many years ago."[95]

THOMAS BROWN—born in Steuben Co., New York, to Alanson Brown and Cynthia Dorcus Hurd, his father was a Mormon who was accused of stealing from non-Mormons in the Missouri period and was later banished from Nauvoo for stealing from the Mormons.[96] Brown was described by a person using the pseudonym "Alpha" that "[Thomas] Brown though scarce twenty-one is notorious in Hancock and the adjoining counties for stealing. He has been in jail in Brown County."[97] Following John Miller's murder, he went into hiding and managed to evade bounty hunters and lawmen. He reconnected with the Mormons near Winter Quarters where he joined with Orrin Porter Rockwell and Return Jackson Redden in hunting and scouting. Hosea Stout noted on February 12, 1847, "Today I learned and reported to Brigham that Tom Brown was threatening the lives of the 12."[98] He made it to the Great Salt Lake Valley in July and, after returning to Winter Quarters was, according to Andrew Jenson, "accidently" shot and killed in February 1848.[99] Historian Wallace Stegner said, "almost as soon as they reached the Missouri, Brown would get himself shot to death in a brawl in Council Bluffs."[100] Edward L. Kimball and Kenneth W. Godfrey additionally explained, "Hickman, [in] *Brigham's Destroying Angel*, 47, wrote that he killed 'a notorious horse thief, who had sworn to take the life of Orson Hyde.' This may have been Brown."[101]

WILLIAM (BILL) HICKMAN—Edward Bonney called him "one of the most notorious rascals unhung." He said Hickman was a "fugitive from justice for several larcenies he had committed in Lee [County, Iowa]"and called him a "notorious scoundrel."[102] The fact Hickman transferred land to help pay lawyers to defend Stephen and William Hodges on June 17, 1845, signifies his membership in the Banditti. His post-Nauvoo atrocities include the brutal murder of two unarmed Native American men in May 1849 "on the banks of the Masouria [*sic*] River." Joseph Young's description of the murders

94. "Trial for Murder," Burlington Hawk-Eye.

95. Andrew Jenson, *Latter-day Saint Encyclopedia* (Salt Lake City: Andrew Jenson Memorial Association and Deseret Press,), 4:709.

96. See "Look Out for Thieves," *Times and Seasons* 2 (December 15, 1840): 256.

97. "Shocking Murder," *Illinois State Register* 6 (May 23, 1845): 3.

98. Brooks, *Diary of Hosea Stout*, 1:236 n. 32.

99. Jenson, *LDS Biographical Encyclopedia*, 4:695.

100. Wallace Stegner, *The Gathering of Zion: The Story of the Mormon Trail: The Story of the Mormon Trail* (Lincoln: University of Nebraska Press, 1964), 126.

101. Edward L. Kimball and Kenneth W. Godfrey, "Law and Order at Winter Quarters," *Journal of Mormon History* 32 (Spring 2006): 126.

102. Bonney, *Banditti of the Prairies*, 230 and 256.

concludes with, "William Hickman is a cold Blooded Murderer and as such he stands Before Every tribunal of Justice in Heaven & on Earth and when the Judge of all the Earth Makes inquisition for Innocent Blood it will be found Dripping from the hands of William Hickman."[103]

RETURN JACKSON REDDEN—he was born on September 26, 1817, at Hiram, Ohio, to George Grant Redden and Adelia Higley Redden and arrived at Nauvoo in 1841. The fact that he transferred land to pay lawyers to represent Stephen and William Hodges on June 17, 1843, connects him with the Banditti at that time. Edward Bonney said he was told by Granville Young, who would be hanged for the murder of Col. Davenport, that he [Young] and Return Jackson robbed a Mormon man of $240.[104]

As previously explained, Return Jackson Redden was charged by Robert Birch in October 1845 with the murder of Ervine Hodges at Nauvoo. Birch, to avoid being hanged, turned state's evidence, and his "confessions" incriminated Grant Redden and sons Return Jackson and William. Grant and William were indicted as accessories before and after the fact and were arrested by a posse at Devil's Creek. Return Jackson was indicted as accessory after the fact, but Rock Island officials realized he would not be given up by the Mormons at Nauvoo because of the violent conflict between the Mormons and anti-Mormons in the countryside. Lyman E. Johnson, a Keokuk lawyer and distant relation of Return Jackson, was deputized by Rock Island officials to assist Sheriff James L. Bradley of Rock Island in arresting Return Jackson at Nauvoo.[105] On October 25, the steamboat *Sarah Ann* steamed up to port at Nauvoo with Sheriff Bradley of Rock Island on board with a warrant for the arrest of Return Jackson. Lyman Johnson met him on the main wharf to "consider arrangements for bailing his father and brother out of jail" when Bradley attempted to arrest him. When a brawl ensued, passengers rushed to help the sheriff, while angry Mormons rushed to protect their own. Bradley and Johnson received serious injuries, and Return Jackson remained at Nauvoo and would later accompany the Mormons to Utah.[106]

Accusations of post-Nauvoo criminal activity include James (Jim) Bridger complaining to Brigham Young in a letter dated July 16, 1848, that, "Jack Redding [*sic*] who Passed two five Dollar Bogus Gold Pieces upon us last fall."[107] In May 1852 *The Humboldt: Highroad of the West*, Dale L. Morgan cited a letter addressed to the

---

103. Joseph Young to Brigham Young, June 26, 1849, Brigham Young Office Files, CR1234 1, box 44, folder 1, Church History Library.

104. Bonney, *Banditti of the Prairies*, 77–93.

105. Bonney, *Banditti of the Prairies*, 217.

106. Shepard and Marquardt, *Lost Apostles*, 258–62.

107. "Mr. President Sir," Brigham Young Collection, July 16, 1848. Brigham Young Office Files. CR 1234 1, box 21 Church History Library.

Commissioner of Indian Affairs, from Major Jacob H. Holeman, which accused "a notorious character by the name of Reading" [*sic*] of being with a group of renegades, deserters and thieves" who plundered emigrants.[108] On June 29, 1854, Heber C. Kimball wrote to his son William, "Jack Redding and Rust are now undergoing their trial before Judge [Elias] Smith for horse stealing." In a postscript he added, "Jack Redding has received his sentence, viz., to be imprisoned three months and pay all expenses."[109] According to an article in the *Salt Lake Daily Tribune*, Return Jackson Redden and Jacob Huffman were indicted for the murder of Ike Potter and Charles Wilson.[110]

Final Thoughts

The criminal association studied in this article apparently began after the arrival of veteran non-Mormon thieves from the defunct William W. Brown and Josh Driscoll gangs in Nauvoo. It is safe to say that a small cabal that had coalesced by 1843 was generally living inconspicuously in the western part of Nauvoo by the Mississippi River. Their commitment to secrecy was successful, and their identities remained uncertain. One partial document found in the Des Moines County Courthouse at Burlington, Iowa, shows that Stephen Hodges was charged with stealing the horse of Robert Wright on September 14, 1842,[111] but this does not prove he was part of the banditti. No records were found documenting stealing by Ervine, Amos, or William. It is possible that Return Jackson Redden, William [Bill] Hickman, and Artemus Johnson belonged to the Banditti at the time of an April 6, 1843 conference and that the Hodges brothers joined thereafter. This possibility is strengthened by the fact that Amos participated in a church mission to New York State in April 1844.[112]

It turned out the Hodges were poor candidates for a secret criminal society because of their apparent mental instability, as reflected by the conduct of Ervine, William, and Stephen Hodges when they confronted Brigham Young and threatened to kill him. Lack of reasoning abilities was apparent when Amos Hodges informed on Judge Fox and Robert Birch, and when Ervine was publicly calling attention to

---

108. Dale L. Morgan, *The Humboldt: Highroad of the West* (New York: Farrar and Rinehart, 1943), 213–18.

109. "My dear son William," June 29, 1854, typescript Kimball Family Organization.

110. See "Criminal Trials," *Salt Lake Daily Tribune* 14 (November 10, 1877): 4. See also Frank Beckwith, "Shameful Friday: A Critical Study of the Mountain Meadows Massacre," HM 31255, Henry E. Huntington Library, San Marino, California.

111. Case File 675, Des Moines Court House, Burlington, Iowa.

112. Joseph Smith, Jr. *History of the Church of Jesus Christ of Latter-day Saints*, ed. B. H. Roberts, 2nd rev. ed., 7 vols. (Salt Lake City: Deseret News, 1932–51), 6:336. John Court testified at the trial of Stephen and William Hodges, "Was acquainted with prisoners in N. York, saw Stephen about a year ago in N. York, Amos was *a Mormon preacher* … Amos and Stephen were living in N. Y. last summer. Amos was preaching there three years ago." "Trial for Murder," *Burlington Hawk-Eye*. Emphasis retained.

his criminal associates. They were terrible role models for their even more mentally fragile brother William. As he was functioning near the lower range of "normal intelligence," William could likely have married, raised a family and lived respectfully with support and modeling but was instead taught to believe he was a bad outlaw. His acting out that fantasy seems to have destroyed him.[113]

The activities of the group of "Gadianton Robbers" or "Banditti of the Prairies" did much to add to the regional and national prejudice against the Mormons. But the group was actually an anomaly. Publication of their real and imagined activities, however, added to the prevailing myth that Nauvoo "was a den of thieves."[114]

And finally, a strange offshoot of the story of the Hodges brothers occurred when the *Cedar Rapids [Iowa] Gazette* printed a statement by seventy-four-year-old Mrs. Mary Hines, of Independence, Iowa, on January 7, 1910, alleging that Stephen and William Hodges had been unjustly hanged. She stated that her deceased husband, John W. Hines, had previously told her that he had been "a very wicked man" and had been a member of Edward Bonney's criminal gang in 1845. This account alleged that John Hines had told his wife that it was he and two accomplices who murdered John Miller and Henry Leiza and not the Hodges gang. Even so, this account is generally regarded as historically baseless.[115]

WILLIAM SHEPARD is a longtime member of the John Whitmer Historical Association and was past president for 2008–09. With H. Michael Marquardt, he has written *Lost Apostles: Forgotten Members of Mormonism's Original Quorum of Twelve*, which was published by Signature Books in 2014.

---

113. There are of course numerous books and articles which speak of the general lack of understanding and treatment for intellectually compromised individuals during this period. I recommend works on reformer Dorotha Dix and a new book by Ron Powers titled *No One Cares About Crazy People: The Chaos and Heartbreak of Mental Health in America* (New York: Hachette Books, 2017).

114. There were other thieves than those labeled the banditti of the prairies in and around Nauvoo. Kenneth W. Godfrey correctly said in "The Nauvoo Neighborhood: A Little Philadelphia or a Unique City Set Upon a Hill, *The Journal of Mormon* History 11 (1984): 96, "It becomes apparent that there was some crime in Nauvoo, perpetuated by Mormons and non-Mormons alike. However, it appears that after its initial settlement, there was probably no more crime in Nauvoo than in other frontier towns of similar size, but only more publicly when a criminal act occurred." See also, Godfrey, "Crime and Punishment in Mormon Nauvoo," 195–227; and my evaluation of the extent of Mormon stealing in "Marshaled and Disciplined for War": A Documentary Chronology of Conflict in Hancock County, Illinois 1839–1845," *John Whitmer Historical Association Journal* 33 (Fall/Winter 2013): 130–31.

115. See, Shepard, "The Notorious Hodges Brothers," 278.

——————— • ———————

The Nauvoo Council of Fifty Minutes

H. Michael Marquardt

Background

I N SEPTEMBER 2016 the LDS Church Historian's Press made available in print the early minutes of the Nauvoo, Illinois, Council or Quorum of Fifty, or King-dom of God of the Church of Jesus Christ of Latter Day Saints. Though the Council was in operation for only a short time in Nauvoo, the release of the minutes now allows scholars access to these vitally important deliberations.

Council meetings were held in Nauvoo during a three-month period in 1844: March, April, and May. They were recorded, copied, and based on memory and on the journal of William Clayton. Though there had been some discussion favoring destruction of the minutes, Clayton made sure that a historical record would con-tain what took place. Willard Richards was the recorder and Clayton the clerk. The organization commenced March 10–11, 1844.

Within the context of American history the Mormon movement was different from and yet the same as other religious organizations. Some thought that a New Jerusalem would be built on the American landscape.[1] In preparing for the second coming of Jesus, the Church of Christ had come to regard itself as the kingdom of God with a mission to spread the latter-day gospel throughout the world.[2] There was thus no need for a kingdom or government separate from this restored church or the US government. But that changed over time as a result of conflict within and outside the church. In 1838 an organization known as the Danites was formed.[3] W. W. Phelps thought it was treasonable "to set up a government within a Government."[4]

---

1. For example see Gershon Greenburg, *The Holy Land in American Religious Thought, 1620–1948* (Lanham, MD: University Press of America, 1994).

2. "Revelations ... A revelation on prayer, given October 30, 1831," *The Evening and the Morning Star* 1 (September 1832): 2, Independence, MO. See LDS and RLDS Doctrine and Covenants 65.

3. Dean C. Jessee, Mark Ashurst-McGee, and Richard L. Jensen, eds., *Journals, Volume 1: 1832–1839* (Salt Lake City: Church Historian's Press, 2008), 231, 293, 464.

4. Missouri General Assembly, *Document Containing the Correspondence, Orders, &c. in Relation to the Disturbances with the Mormons; and the Evidence Given before the Hon. Austin A. King, Judge of the Fifth Judicial Circuit of the*

During the Nauvoo period of church history there developed an inclination to form secret organizations. One such group was the Council of Fifty. Some thirty-five years ago two studies of this council were published but were limited to available historical records[5] because these three volumes of minutes were not available at the time. Although there seems to have been a problem in keeping the topics discussed in the meetings confidential, such is no longer the case.

Several early programs were commenced at Nauvoo by Joseph Smith in 1844. They included plans for westward migration of church headquarters toward the general areas of Texas, Oregon, California and the Rocky Mountains. After writing letters in November 1843 to a few presidential candidates on their views of the Mormons, Joseph Smith decided to become a candidate himself for president of the United States. His main publication on the subject, written for him by W.W. Phelps, was titled, *General Smith's Views of the Powers and Policy of the Government of the United States*, and was first published in Nauvoo in February 1844. Sidney Rigdon became Smith's running mate for the office of vice president.

Latter Day Saints still continued to view themselves, especially in Nauvoo, in a persecution mode, envisioning their actions as a defense of their rights under the Nauvoo Charter. Their view was that the US government was as much responsible for actions against them as were the states of Missouri and Illinois. As such, survival became an existential objective in the quest to protect their church and their leader Joseph Smith.[6]

Joseph Smith as Chairman of the Council

The council consisted of about fifty men who were bound by secrecy and sworn in allegiance to chairman Joseph Smith. Members of the Kingdom of God were forming a theocracy wherein the voice of God was to become the voice of the council. They envisioned their group as the kingdom that Daniel of the Old Testament saw coming out of a mountain and filling the earth. As recorded in the minutes, the name of the select organization was the result of a revelation pronounced by church president Joseph Smith on March 14.

> The name of the council was discussed and the Lord was pleased to give the following Revelation; Verily thus saith the Lord, this is the name by which you shall be called, The

---

State of Missouri, at the Court-House in Richmond, in a Criminal Court of Inquiry, begun November 12, 1838, on the trial of Joseph Smith, Jr., and others, for High Treason and Other Crimes Against the State (Fayette, Missouri: Printed at the office of the Boon's Lick Democrat, 1841), 122.

5. See D. Michael Quinn, "The Council of Fifty and Its Members, 1844–1945," *BYU Studies* 20 (Winter 1980): 163–97 and Andrew F. Ehat, "'It Seems Like Heaven Began on Earth': Joseph Smith and the Constitution of the Kingdom of God," *BYU Studies* 20 (Spring 1980): 253–79.

6. See Bill Shepard and H. Michael Marquardt, "Mortal Enemies: Mormons and Missourians 1839-1844," *John Whitmer Historical Association Journal* 36, no. 1 (Spring/Summer 2016): 35–80.

Kingdom of God and his Laws, with the keys and power thereof, and judgment in the hands of his servants. Ahman Christ.[7]

At a church conference on April 5, Sidney Rigdon of the First Presidency mentioned in his discourse: "When God sets up a system of salvation, he sets up a system of government; when I speak of a government I mean what I say; I mean government that shall rule over temporal and spiritual affairs."[8] Six days later, at a meeting of the Council of Fifty, Rigdon presented a history of the council and said, "The design was to form a Theocracy according to the will of Heaven, planted without any intention to interfere with any government of the world. We wish to have nothing to do with them. . . . It is nevertheless necessary to be careful and prudent inasmuch as there is so much disposition in the minds of men to cry treason at every thing we do." Rigdon "said further that we had chosen our beloved Prest. Joseph Smith as our standing chairman, and our mouth between us and our God."[9]

Joseph Smith Received as Prophet, Priest and King

It was also in this secret group of men where they received "from this time henceforth and forever, Joseph Smith, as our Prophet, Priest & King, and uphold him in that capacity in which God has anointed him." The council adjourned the morning meeting "with shouts of Hossanna [sic] to God and the Lamb Amen and Amen."[10] This occurred on April 11, 1844, at a meeting in the Nauvoo Masonic Hall, but the action did not remain a secret for long. A report published in New York from an individual who visited Nauvoo read:

> In many respects, Joe [Smith] has the advantage over his illustrious predecessor [Mahomet]: he, Joe, is not only Prophet, but is also Mormon King, and in his triune function of Prophet, Priest and King, he lords it over God's heritage with such a strict eye to the Lord's treasury, that he will by and by be enabled to present the world with a faint imitation of the outward glories of Solomon's temple.[11]

At the April 18 council meeting Elder David Yearsley (1808–49), a merchant and council member, commented on setting up the kingdom:

---

7. Council of Fifty, Minutes, March 14, 1844, in Matthew J. Grow, Ronald K. Esplin, Mark Ashurst-McGee, Gerrit J. Dirkmaat, and Jeffrey D. Mahas, eds., *Council of Fifty, Minutes, March 1844–January 1846*, vol. 1 of the Administrative Records series of *The Joseph Smith Papers* (Salt Lake City: Church Historian's Press, 2016), 48–49 (hereafter as *Council of Fifty, Minutes*). The minutes are located in MS 30055, Council of Fifty record books, 1844–1846, LDS Church History Library, Salt Lake City.

8. "Conference Minutes," *Times and Seasons* 5, no. 9 (May 1, 1844): 524.

9. *Council of Fifty, Minutes*, April 11, 1844, 88–89.

10. *Council of Fifty, Minutes*, April 11, 1844, 95–96.

11. "Life in Nauvoo," April 25th, 1844, in *New-York Daily Tribune* vol. 4, no. 41, whole no. 975, May 28, 1844, p. 4, column 1.

We can try to elect our president for a scare crow, but how can a man be elected president when he is already proclaimed king. Can he give up his office for a smaller one.[?] He is perfectly willing to go and electioneer, to blind the eyes of the people, but he wants to see our king upheld in his office here.[12]

Joseph Smith was careful in cautioning council members, "It is not wisdom to use the term 'king' all the while. Let us use the term 'proper source' instead of 'king' and it will be all understood and no person can take advantage."[13]

Excommunication of William Law, Jane Law and Others

There was pressure from within the church by stalwart William Law, recently a member of the First Presidency, against what he regarded as secret practices not included in the teachings found in the Book of Mormon or the Doctrine and Covenants. The April 18 Council of Fifty meeting ended about 5:30 p.m., followed by a special "council of the authorities"[14] at 6:00 p.m. While six members of the Quorum of Twelve and seven of the Nauvoo High Council were present, this was neither a High Council meeting nor a council under Bishop Newel K. Whitney, who was also in attendance. Of the thirty-two men present at the meeting, twenty-three were members of the Council of Fifty.[15] Notably, neither Joseph Smith nor Sidney Rigdon attended. William and Jane Law and three other church members were excommunicated, and a notice to that effect was printed in the *Times and Seasons*:

> Nauvoo, April, 18, 1844.
>
> Robert D. Foster, Wilson Law, William Law, and Jane Law of Nauvoo; and Howard Smith, of Scott county, Illinois, for unchristian like conduct, were cut off from the Church of Jesus Christ of Latter Day Saints, by the authorities of said church, and ordered to be published in the Times and Seasons.
>
> W. RICHARDS,
> Church Recorder.[16]

Even after this event there was still time for negotiation and reconciliation between the church and the Law family. At the May 6, 1844 Council of Fifty meeting Sidney Rigdon "reported that he had a labored with the Laws without accomplishing any thing, but judged that they had taken a course which they never would

---

12. *Council of Fifty, Minutes*, April 18, 1844, 125.

13. *Council of Fifty, Minutes*, April 18, 1844, 128.

14. Willard Richards Journal, April 18, 1844, MS 1490, Church History Library.

15. See Joseph Smith Journal, kept by Willard Richards, April 18, 1844, Church History Library; also in Andrew H. Hedges, Alex D. Smith, and Brent M. Rogers, eds., *Journals, Volume 3: May 1843–June 1844* (Salt Lake City: Church Historian's Press, 2015), 231–32.

16. *Times and Seasons* 5, no. 8 (April 15, 1844): 511, printed circa April 20, 1844.

become reconciled." The Council of Fifty turned the offenders over "to the buffetings of Satan."[17] William Law afterwards helped establish the *Nauvoo Expositor*, a newspaper that would soon publish negative articles against both the church and the Nauvoo city charter.[18] Soon afterwards William Law would become a leader in a reformed church.

Constitution of the Kingdom of God

A committee was appointed to write a constitution and bylaws of the Council of Fifty but had been unable to complete the assignment. Accordingly, Joseph Smith proclaimed a revelation on April 25 as follows:

> Verily thus saith the Lord, ye are my constitution, and I am your God, and ye are my spokesmen. From henceforth do as I shall command you. Saith the Lord.[19]

Sidney Rigdon, Joseph Smith's vice presidential running mate, said on May 6 "as the Lord God lives Joseph shall be President next term and I will follow him."[20] Six days later Smith proclaimed in a speech near the Nauvoo temple, "I calculate to be one of the Instruments of setting up the Kingdom of Daniel, by the word of the Lord, and I intend to lay a foundation that will revolutionize the whole world."[21]

The last meeting of the fifty was held on May 25, 1844, with Joseph Smith in attendance. Shortly thereafter on June 7, the only issue of the accusatory *Nauvoo Expositor* was published, and twenty days later Joseph and Hyrum Smith lay dead of murder at Carthage jail.

Brigham Young as Chairman of the Council

The first meeting of the Council of Fifty following the death of Joseph Smith was held on February 4, 1845. This initiated three clusters of meetings that would be held in Nauvoo: February 4–May 10, 1845; September 9–October 4, 1845; and January 1846. Wanting nothing to do with the US government, members instead focused on five topics: (1) Brigham Young as successor to Joseph Smith; (2) the gentiles' rejection of the gospel; (3) confirmation of Brigham Young as prophet, priest and king; (4) plans for deputizing Indians to assist in the mission; and (5) plans for the western migration.

---

17. *Council of Fifty, Minutes*, May 6, 1844, 152, 154.

18. [No title], *Nauvoo Expositor* 1 (June 7, 1844): 2, column 3.

19. *Council of Fifty, Minutes*, April 25, 1844, 136–37.

20. *Council of Fifty, Minutes*, May 6, 1844, 158.

21. Discourse reported by Thomas Bullock, May 12, 1844, Joseph Smith Collection, MS 155, box 4, folder 6, Church History Library.

In early 1845 the first copies of a *Proclamation of the Twelve Apostles of the Church of Jesus Christ, of Latter-Day Saints. To all the Kings of the World; To the President of the United States of America; To the Governors of the several States; And to the Rulers and People of all Nations: Greetings* were published in New York. The proclamation was composed by Council of Fifty member Parley P. Pratt and proclaimed, "Know ye:— That the kingdom of God has come: as has been predicted by ancient prophets, and prayed for in all ages; even that kingdom which shall fill the whole earth, and shall stand for ever."[22]

Brigham Young the Successor to Joseph Smith

At the first council meeting after Joseph Smith's death, held on February 4, 1845, it was confirmed that Brigham Young was "president of this quorum" and "president of the Kingdom of God."[23] Orson Pratt said it was "self evident that the president of the church stands as the head of this council."[24] Willard Richards told Council members, "Instead of saying K-i-n-g say chairman." As indicated by William Clayton in the minutes, Young was the "legal successor of president Joseph as our head."[25]

Members of the council knew there were leaks of what was discussed in their meetings. W. W. Phelps commented, "'Tis not yet a year since this council was first organized, yet, some have told what has passed here although under the most solemn obligations of secrecy."[26] Orrin Porter Rockwell said "those [who] leaked out shall pay the forfeit by the loss of his head; if I find them."[27]

The minutes of the special conference for April 7, 1845, included the proposal by Apostle George A. Smith "that we acknowledge President Brigham Young as the President of the Quorum of the Twelve Apostles to this Church, and nation, and all nations, and also the President of the whole Church of Latter Day Saints," which vote was carried unanimously.[28] The minutes were edited for publication in the *Times*

---

22. *Proclamation of the Twelve Apostles of the Church of Jesus Christ, of Latter-Day Saints. To all the Kings of the World; To the President of the United States of America; To the Governors of the several States; And to the Rulers and People of all Nations: Greetings* (New York, April 6, 1845), 1.

23. *Council of Fifty, Minutes*, February 4, 1845, 221.

24. *Council of Fifty, Minutes*, February 4, 1845, 223.

25. *Council of Fifty, Minutes*, February 4, 1845, 224–25.

26. *Council of Fifty, Minutes*, February 4, 1845, 220.

27. *Council of Fifty, Minutes*, February 4, 1845, 224.

28. General Church Minutes, CR 100 318, box 1, folder 32, April 7, 1845, Church History Library. Other individuals mentioned Brigham Young as church president. See Samuel James to S[idney]. Rigdon, January 28, 1845, *Latter Day Saints' Messenger and Advocate* 1, no. 9 (March 1, 1845): 130, column 2, Pittsburgh, PA; Daniel Davis Diary, MS 1676, folder 1, 12, Church History Library; Appointment of David Candland to a mission in England, January 22, 1846, signed by Brigham Young "President of the church of Jesus Christ of Latter Day Saints," copy in my possession. See also D. Michael Quinn, *The Mormon Hierarchy: Origins of Power* (Salt Lake City: Signature Books in association with Smith Research Associates, 1994), 178, 648, 650–51.

and Seasons, eliminating the phrase, "nation, and all nations, and also the President of the whole Church of Latter Day Saints" and adding the word "generation" to read "that we acknowledge President Brigham Young is the president of the quorum of the Twelve apostles to this church and generation."[29]

The Gentiles Have Rejected the Gospel[30]

Mormon scriptures predicted a time when the fullness of the gospel would be rejected by the gentiles. From that point the gospel would go to the house of Israel, of which the American Indians were alleged to be a remnant. This would be considered in prophetic words that "the times of the Gentiles be fulfilled."[31] The concept of the gentiles' rejection was discussed in Council of Fifty meetings.

William Clayton did not attend the meeting of February 27, 1845, as he was ill. In separate minutes of the "Meeting of the Twelve & others," recorded by clerk Thomas Bullock, it included the comment of W. W. Phelps that "the Kingdom is <now> rent from the Gentiles."[32] Two days later council president Brigham Young explained, "The gentiles have rejected the gospel and we will carry it to the branch of the house of Israel in the west. Let the gentiles remain in ignorance unless they will come to the standard."[33]

This discussion continued in the month of March through the next four meetings of the Council. George Miller said the "gentiles have rejected every thing that belongs to salvation" and "the fullness of the gentiles has come in."[34]

At the March 11 meeting Brigham Young said, "He don[']t care about preaching to the gentiles any longer" but "feels as Lyman Wight said let the damned scoundrels be killed, let them be swept off from the earth, and then we can go and be baptized for them." Young continued, "The gentiles have rejected the gospel, and where shall we go to preach. We cannot go any where but to the house of Israel ... This is the last call we will make to them and if they don[']t listen to it we will sweep them out of existance [existence]." Heber Kimball agreed.[35]

---

29. "Conference Minutes," *Times and Seasons* 6, no. 7 (April 15, 1845): 870.

30. See William Shepard, "The Concept of a 'Rejected Gospel' in Mormon History, Part 1," *Journal of Mormon History* 34, no. 2 (Spring 2008): 130–81.

31. *Book of Mormon* (Palmyra [New York]: E. B. Grandin, 1830), 487–88; A Book of Commandments, for the Government of the Church of Christ (Independence [MO]: W. W. Phelps & Co., 1833), 4:5–6 (March 1829); 48:25–27 (March 1831).

32. *Council of Fifty, Minutes*, in printed Appendix 1, February 27, 1845, 533, angle brackets indicate words above the line. See also Jedediah S. Rogers, ed., *The Council of Fifty: A Documentary History* (Salt Lake City: Signature Books, 2014), 83.

33. *Council of Fifty, Minutes*, March 1, 1845, 255.

34. *Council of Fifty, Minutes*, March 4, 1845, 289.

35. *Council of Fifty, Minutes*, March 11, 1845, 299–301.

On March 18 Young confirmed what he had stated the previous week. Orson Spencer expressed his feelings, "Our salvation is the destruction of the gentiles and their destruction will be our salvation."[36] Young stated, "The kingdom is rent from the gentiles, and has been ever since this council was organised."[37]

At the church conference of April 8 Heber C. Kimball "proposed to withdraw fellowship from the Gentiles' eniquity [iniquity], which was done by a unanimous vote" and it was explained: "Now they are disfellowshipt."[38] Brigham Young said "that, by martyring the Prophet and Patriarch, the Gentiles have rejected the gospel."[39] During the next conference in October, Apostle Kimball mentioned, "At the last conference, a vote was passed that the Gentiles were cut off; and now, why do you want to labor for them. Inasmuch as the Gentiles reject us, lo! we turn to the Jews."[40]

Brigham Young Confirmed as Prophet, Priest and King

Some new members were inducted into the council on March 1. They voted in the affirmative to "receive Prest. B. Young as successor of Prest. Joseph Smith and prophet, priest, and king to this kingdom forever after."[41] On March 4 those present "all voted to sustain Prest Young in his place as standing chairman, Prophet, Priest, and King." Heber C. Kimball, filling in as chairman for this meeting, "said that this was the kingdom which Daniel saw would be set up in the last days which would overthrow and subdue all other kingdoms."[42]

Beyond the Rocky Mountains

Discussions during the next three March meetings included harsh words of Brigham Young as summarized by the clerk: "in regard to going beyond the rocky mountains, he don[']t feel like it, it is so far to go there, and have to come back to kill off these cursed scoundrels."[43] Orson Pratt thought "to read the minutes seems to him to be a waste of time."[44]

It was not always clear where President Young intended the Mormons to place their new home. He said "it was Joseph[']s mind that the head of California Bay was

---

36. *Council of Fifty, Minutes,* March 18, 1845, 335.

37. *Council of Fifty, Minutes,* March 18, 1845, 338.

38. "Speech Delivered by Heber C. Kimball," April 8, 1845 in *Times and Seasons* 6, no. 13 (July 15, 1845): 973.

39. "The Conference," *Nauvoo Neighbor* 2, no. 50 (April 16, 1845): 2.

40. "Conference Minutes," April 8, 1845, *Times and Seasons* 6, no. 16 (November 1, 1845): 1012.

41. *Council of Fifty, Minutes,* March 1, 1845, 256.

42. *Council of Fifty, Minutes,* March 4, 1845, 278.

43. *Council of Fifty, Minutes,* March 11, 1845, 303.

44. *Council of Fifty, Minutes,* March 18, 1845, 325.

the place for us where we could have commercial advantages, but he also proposed other places for our consideration."[45] John Taylor said "We ask no favors of the United States of any kind nor never mean to."[46] Concerning the command to build the Nauvoo House, Young explained:

> It is a commandment from God through the prophet Joseph to build that house and shall we say we can[']t build it? no. If we say we can build it, we can do it. There are sacred records deposited in the foundation of that house and it is our duty to build the house and cover up those records.[47]

After hearing a report from John M. Bernhisel, counselor John Taylor said he was much pleased:

> Sufficient information has been given to prove that it is a good place for the saints to make a location, that they may build a City on the Coast of the Pacific and carry the gospel to the other part of the globe. This would be a good place for the time being, there is plenty of cattle and provisions of every kind. We will soon be independent of this nation, and we will be the head and not the tail.[48]

Shod with the Preparation of the Gospel of Peace

Apostle Heber C. Kimball said in his discourse at an April 8 church conference that he wanted the church members to finish the Nauvoo Temple and take stock in the Nauvoo House. He quoted Ephesians 6:15 (KJV), "And your feet shod with the preparation of the gospel of peace." But in this case the reference was to having weapons, like knives, guns and rifles that could be used against others. Kimball asked and answered:

> What is the object do you suppose of making the proclamation for all the saints to gather in, from all the United States, if we want to send them back again? We want them here, that they may help us to build the Temple, and the Nauvoo House; and want them to bring their firelocks, and learn to use them, and keep them well cleaned and loaded, and primed, so that they will go off the first shot, that every man may be in

---

45. *Council of Fifty, Minutes*, March 18, 1845, 328.

46. *Council of Fifty, Minutes*, March 18, 1845, 330.

47. *Council of Fifty, Minutes*, March 18, 1845, 344. The list of items deposited in the cornerstone of the Nauvoo House on October 2, 1841 included the original Book of Mormon manuscript. Recorded in the Book of the Law of the Lord under the date of December 29, 1841, see Andrew H. Hedges, Alex D. Smith, and Richard Lloyd Anderson, eds., *Journals, Volume 2: December 1841–April 1843* (Salt Lake City: Church Historian's Press, 2011), 19–20.

48. *Council of Fifty, Minutes*, March 22, 1845, 352.

readiness, and prepared, that is, every man shod with the preparation of the gospel of peace; (holding up his cane as a sample;) that is the way.[49]

What Kimball was referencing in this passage was clarified in the Council of Fifty minutes. At the first Council meeting after the April conference Peter Haws "said he had long contemplated the means whereby cousin Lemuel could be shod with the preparation of the gospel of peace." "Preparation of the gospel of peace" was explained in a footnote: "This phrase was used by Latter-day Saints at this time to describe being armed."[50] Haws commented, "The Indians think nothing of going two or three thousand miles, and whenever it is made known to them, that they can have a preparation of the gospel to administer to this nation they will go into it."[51] The idea was to give weapons to the American Indians.

The minutes reported that John Taylor "believes in every one of the Indian tribes being shod with the preparation of the gospel."[52] Charles C. Rich said, "we should have the pulling of the strings, and that we should have the influence with the Indians and not any other nation. He would be glad to have the Indians put in possession of the arms, but let us have the influence of dictating and controlling the whole matter."[53]

Theodore Turley, who had been commissioned on March 18 to make Bowie knives and fifteen-shooters (rifles), "said he had been appointed to go to work and make some tools for the preparation of the gospel" and needed a larger shop.[54]

In May Thomas Bullock recorded Brigham Young as saying:

I want you all to be shod with the preparat[ion]n. of the Gospel – have your firelocks clean – be ready at a moments warning – to slaughter all that come – they will find death here – c [and] hell will follow after – our enemies if they tho[ugh]t. we were not prepared, wo[ul]d. be upon us – we have influence in the world – every one be peaceable, atte[n]d. to their own bus[iness]: c [and] if an enemy comes to destroy me or my family I wo[ul]d. send them to hell across lots.[55]

---

49. "Speech Delivered by Heber C. Kimball," April 8, 1845, *Times and Seasons* 6, no. 13 (July 15, 1845): 971. The local newspaper made an interesting reference to the Nauvoo cane, "It is becoming quite fashionable for gentlemen to possess *a Nauvoo cane*; and the good people of this city of peace, also use *a cane*,—but the point of the staff, is, to have it 'shod with the preparation of the gospel.'" "Nauvoo Canes," *Nauvoo Neighbor* 2, no. 52 (April 30, 1845): 2, column 5, emphasis retained. Kimball's speech was reprinted in the *Warsaw Signal* 2 (October 22, 1845):1.

50. *Council of Fifty, Minutes,* April 11, 1845, 403, and note 665.

51. *Council of Fifty, Minutes,* April 11, 1845, 408.

52. *Council of Fifty, Minutes,* April 11, 1845, 406.

53. *Council of Fifty, Minutes,* April 11, 1845, 408.

54. *Council of Fifty, Minutes,* April 11, 1845, 416.

55. General Church Minutes, CR 100 318, Box 1, folder 33, May 4, 1845, Church History Library.

At the May 10 Council meeting Heber C. Kimball "moved that we declare ourselves an independant [*sic*] nation," and Orson Pratt "said he did not think it necessary, inasmuch as the nation has already made us independant." Brigham Young "stated that through his advise brother Turley has commenced making fifteen shooters, and has one here for a sample. He wants some of one of the brethren to buy it, that Turley can send to St Louis and get some more barrels. The Gun was sold to W. [Willard] Richards."[56]

More Plans for the Western Migration

At the first meeting in September Brigham Young indicated "that there is not much difficulty in sending people beyond the mountains. We have designed sending them somewhere near the Great Salt Lake and after we get there, in a little time we can work our way to the head of the California Bay, or the Bay of the St [San] Francisco."[57] Six days later Young wrote in a letter to Samuel Brannan, "I wish you together with your press[,] paper and ten thousand of the brethren were now in California at the Bay of St. Francisco, and if you can clear yourself and go there do so and we will meet you there."[58]

The Council of Fifty was still making considerations on where to locate in January 1846. In their next-to-last meeting William Clayton recorded in the minutes concerning Brigham Young, "When we leave here his mind is to go just beyond the Rocky mountains, somewhere on the Mexican claim and the United States will have no business to come there and if they do we will treat them as enemies."[59]

Summary

We have learned from the minutes that both Joseph Smith and Brigham Young were accepted in their chairmanships as prophet, priest and king in this latter-day "Kingdom of God." Many of the ideas planned in Council meetings, thought to be important at the time, would never occur. William Shepard explained:

> After the deaths of Brigham Young in 1877 and Orson Pratt in 1881, the doctrine of Gentile rejection was rarely mentioned. Reasons for its decline include the Church's distancing itself from doctrines which antagonized non-Mormons, a transition away from teaching that the millennium was imminent, and the fact that the doctrine impeded

---

56. *Council of Fifty, Minutes*, May 10, 1845, 454.

57. *Council of Fifty, Minutes*, September 9, 1845, 472.

58. Brigham Young office files, Brigham Young to Samuel Brannan, September 15, 1845, retained copy, CR 1234 1, box 16, folder 4, Church History Library. Printed in Will Bagley, ed., *Scoundrel's Tale: The Samuel Brannan Papers* (Spokane, WA: Arthur H. Clark Company, 1999), 91–92. The words "and we will meet you there" were omitted when the Manuscript History of Brigham Young was compiled.

59. *Council of Fifty, Minutes*, January 11, 1846, 513.

the missionary program. Another important reason was that the Church was beginning its slow transition from a posture of confrontation with the United States to an attitude that supporting the nation in times of crisis was a patriotic and religious duty.[60]

The minutes indicate the existence of big projects that would never take place. The death of Joseph Smith would abruptly terminate his presidential campaign. Under Brigham Young's leadership there would be no alliance with the American Indians to form a force against the US government. Missionaries would not depart to the Pacific Islands as planned. But such outcomes would hardly be problematic to council members since the "Kingdom of God" would be moving forward regardless. The plan to move west was to them the overriding concern. But conflict with the United States government would yet resume years later.[61]

With the publication of the Nauvoo Council of Fifty minutes by the Church Historian's Press, one might now hope that further advances in scholarship and history would follow with the publication of additional historical records, such as the remaining minutes of the Council of Fifty and the Nauvoo journals of William Clayton. A recent compilation of articles using the Nauvoo minutes has started the process.[62] In the final analysis, we should be grateful to those who have made this wealth of documentary records of the Latter Day Saint movement available for professional study.

H. MICHAEL MARQUARDT (research@xmission.com) is an independent historian and research consultant. He is on the editorial board of the *John Whitmer Historical Association Journal*. He is the compiler of *Early Patriarchal Blessings of The Church of Jesus Christ of Latter-day Saints* (Smith Pettit Foundation, 2007); *Later Patriarchal Blessings of The Church of Jesus Christ of Latter-day Saints* (Smith Pettit Foundation, 2012); author of *Joseph Smith's 1828–1843 Revelations* (Xulon Press, 2013) and co-author with William Shepard of *Lost Apostles: Forgotten Members of Mormonism's Original Quorum of Twelve* (Signature Books, 2014).

---

60. William Shepard, "The Concept of a 'Rejected Gospel' in Mormon History, Part 1," *Journal of Mormon History* 34, no. 2 (Spring 2008): 153.

61. See William P. MacKinnon, ed., *At Sword's Point, Part 1: A Documentary History of the Utah War to 1858* (Norman, OK: Arthur H. Clark Company, an imprint of the University of Oklahoma Press, 2008) and *At Sword's Point, Part 2: A Documentary History of the Utah War, 1858-1859* (Norman, OK: Arthur H. Clark Company, an imprint of the University of Oklahoma Press, 2016).

62. Matthew J. Grow and R. Eric Smith, eds, *The Council of Fifty: What the Records Reveal about Mormon History* (Provo, UT: Religious Studies Center, Brigham Young University, in cooperation with Deseret Book, 2017).

The Historical Attachment of Nauvoo for Community of Christ

Mark A. Scherer

I N MID-APRIL 2002, I walked over to a nice podium on a rostrum in a large hotel complex in Pasadena, California. The invitation to be there came from the good folks of Sunstone West, and they asked me to provide a banquet keynote. To frame my talk, they presented interesting questions asking about what the Community of Christ/Reorganized Church[1] position was on events in Nauvoo during the time of Mormon occupation. They wanted to know about our view of Joseph Smith Jr. and Emma Hale Smith, polygamy, John C. Bennett, how we viewed events at the Carthage jail, and William and Jane Law. They provided a number of other questions—far more than I could reasonably address given the amount time allocated for my keynote.

These excellent discussion topics were presented to me in the form of questions. As I surveyed their inquiries, it occurred to me that these had not been asked of me from within my own leadership during my then eight-year tenure in the church historian's office. From my musing at their insightful questions, the title of presentation emerged: "Answering Questions No Longer Asked." *Sunstone Magazine* eventually published the talk.[2] Now, some fifteen years later, these questions are posed again here at the JWHA conference.

Before I go any further, let me state that Community of Christ does not take "official positions" in matters of church history. Rather, today on the World Church website are a list of nine principles that assist the members in dealing responsibly in matters of church history.[3] Hopefully, therefore, you will not assume that the thoughts I present today have any official authority other than that which comes

---

1. At the time of the invitation, the official name change was effectuated just a few months earlier.

2. Mark A. Scherer, "Answering Questions No Longer Asked: Nauvoo, Its Meaning and Interpretation in the RLDS/Community of Christ Church," *Sunstone: Mormon Experience, Scholarship, Issues, & Art* 123 (July 2002): 28–32.

3. The church's official statement on the institution's philosophical approach to matters of its history can be found on the website at http://www.cofchrist.org/church-history-principles.

from a twenty-year perspective from the retired occupant of world church historian's chair.

Evolution of Thought

There has been a noticeable evolution of thought on the connection of Nauvoo within the Reorganized Church/Community of Christ tradition. Early in the Reorganization, church historian Heman C. Smith addressed the Nauvoo Era and its perceived heresies with emotion. The only temple ordinance embraced by the Reorganization was baptism for the dead, but then only for the opening five years. The "Prairie Saints" saw polygamy as the great evil emerging from Nauvoo and laid blame for the aberrant marital practice squarely at the feet of pariah John Cook Bennett.[4] A generation later his daughter, Inez Smith Davis, in her *The Story of the Church*, redirected fire away from Bennett and instead toward Brigham Young.[5]

Until the second half of the twentieth century the Reorganized Church understood Nauvoo in binary terms: good (Joseph Smith Jr.) versus bad (Brigham Young). For the church headquartered in Salt Lake City, Nauvoo represented the crowning achievement of Latter Day Saintism, and for the one headquartered in Independence, Nauvoo represented the movement's "dark and cloudy days." Thus, events of the Nauvoo era, from 1839–45, had become ground zero in the historical and theological boundary separating the two major faith traditions of Latter Day Saintism.

Reorganized Church member Robert Bruce Flanders, in his *Nauvoo: Kingdom on the Mississippi*, that first appeared in November 1965, exploded the binitarian approach as he offered a far more scholarly synthesis that exposed the complexity of Nauvoo.[6] The Flanders work had a considerable impact among church leadership when they met in a series of Joint Council Seminars starting in 1967. Some among the leadership rose up in protest as the reverberations of the Flanders writing spread across the North American church.[7]

Although widely appreciated among the community of history scholars and just plain history buffs within the Reorganized Church tradition, the passing of time saw a declining relevance of Nauvoo (and church history in general) to the overall church program. The value of Nauvoo went into a glide path as it became a battleground

---

4. Joseph Smith and Heman C. Smith, *History of the Church of Jesus Christ of Latter Day Saints*, Vol 2, (Lamoni, IA, Board of Publications of the Reorganized Church of Jesus Christ of Latter Day Saints), 732.

5. Inez Smith Davis, *The Story of the Church*, , (Independence, MO, Herald Publishing House, 12th ed, 1981), 489.

6. Robert Bruce Flanders, *Nauvoo: Kingdom on the Mississippi* (Urbana: University of Illinois Press), 1965.

7. Even before the release of *Kingdom on the Mississippi*, Flanders received resistance from Graceland president Harvey Grice. Then in the spring of 1966, shortly after the release of *Kingdom on the Mississippi*, author Flanders was pressed for his interpretative approach by church officials. For a discussion of the difficulties that Flanders endured because of his writings see Robert Bruce Flanders, "Nauvoo on My Mind," *John Whitmer Historical Association Journal* 23 (2003): 14–15.

for church docents who defended the primacy of the Reorganized Church against all comers, especially LDS Mormons, as "the only true church." When the Reorganization moved into international cultures the glide path steepened even more. For some in the next generation of church leadership, events of Nauvoo made possibly for an interesting story while others viewed Nauvoo as source of contention only to be avoided. Neither did anything to reverse the glide toward irrelevance.

Fast forwarding to 2010, Community of Christ sponsored a church heritage reunion on the church campgrounds up the hill here in Nauvoo. The event was timed to commemorate the 150th anniversary of the Reorganization. As world church historian, it behooved me to guide the reunion planning committee. We structured the week around the theme of the University of the City of Nauvoo, and the response was huge. With hundreds present, this was the largest reunion I have ever attended, with participants from all over the United States, including Hawaii and Canada. Guest instructors were appointed faculty members and taught classes through the week while I served as Nauvoo University Chancellor. President-emeritus Wallace B. Smith, Community of Christ seminary dean Don Compier, and scholar-historian Dan Vogel served on the faculty teaching classes. Those who finished their classes received a diploma for their efforts. On commemorative occasions such as this reunion, Nauvoo retained its allure.

Moving to Today

So what place does Nauvoo occupy within Community of Christ today? It would be hazardous for any responsible historian to summarize in just a few words the impact of Nauvoo on today's members of Community of Christ—the spectrum of opinion is far too broad. Some communitarians approach Nauvoo with the same affection as their Salt Lake cousins. Some communitarians see Nauvoo as the citadel for theological radicalism that veered the movement out of the Christian mainstream. I would estimate that the rest of the church membership views Nauvoo somewhere between the two extremes.

Today all Community of Christ historic sites, including Nauvoo, are administered as an "affiliate organization." The church obviously owns them, but our historic sites program is intended to be mostly self-funding, that is, not covered in the world church budget. A corporate body of the church leadership appoints a historic sites foundation board to provide overall direction with each site having its own program. For twenty years I served mostly in an *ex officio* capacity.

You have never met a group of people more dedicated to the preservation of the Community of Christ historic sites than the Historic Sites Foundation Board. Their mission supports preserving and sharing the Community of Christ historic sites with present and future generations. They raise funds and resources for the preservation and development of the sites. They assist in the acquisition of appropriate artifacts for use at each site. They raise awareness of the benefits and needs of each site. The board recruits volunteers for guiding, site maintenance, and provision of ongoing needs. They advise site staff on such things as interpretation and development of educational programs.[8]

I mention the Historic Sites Foundation because it will have a crucial role in the future disposition and contribution of Nauvoo to the overall church program. But going forward, the greatest challenge that Nauvoo faces is not in its care and keeping. Physically the site is in good condition, thanks to the support of the foundation board and the excellent onsite administration. The site historical interpretation is strong.

Rather, the greatest challenge may be an intangible. Since Nauvoo has always been in search of relevance to many Community of Christ leaders and members, it has become vulnerable. Nauvoo cannot expect to generate relevance simply by being a summer vacation stop for only handfuls of Community of Christ members and busloads full of Mormons.

Haun's Mill: Nauvoo's Cautionary Tale

Let me be clear. My thoughts today are not an indictment but for me just a statement of an obvious reality. The lack of relevance to the world church program lingers as a specter hovering over Nauvoo. The relevance vacuum prompted the sale in May 2012 of Haun's Mill and other church properties to the LDS Mormons who considered the properties anything but irrelevant. I take some blame for this because as world church historian it occurred on my watch. I failed in my duties to convince decision makers that Haun's Mill was the physical representation of the banality of violence, a place made sacred by the deaths of at least seventeen of its forebears.

Haun's Mill should have fit squarely within the world church program as an ensign of peace and where opposition to retribution and violence could be lifted up. My failure to accomplish this is a heavy burden that I must carry but possibly made lighter by its new owners who will hopefully develop a program that Community of Christ did not do—one that memorializes the lives of those who made the ultimate sacrifice for their beliefs. Hopefully Haun's Mill will become that hallowed "place of peace" that it has always deserved to be.

Spending this short time covering the Haun's Mill experience is intended to be a cautionary tale to Nauvoo. The Nauvoo story must find relevance to the Community of Christ mission today. Priorities must be put in order. Researching the minute

---

8. For more information on the Community of Christ Historic Sites Foundation Board see their website. For their missional goals see http://www.historicsitesfoundation.org/page.do?act=lo&page=Our_Mission_And__Goals

details of Nauvoo history is quite important, but so were the days on end spent at Haun's Mill searching for the newly dug well that served as the sacred burial site. Spending considerable resources on aerial overflights, infrared photo imaging, and magnetometer readings contributed very little to the larger world church program.

Here at Nauvoo material cultural explorations and interpretation are also necessary. For example, it can be lots of fun to discover adze marks in roughhewn floor joists or to painstakingly analyze porcelain pottery chards in an archeological dig near the Homestead. But totally focusing on that is what caused the sale of Haun's Mill. It simply is not enough. If we had spent just as much time exploring how the Haun's Mill historic site could move forward the mission of the church, perhaps there would have been greater appreciation among world church leaders. Left unaccomplished, the site's fate was sealed.

Researching to discover the meaning of Nauvoo to the world church mission must be the priority today. Appropriate questions must be asked and must get forthright answers. For example, how does the Nauvoo Mansion House located on the western Illinois frontier in the early 1800s speak to a completely international church in the twenty-first century? And, how do events that led to the demise of church founder Joseph Smith communicate the need for embracing social norms rather than violating them? Here should be where scholars place their efforts.

The timeworn binary good v. bad argumentation in the messaging is a fatal trap to be avoided at all costs. Instead, an in-depth exploration of Nauvoo's stewardship model of community should receive primary focus. In the early church, Nauvoo was the fourth attempt to establish a "signal community" (to use current language), with Kirtland, Independence, and Far West being the other three. All four were variations on a theme of living in community. What lessons can be learned?

Today for Community of Christ the Nauvoo story should focus on what it means to become a people of peace. Inclusiveness in denominational beliefs and practices is preferable over exclusiveness. The Nauvoo narrative communicates the need to embrace other faith traditions as equally legitimate. Also, the Nauvoo experience speaks to the importance of seeing all people as being of inestimable worth. This Community of Christ enduring principle finds validation as Nauvoo's central lesson.[9] Investing inordinate amounts of time, talents, and treasures in matters of low priority, although well-intentioned, ignores the hazards told in Nauvoo's teachings.

---

9. There are nine "enduring principles" of Community of Christ: Grace and Generosity, Sacredness of Creation, Continuing Revelation, Worth of All Persons, All Are Called, Responsible Choices, Pursuit of Peace (Shalom), Unity in Diversity, and Blessings of Community. For an explanation of each principle, see: http://www.cofchrist.org/enduring-principles.

Conclusion

It is accurate to say that in September 2017, just as it was back in April 2002, the Community of Christ leadership is focused not so much on Nauvoo as it is on Nairobi and Nepal; not some much on Palmyra as it is on Papeete and Peru; not so much on Far West as it is on France and the Federal Republic of Germany; not so much on Independence as in India, Ikot Oku Mfang, and Indonesia; and, not even so much on Kirtland as it is on Kinshasa, Kenya, and the Ukraine. Today's Community of Christ is a world church with many more active participants living outside North America than inside and speaking far more international languages than in English. Our historic sites generally, and Nauvoo specifically, must speak resoundingly in those international languages and find multicultural relevance.

Today's Community of Christ historic sites leaders need to read Apostle Charles D. Neff's seminal November 1967 *Saints' Herald* article entitled "What Shall We Teach?"[10] This is the most foretelling work of this period. Neff challenged prevailing views that church mission should be all about superimposing the North American church into international cultures that would find virtually no meaning. Missionaries were proselytizing with explanations that had no relevance to their listeners. They were presenting answers to questions that people simply were not asking. The Nauvoo message must provide answers that people are asking. We must see the parallels.

There are significant opportunities to make relevant our historic sites to an international church. Although there are many opportunities, two come to mind. First, through the wonderful Community of Christ internship and guide service program, our historic sites leaders have made quite a contribution by expressing this international characteristic. Within resources this program should be expanded dramatically.

Second, today's Community of Christ historic sites are found all along the Restoration Trail that wends its way along the navigable rivers and canals, the early national roads, and the well-worn and newly blazed wagon trails of North America. But the Restoration Trail ranges far beyond just one continent into Australia, French Polynesia, Mexico, Central and South America, Asia, and Europe. A true world church should be reflected in its historic sites and not in symbolic or cursory ways.

So, you ask what is the attachment of Nauvoo to Community of Christ? The financial challenges of today place inordinate pressure on all our historic sites but especially Nauvoo, the most vulnerable. I think in the days soon to come we will find Nauvoo's worth and importance to Community of Christ. Hopefully it will not be too late.

---

10. Charles D. Neff, "What Shall We Teach?," *Saints' Herald* 114, no. 21 (November 1, 1967): 726–27, 739.

MARK A. SCHERER became the Community of Christ World Church historian in 1995 and retired from these responsibilities in 2016. He has been an associate professor of history with Graceland University and continues as an adjunct faculty member of Community of Christ Seminary. Currently he serves as Archivist for Unity Village, Missouri, a full time position that he enjoys immensely.

--- • ---

Book Review Article

Michael W. Homer. *Joseph's Temples: The Dynamic Relationship Between Freemasonry and Mormonism*. Salt Lake City: University of Utah Press, 2014. 448 pp. Hardback: $34.95. ISBN: 978-1-60781-344-6.

Angela Pulley Hudson. *Real Native Genius: How an Ex-Slave and a White Mormon Became Famous Indians*. University of North Carolina Press, 2015. 270 pp. Illustrated. Paperback: $32.50. ISBN: 978-1-4696-2443-3.

By Newell G. Bringhurst

TWO CAREFULLY RESEARCHED and written volumes make for essential reading on the highly controversial topics of freemasonry, temple worship, and race relative to their impact on The Church of Jesus Christ of Latter-day Saints.

The first, Michael W. Homer's long-awaited *Joseph's Temples: The Dynamic Relationship Between Freemasonry and Mormonism* is an incisive account of the changing, often-troubled relationship between Mormonism and Freemasonry from the time of Joseph Smith down to the present. This topic is considered within the context of evolving Mormon temple worship, asserting a direct relationship between such sacred rites and Masonic ritual.

The bulk of Homer's work focuses on the impact of Freemasonry on Mormonism during Joseph Smith's lifetime. Building on the findings of earlier authors who have broached this topic—most especially, D. Michael Quinn, John R. Brooke, and Clyde Forsberg—the author asserts that Smith drew from varied aspects of Freemasonry. Such influences affected the evolution of LDS doctrine and practice following Smith's death.

Smith's actions and behavior reflected the fact that Mormonism's founder, like many of his contemporaries, shared the "mistaken belief ... that Freemasonry had ancient origins and that it could trace its rituals back to Solomon's Temple." The parallels between Mormonism and Freemasonry were pervasive, indeed "much broader than the strains of anti-Masonry in the Book of Mormon, or the similarities that have been noted between Masonic and Mormon temple rituals" (2).

The connection between Mormonism and Masonry began in New York and continued in Ohio, Missouri, Illinois, and Utah. The Masons, Smith asserts, "practiced an 'apostate endowment' just as sectarians practiced 'apostate religions,'" whereas Latter-day Saints "restored the original ritual" (3). Similarly, the Nauvoo Female Relief Society, founded by Smith in conjunction with "his expansive ideas concerning marriage, also contained a specter of Masonry." Through this organization, Smith taught "the Mormon sisters to keep a secret through that society"—an essential precursor for indoctrinating these "same women into temple rituals that included explicit vows of secrecy" (3–4). This, in turn, affirmed the Mormon leader's introduction of plural marriage with its vows of absolute secrecy.

Among the most provocative aspects of Homer's volume is his assertion of a direct connection between Freemasonry and evolving LDS racial concepts and practices adversely impacting African-American Mormons. The author claims that "Smith's attitudes concerning race were probably influenced by the legends and policies of American Freemasonry"—this based on the assertion that "Masons believed that Africans were descended from Cain and Ham and that they had perverted pure Freemasonry and established a spurious form of the Craft" (113). Masonic racial influences, in turn, informed Smith's scriptural writings, specifically, his transcription of the Book of Moses and the Book of Abraham. Through the latter work, Smith "may have [been] influenced by Masonic fascination with Abraham [that] spanned the history of the Craft" (133). The Book of Abraham "notion that Ham's descendants were cursed [i.e. were ineligible to receive the priesthood] was consistent with Masonry's two-race theory, which prevented all African Americans from being initiated, passed, and raised in Masonic temples" (361). Homer, however, concedes that "there is no evidence that Smith…during his lifetime insisted that African men could not be ordained to the Mormon priesthood or participate in the temple [and] in fact…announced that a new temple in Nauvoo…would be open to 'all languages, and of every tongue, and of every color'" (362).

Such was not the case with Brigham Young who implemented Mormonism's prohibition on black priesthood ordination and temple rites following Smith's death. Homer asserts a direct connection between the expansion of Mormon temple ritual, wherein males and females interacted "in close proximity," and the concurrent prohibition of blacks from such activities (369). The author further suggests that this ban resulted from Young's continuing embrace of Freemasonry. Specifically, the Mormon leader "may have believed that Masonry's ancient landmarks were remnants of qualifications to enter the temple, and that just as Africans were ineligible to enter Solomon's Temple (and successor Masonic temples), that the policy should be extended to Joseph's temples" (369–70). In sum, Young's prohibition on "blacks from holding priesthood powers and participating in Mormon temple rituals had parallels with American Masonic practice" (4).

Informative is Homer's discussion of the changing dynamics between Mormonism and Freemasonry from the time of Brigham Young down to the present. During the pioneer period, "Mormon Masons remained surprisingly loyal to the Craft. Young wore a Masonic pin while sitting for a photograph…The church also held 'Masonic Schools' and continued to use and display Masonic symbols on church buildings, cooperatives, grave markers, newspaper mastheads, hotels, residents, coins, logos, and seals" (265). Mormon leaders, moreover, publicly affirmed "the parallels between the endowment and Masonic ritual …" (273).

By the mid-1860s, however, Mormon leaders began to distance themselves from Freemasonry, prompted by the formation of the Utah-based Mount Moriah Lodge, organized by local non-Mormon merchants. The lodge prohibited Mormons from joining, pointing to their practice of plural marriage—recently outlawed by Federal statute. Non-Mormon Freemasons also involved themselves in "the legal battles to force the Mormons to eradicate polygamy…" (283).

At the same time "both Mormons and non-Mormons continued to acknowledge the connection between Masonry and Mormonism" (286). Throughout the late nineteenth century and into the early twentieth, Mormon leaders continued to affirm "the similarities between the endowment and Masonic ritual" noting that "both rituals had a common connection with the Temple of Solomon" (299).

By the beginning of the twentieth century, LDS leaders became "increasingly uncomfortable with the connections that had been noted between Masonic ritual and the Mormon temple" (307). As those Mormon Masons initiated in Nauvoo died out, there were fewer voices espousing such connections (317). Ultimately, in 1900, church leaders issued a statement declaring strong opposition "'to secret societies' and that those who continued to go into them would be denied admission to the Temple for ordinance work." The statement further characterized secret organizations—including the Masons—as "institutions of the evil one…snares that are set to entrap our feet and to win our affections from the Kingdom of God" (319). Later church leaders and spokesmen subsequently disavowed any connection between Freemasonry and Mormon temple ritual, claiming that "Smith [had] received the entire endowment… by revelation from God…before he became a Freemason." This assertion was clearly designed to counter "Masonic claims that the Mormon prophet borrowed portions of the Masonic ritual" (331–32).

Utah Masons continued to prohibit Latter-day Saint males from joining their lodges—such prohibition remaining in place for most of the twentieth century. This restriction applied only to lodges in Utah, whereas Mormon males could join lodges elsewhere. Finally, in 1984 the Grand Lodge of Utah repealed its unique exclusionary policy. Five years later, the LDS church lifted its own ban on joining secret societies, specifically removing from its *General Handbook of Instructions* a provision that discouraged members from joining "any organization that …is secret and oath-bound" (397–38).

Michael W. Homer's *Joseph Temples* is an important work, deserving the attention not only of scholars but of interested laypersons as well. It stands alone as the most complete scholarly work to trace the evolving relationship between Mormonism and Freemasonry. A second attribute is the thoroughness with which the volume contextualizes the changing dynamics between Mormonism and Freemasonry relative to larger historical developments. A third quality is the volume's extensive documentation through a wide range of both primary and secondary sources, specifically its extensive footnotes and impressive bibliography. Most convenient is a seven-page chronology outlining the significant events involving the dynamic relationship between Mormonism and Freemasonry.

But at the same time the volume is deficient in several respects. The chapter on "Legends and Folklore" (360–92) is overwritten. Specifically, its discussion of the rise and fall of Mormonism's black priesthood and temple ban deals less with Masonic influences than with the myriad of other factors influencing Brigham Young to implement the ban in the first place. This development is discussed more comprehensively in the previously-published works of Lester E. Bush, Armand Mauss, and this reviewer.

A topic meriting greater discussion is the evolving relationship between the Reorganized Church of Jesus Christ of Latter Day Saints (now Community of Christ) and Freemasonry. Homer provides tantalizing insights into this topic through his mention of the fact that RLDS president Frederick M. Smith, as a Freemason, became "worshipful master of Orient Lodge 546 (Kansas City, Missouri) in 1934 and served as grand chaplain of the Grand Lodge of Missouri in 1940 and 1942–1945" (338). Such issues notwithstanding, Michael W. Homer's *Joseph Temples* stands as the most comprehensive work on the evolving relationship between Mormonism and Masonry.

* * *

Equally insightful is *Real Native Genius: How an Ex-Slave and a White Mormon became Famous Indians* penned by Angela Pulley Hudson, a professor of history at Texas A & M University. The volume vividly traces the exploits of two controversial nineteenth-century characters, Warner McCary—an ex-slave born in Mississippi and his wife Lucy Stanton—a divorced white Mormon woman originally from New York. Skillfully intertwining the histories of slavery, Mormonism, popular culture, and American medicine, Hudson's compelling tale of ingenuity, imposture, and identity is literally stranger than fiction.

Warner McCary, born into slavery in Natchez, Mississippi, suffered all of its indignities—made worse when the rest of his immediate family was freed, whereas he remained enslaved. No ordinary slave, McCary honed his skills as a performer, imitating animal sounds, whistling tunes, and later by playing the fife and drum. Following his escape to the North, McCary utilized his talents as an engaging musical entertainer in a wide variety of forums. In the process he assumed a shifting Indian identity both on and off-stage.

Lucile (Lucy) Celesta Stanton, McCary's future wife, was born in central New York State and later moved to Kirtland, Ohio, in the wake of her family's conversion to Mormonism in 1830. Deeply devout from a young age, Lucy later claimed to have had her first visionary experience at age two (51), "As a young lady, she was among several white women who were captivated by the African-American Mormon known as 'Black Pete'" and reportedly chased him about. Such experiences anticipated her later involvement with William McCary (53). In 1833, following her migration to Independence Missouri, Lucy met and married her first husband, Oliver Harmon Bassett. They subsequently became the parents of three children. In the wake of the Mormon expulsion from Missouri, the family settled in Quincy, Illinois. In 1843 Lucy and Oliver divorced, allegedly over the latter's loss of faith in Mormonism.

Some two years later, in 1845, Lucy met Wilhelm McCary, following his arrival in Iowa. McCary, who presented himself as an Indian, captivated Lucy with his charismatic demeanor and musical talent. He immediately proposed marriage. She accepted on the spot. Apostle Orson Hyde married the pair "for time and eternity" following McCary's baptism and ordination into the LDS priesthood (65–67).

This set the stage for McCary's emergence as a schismatic Mormon leader, ably assisted by his wife. After migrating to Cincinnati in early 1846, the dynamic duo established a new "fanatical sect" consisting of some sixty members. McCary presented himself as a "Pretended Lamite [Lamanite or Indian] Prophet ... (71). Lucy "adopted an Indian persona" calling herself "Luceil Bsuba," McCary's "Delaware wife" (73).

The McCarys left Cincinnati in early 1847, moving on to Winter Quarters, near Florence, Nebraska, where the main body of Mormons were encamped under the leadership of Brigham Young. Initially McCary entertained the Latter-day Saints with his musical talents. He sought to convince Young and other Mormon leaders of his "Indianess" while obscuring his African-American ancestry—albeit with limited success (83–87). Wilhelm and Lucy boldly asserted their own doctrines and practices, forming their own schismatic group. At its heart was "their own sealing ceremony… a form of plural marriage [involving] group sex, or at least a shared sexual experience" (87–89). The McCarys' small but committed group included Lucy's immediate family. Most important was her father, Daniel Stanton, who allowed their meetings to be held in his house (90). In October 1847 Wilhelm was compelled to flee to Missouri following the disclosure of his "sexual ceremonies and unorthodox beliefs" (90).

McCary's Winter Quarters activities had long-lasting consequences. Specifically, "The role of interracial marriage—and by extension the McCary's [own] union" was a factor in the emergence of Mormonism's long-standing black priesthood ban. Beginning in 1847 Church leaders had taken steps towards the establishment of the ban, ultimately publicized as doctrine by the early 1850s (91).

Meanwhile, Wilhelm and Lucy McCary moved on, travelling east and becoming in the words of Hudson, "Professional Indians." They performed before enthusiastic audiences in Washington, DC, Baltimore, New York City, Concord, New Hampshire, and Boston. Wilhelm initially adopted the name "Mr Chubbee" calling himself "the long-lost flute-playing son of a Choctaw chief." Lucy, in turn, "resumed her Native guise" (93). Lucy's whiteness, notwithstanding "she was 'tawny' enough in her features to conjure up something like the popular antebellum images of Pocahontas, the Algonquian heroine…" (98–99).

Chubbee, beginning in 1852, assumed yet another new name, "Chief Okah Tubbee." Further burnishing the couple's Indian persona, Tubbee's resourceful wife produced his "autobiography" published as *A Thrilling Sketch of the Life of the Distinguished Chief Okah Tubbee, of the Choctaw Nation of Indians*. Based on a series of biographical letters written by Lucy, the volume sought to "authenticate" the couple's "new identities" and "capitalize on their recent stage success" (102). It also attempted to convince readers that Okah Tubbee "was not just any Indian, but a chief endowed at birth with remarkable talent and chosen for divine purposes" (104).

In March 1849 the pair returned to the Midwest, initially settling in St. Louis, where Laah Ceil Manitoi Elaah Tubbee (the name she now assumed) gave birth to the couple's child, Mosholeh, named for her husband's "putative Choctaw grandfather." (114) The family subsequently moved to Independence, Missouri, where Okah Tubbee "established himself as a doctor" of Indian medicine.(117) As self-proclaimed Indian physicians, the Tubbees capitalized "on their audiences' needs, desires, and expectations." (124).

In the spring of 1851, the Tubbees moved yet again, this time to Terre Haute, Indiana where they staged "musical entertainments" and hawked Indian medicine. Assuming the title, "Dr. Okah Tubbee," he billed himself a "musical physician." (122-23) The couple along with their young son performed together in various Indiana communities. They "presented themselves as examples of civilized Indianess [and] exotic otherness." (123) Their talents earned them widespread fame, making them national celebrities, meriting media attention as newspapers throughout the country. This, however, proved a mixed blessing as Okah Tubbee found it increasingly difficult to conceal his status as an escaped black slave. Further undermining his situation was the punitive Fugitive Slave Act of 1850, authorizing the capture of black slaves who had fled north (130–31).

Okah Tubbee further compromised his status when in August 1851 he took a second wife, Sarah Marlett, after moving to Buffalo, New York. He justified his "apparent infidelity and bigamy," by asserting that, "taking multiple wives was an 'Indian custom'" (139). McCary's relationship with Marlett quickly disintegrated. To escape both Sarah Marlett and the resulting uproar, Okah and Laah Ceil fled to Canada. They resumed their stage performances, providing musical entertainment to audiences throughout Ontario. By March 1852, the Tubbees stopped their stage performances, becoming full time medical practitioners. Taking up residence in Toronto, the Tubbees advertised themselves as experts in treating "Chronic Diseases, and those of a private nature" (140).

By August 1852 Okah Tubbee's "fortunes were on the decline" due to accusations of bigamy resulting from the Sarah Marlett affair. The scorned woman sought to sue him in the Ontario Court of the Queen's Bench, resulting in his arrest and subsequent trial. Although acquitted, the case was widely reported. Such revelations hurt "efforts to establish his trustworthiness as a physician" (142). Further complicating his situation were accusations of malpractice, combined with expenses accrued in the wake of his legal troubles. All this prompted the couple to prepare and issue a second edition of his autobiography, published in 1852 under the title, *A Sketch of the Life of Okah Tubbee, (called) William Chubbee, Son of the Head Chief, Mosholeh Tubbee, of the Choctaw Nation of Indians, by Laah Ceil Manatoi Elaah Tubbee, His Wife.* Further attempting to reverse their declining fortunes, Okah Tubbee embarked on a medical tour during the winter of 1853, treating patients and visiting First Nation settlements.

His reputation was further damaged by negative publicity resulting from the death of a patient under his care. Further disrupting their business were marital difficulties. By 1856 the Tubbees had separated, Okah returning to Boston alone. His estranged wife remained in Toronto where she continued to practice medicine under the name, "Okah Leeheeil Tubbee, Indian Doctor." Concurrently, the elusive Okah Tubbee or Wah Bah Goosh—as he now called himself, simply disappeared, no trace of him found after 1856 (151).

Okah Leeheeil Tubbee eventually returned to the United States. By 1861 she had established a "successful business" as an "Indian doctress" in Buffalo, New York" (153). Madame Leeheeil—as she now identified herself, "was typically a fortune teller or a botanic physician (and sometimes both), identifying herself as an "Indian doctress." She specialized in what were dubbed "'cases of a delicate nature,' or unwanted pregnancies" (156). Not surprisingly, Madame Laahceil's medical practice as an "alleged abortionist ... raised concerns"—particularly following the death of a patient, thus leading to her arrest "on suspicion of manslaughter" (157). The death of a second patient led to her trial for manslaughter in the second degree. The jury found her guilty and sentenced her to seven years hard labor at the New York State Women's Prison at Sing Sing (166).

Following release from prison in 1869, her life took yet another unexpected turn. She migrated to Utah, rejoining her Mormon family in Springville—a small rural town some sixty miles south of Salt Lake City. In the process she shed "her Indian persona and resumed her life as Lucy Stanton." She once more worked as a midwife, though whether she provided abortions is unclear," notes Hudson (168). In 1873 she married yet a third time—none other than Heman Bassett—the brother of her first husband Oliver. She "was rebaptized and reconfirmed as a member" of the LDS church, completing "her reentry into the fold ..." (169). But she suffered poor health, complicated by "intermittent paralysis." She died in 1878 and was buried in the Springville City Cemetery next to her three oldest children.

Among the strengths of Hudson's *Real Native Genius* is the incredible breadth of research. The author utilized manuscript collections from fifteen different archives and/or libraries in all parts of the United States and Canada. She also drew information from some one hundred newspapers, and dozens of published books, articles, and essays.

A second attribute is the effectiveness with which Hudson places her account of Warner McCary and Lucy Stanton within the larger context of nineteenth-century American history. Particularly well developed is the author's discussion of popular perceptions relative to Native Americans. She effectively places McCary and Stanton as medical practitioners within the saga of the evolving medical profession. Also insightful is Hudson's evocative discussion of gender, specifically the role of women in the evolving medical field.

From my own personal perspective, Hudson's recounting of Warner McCary's strange odyssey assumed a personal relevance in that I first encountered the eccentric African American some forty-five years ago in producing my own study on LDS race relations, *Saints, Slaves and Blacks: The Changing Place of Black People within Mormonism* (1981). Hudson, however, has moved far beyond my preliminary findings. Her account is by far the most complete account of McCary and his bizarre exploits. Hudson carefully acknowledges the work of previous scholars, namely Daniel F. Littlefield, Patrick Polk, Connell O'Donovan, John Turner, and W. Paul Reeve.

Enhancing Hudson's volume is her skillful discussion of Lucy Stanton, making it truly a first-rate dual biography. McCary was clearly affected by his extremely talented, resourceful wife, who was certainly his equal. In the words of Hudson, Stanton played "a far more central role in administering medical advice and therapies than was apparent from the advertisements [for their medical practice], drawing on a familiarity with both folk medicine and midwifery that was common among frontier women, as well as her particular interest in faith healing" (144). Stanton further enhanced her role through authorship of two versions of Okah Tubbee's "autobiography."

The volume's strengths notwithstanding, it is plagued by two major shortcomings. Particularly fundamental is the style of writing. The narrative throughout tends to be overly repetitive. The author provides excessive foreshadowing in her "Prologue," in outlining the contents of each of the chapters to follow (11–14). The volume's excessive repetition is also evident in the author's tendency to over-describe certain events and actions, which slows down the pace of her fascinating tale.

Second, the text is marred by a series of misstatements and factual errors. Incorrect is the author's assertion that "William Miller [was the] founder of the millennialist Seventh-day Adventist Church" (47). Ellen G. White was the denomination's founder, known in Adventist circles as its "Prophetess of Health." Incorrect is the author's assertion that "the early Mormon movement welcomed the equal participation of men, women, and people of color, rich or poor, as did many other popular sects during the Second Great Awakening" (47).

Misleading is Hudson's discussion of the "succession crisis" following the death of Joseph Smith. She is incorrect in stating: "Ultimately, church authority was determined to rest with the Quorum of the Twelve under the leadership of Brigham Young, who dismissed other claimants" (70). Actually, the question of Mormon church authority has been a point of contention from Joseph Smith's time down to the present. Over that period, some four hundred different LDS sects have emerged—each tracing its authority back to Mormonism's founder.

Incorrect is the author's assertion that Mormon apostle Orson Hyde was "another contender for church leadership" (71), along with her statement that "Nelson Whipple [was a] member of the Quorum of Twelve" (87). Overly simplistic is the author's discussion of plural marriage, in particular her assertion: "'Celestial' or plural marriage had first been introduced when Joseph Smith revealed its importance to the faith in 1843. He had a revelation that men and women could be 'sealed' together for eternity in the temple, a union distinct from 'carnal' marriage, but he also asserted that men could take multiple wives, a 'return to the practice of Old Testament patriarchs'" (88).

Such problems notwithstanding, Angela Pulley Hudson's *Real Native Genius* is an important work, well worth the attention of scholars and laypersons alike. Most illuminating are its insights relative to race, gender, medicine, and religion within the context of nineteenth-century American society.

NEWELL G. BRINGHURST (newellgb@hotmail.com) is a retired professor of history and political science at the College of the Sequoias in Visalia, California. He is widely published in Mormon studies and is a former president of both the John Whitmer Historical Association and the Mormon History Association.

Book Reviews

Gregory A. Prince. *Leonard Arrington and the Writing of Mormon History.* Salt Lake City, University of Utah Press and the Tanner Trust Fund, 2016. 540 pp. End notes, index, bibliography, illustrations. Cloth, $39.95. ISBN # 978-1-60781-479-5.

Review by Paul M. Edwards

ONE MUST EITHER be a great admirer of the subject or hold the author in the highest respect in order to commit oneself to reading a 540-page biography of someone they think they already know. I happen to fall within such a category. Having known Leonard Arrington for nearly thirty years, I was privileged to have identified him as friend, mentor, and occasional colleague. I have known Greg Prince for nearly as long and, while I did not have the opportunity to be around him much, I had learned to appreciate him for the man he is and to admire him as a uniquely gifted scholar and author. It is with the acknowledgment of such bias that I approach this review.

Rich in original research and illustrated with the words of those who knew him best, Prince's tome has been able to draw Leonard down from the lofty perches of appreciation just long enough to introduce him to us as the child, the boy, and the man. Aware of the continuity as well as the contingences of a person's existence, Prince paints a graphic picture of the development of this man and the execution of his signification life.

Prince is at his very best when presenting Arrington's incredible use of words in his historical writing, and also in the articulation of relationships by which he opened his world to the reader. From the precision of words to identify, to the vagueness of words to pacify, Arrington could talk with just about anyone and come away having been both informed and enlightened. One of the brightest, most intelligent and complex of men I have ever known, Arrington could be childishly simple in the presentation of the difficult.

At the most I am one of many who saw him as a special friend and to a small extent felt a bonding built on a shared healthy dose of existential idealism in which he had molded his life essence with the most significant of results. We did have the chance to talk at some length about history's great paradoxes and values, as well as the responsibility, of allowing any meaning to emerge from their disunity. He was the eternal optimist who found, or created, beauty in whatever he did. I, who never overcame the realization that Superman shaved every morning, was able to share with him at least the fact that meaningfulness was not fully found in history, nor totally acceptable in religion.

Long after General McArthur adopted Aristotle's view that there is no substitute for victory, Arrington had adopted his own awareness that while victory can be interpreted in many ways, there is no substitute for integrity. The price of this was often high, significantly so for Leonard, but he could do little else but pay it. Never a director but always as a guide, he faced Mormonism as more than a historian in a manner that cries out for completion. Had his very presence not been seen as a threat to institutional integrity, and he had been allowed to work his way in the understanding and presentation of the past, God only knows what might have been accomplished.

Prince has not written the traditional biography providing a thread of development through chronology, but has rather dealt with his life via a series of themes reflecting his subject's major roles and contributions. I rather like this format but do acknowledge the gaps of understanding it creates when separating imaging and events. Like all persons, Arrington was a product not only of the significant events in his life, but also of the numerous contingencies that bombarded him and which generally were most often exposed in chronology. A second problem is that the assigning of themes and projections to Arrington's ideas and work limits us to Prince's imposed interpretation and order.

The "Happy Warrior" was, I believe, not all that happy when at war. I think it possible here to diverge from Prince without being either disagreeable or any more sure of my position than he is of his. Greg knew Leonard as well as me and certainly has captured much of the man as church member, historian, leader, and asset. But I am not sure Prince and I knew him, or looked to him, in the same manner. While Leonard never complained, I often had the feeling that he was sad. Not so much the sadness of poor relationship or fear or even isolation, but the sadness of *The Stranger*; the man who knew that dreams died primarily from the pursuit of them.

If you do not see the sadness, it is possible to miss the quandary of his bifurcated soul. Prince beautifully recounts three experiences in which the validation of the divine was made apparent. He was not so clear to identify those series of experiences in which the intellectual and rational challenged the affirmations of the hierarchical base of official belief. Arrington displayed the ultimate courage, for he moved ahead while being afraid.

As a major recipient of the effort, I am most appreciative of Prince's comments regarding Arrington's bridge-building with RLDS. Prince, like Arrington, was cautiously aware of how significant this was, at least to the RLDS, and has codified Arrington's special role in making this happen. For many of us, raised on Mormon horror stories, Leonard became the calm and loveable standard against which all such stories were reconsidered.

This is not only an excellent biography; it is a wonderful story. Such a man who built himself from scratch and who personified intelligence and wisdom did so throughout an interesting and often intriguing life. The recount of this life, well told and evenly divided between formation and outcome, gives us a beautifully written account of a highly engaging man. Even if you think you knew the man well, you will know him even more intimately after finishing Prince's book.

PAUL M. EDWARDS, a past president of the JWHA and the MHA, is currently senior fellow at the Center for the Study of the Korean War in Independence, Missouri.

97032814R00115

Made in the USA
Columbia, SC
06 June 2018